# COOKING WITH ANTOINE
## AT
# LE PÉRIGORD

# COOKING WITH ANTOINE
## AT
# LE PÉRIGORD

### ANTOINE BOUTERIN

**with Elizabeth Crossman**
*Illustrations by Antoine Bouterin*

G. P. Putnam's Sons
New York

G. P. Putnam's Sons
*Publishers Since 1838*
200 Madison Avenue
New York, NY 10016

Library of Congress Cataloging-in-Publication Data

Bouterin, Antoine.
Cooking with Antoine at Le Périgord.

1. Cookery, French.   I. Crossman, Elizabeth.
II. Title.
TX719.B746   1986       641.5944        85-24561
ISBN 0-399-13135-3

Printed in the United States of America

1   2   3   4   5   6   7   8   9   10

To my friend
Yanou Collart
To George Briguet,
who gave me the opportunity to practice
my culinary ideas in the United States
and
To my grandmother Marguerite

# CONTENTS

INTRODUCTION · 9

CANAPÉS · 15
APPETIZERS · 21
TRUFFLES, CAVIAR AND FOIE GRAS · 31
SOUPS · 37
EGGS · 53
FISH · 57
SHELLFISH · 93
CHICKEN AND OTHER DOMESTIC FOWL · 109
MEAT · 127
GAME · 139
VEGETABLES · 153
VINAIGRETTES, OILS AND BUTTERS · 171
HERBS, SPICES AND FLOWERS · 179
DESSERTS · 183
BREAD · 197
JAMS · 203
WINES AND OTHER DRINKS · 209
STOCKS · 217
SAUCES · 225
MENUS · 241

INDEX · 245

# INTRODUCTION

I was born in Saint-Rémy in the south of France. Saint-Rémy is a small town full of charm situated in the heart of Provence where, although the old traditions are slowly disappearing in the whirlwind of progress, there is still a certain sweetness of life and a fondness for the past ways.

The cooking of Provence is scented with thyme, basil and rosemary, all mixed with the sublime perfume of garlic and parsley. These sweet smells of my childhood drew me into the kitchen, and because of them I knew I wanted to become a cook. Today fresh herbs play a major part in my cuisine. My grandmother Marguerite lived near us, and she is the person whose cooking influenced me the most. She was a top *cordon bleu* as we say in France, that is, an excellent cook. Like an alchemist, she knew the magic to transform practically nothing into a sublime and succulent dish. Every Sunday I watched her bustle about her wood stove and admired her preparations for the weekly family dinner.

I was four years old when I first made my very own culinary creations, pâtés of sand mixed with leaves and flowers from the garden. A year and a half later I made a chocolate cake for my sister's seventh birthday. It was very good and I received many compliments.

The closer I came to being old enough to choose my life's work, the more clearly I knew that I would become a cook. Whenever people asked me what I wanted to be when I grew up, I always replied proudly, "A chef de cuisine."

And so it happened: at the end of my primary school when I was fourteen years old, I started my apprenticeship (what we call *l'apprentissage* in France) at La Riboto de Taven, a two star restaurant in Les Baux de Provence, not many kilometers from my family's farm. For the next ten years I worked to learn my art in many restaurants, including those belonging to the well-known Relais Châteaux and Relais Gourmands Association. The chef who most inspired me during my training period was Chef Charles Berot. I spent two summer seasons cooking at his two star restaurant, L'Escale, on the coast of the Mediterranean near Marseilles, and I will tell you more about him in the introduction to the fish chapter.

The formation of a cook usually starts with an apprenticeship or attendance at a cooking school. In France the C.A.P., Certificate of Professional Aptitude, is the first degree, which students then follow with a master's degree or *"le bac hôtelier,"* a baccalaureate of hotel-keeping. I have earned both these diplomas myself, but in my opinion cooking is an instinct, a gift, something subtle and personal, that must come from inside. Cooking school is followed by a training period during which young cooks work in restaurants under the great chefs to learn how to apply their learning, their imagination and their talent.

It was not easy. At the time I started, apprentices were barely paid and were expected to work twelve or thirteen hours a day. But I made myself work very hard and endure the harshness of my chefs with the happy result that I have attained my ambition.

I first came to the United States in 1980, when La Varenne Cooking School in Paris sent me on a tour of cooking schools that took me to New York, Ohio, Texas and California. At the end of my trip, I had fallen in love with this country, especially with "the Big Apple."

I have always let my own inspiration influence my style of cooking. I love to create, but it is important to me that I respect the integrity of the food. As the seventeenth-century moralist La Bruyère said: "sometimes art spoils nature in seeking to perfect her." My food follows the seasons, and so I change my menu at Le Périgord four times a year.

It gives me great pleasure to teach my cooks my knowledge of cooking and the art of my cuisine. In the same way I am very proud to be able to write this book, with the invaluable help of Elizabeth Crossman, so that I can share my knowledge with you. I will feel I have succeeded if the book makes you happy in your cooking and becomes a base from which you may create your own culinary taste and originality.

I hope many young people will choose the profession of chef so that taste, the most elegant of senses, will survive in the future.

### My Philosophy of Cooking

Cooking should have great simplicity. I believe in maintaining a respect for the ingredients and yet creating a marriage of tastes and flavors. The classic foundations of French cuisine are a natural beginning from which we can create dishes with their own lightness, elegance and honesty.

### Presentation

Food presentation is extremely important because the visual effect of food plays a large part in our enjoyment of a meal. We use the word *dresser* in French to describe this process by which you personalize a recipe and present it so that it reflects your own taste.

It was not so long ago that both hot and cold dishes demanded a rich, even fantastic presentation. Today we believe more in simplicity and elegance, in the marriage of tastes and colors. You may have noticed the change in restaurant service from platters to individual plates, each with the food artfully arranged so as to whet your appetite and entice your eye.

In recent years food presentation in French cuisine and in the new American cuisine has been inspired by the Japanese and Chinese who are masters of clever combinations. For myself, I like a variety of vegetable colors and textures to enhance the main dish and simple, colorful decorations like the tomato-peel rose or carrot tulip illustrated here.

### Kitchen Equipment

"A workman is as good as his tools," the old proverb says, and so it is for cooks. I do not think there is any need to buy a lot of expensive kitchen equipment and gadgets, but I do recommend the following items for a well-stocked kitchen.

A *tall (stock) pot* for boiling vegetables, large pieces of meat, chicken, stock, etc.

A *sauté pan* for lightly frying or browning food, for stews and fricassees, for cooking fish and meat in butter.

A *frying pan* for frying and browning food.

*Pots (saucepans)* for heating, cooking or blanching food.

A *three-piece steamer* for steaming vegetables, fish, chicken, fruits, etc.

A *fish cooker* to poach a whole fish.

A *gratin dish* of metal, porcelain or oven-proof glass for cooking in the oven.

A *metal plate or platter* for roasting chickens, meat or fish in the oven.

A *colander* for draining food and refreshing it under cold water.

A *strainer* for straining and purifying bouillons, sauces, etc. The conical-shaped chinois is particularly useful.

*The little utensils:* a whisk, knives, a ladle, a skimmer, a small flat paintbrush (pastry brush), tongs, wooden spoons, a grater, measuring cups and spoons.

A *mandoline*. I particularly recommend this useful instrument to you because with it you can do so much so easily. The top blades cut vegetables into julienne strips, large julienne, cubes, etc. You can use it to make French fried potatoes, vegetable slices and potato chips—the bottom teeth will produce waferlike slices. (See illustration.)

A *food processor and an electric mixer*. While these two machines are not necessities, they are certainly valuable additions to your kitchen.

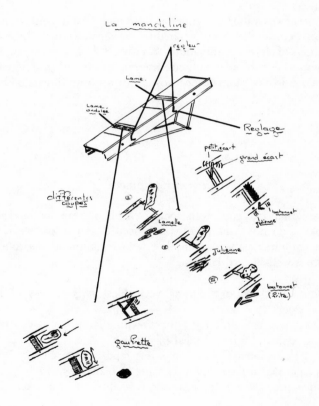

## A Culinary Vocabulary

Here is a list of culinary terms, some of which may be new to you. I hope you will take time to read these brief descriptions before you begin to cook.

*Blanch (blanchir)*: consists of throwing an ingredient in boiling water for a few seconds in order to tenderize or soften it.

*Bouquet garni*: a little bunch of fresh herbs (basil, thyme, parsley, bay leaves) used to flavor stocks sauces and stews. (See p. 182.)

*Deglaze (déglacer)*: to pour a liquid (stock or wine) on the caramelized sugars produced in a pan in the course of cooking. It is thus that one obtains juice or the base of a sauce. Before deglazing a pan, pour off any fat remaining from the cooking.

*Egg wash or glaze (dorure)*: the yolk of an egg beaten with 2–3 tablespoons of cold water and painted over food or pastry in light layers to create a golden color when cooked.

*Finish a sauce with butter (monter au beurre)*: When butter is added to a sauce just before serving, it makes the sauce smooth and glossy. It is very important that you do not stir the butter into the sauce with a spoon—this might make the sauce greasy. The procedure is to drop pieces of softened butter into the sauce and agitate the pan back and forth over the heat to incorporate the butter. You can, of course, omit the butter entirely as it is not integral to the taste, but the sauce will not be as elegant.

*Hot water bath (bain-marie)*: a container of boiling water in which another pot is set, as in a double boiler, on top of the stove or a pan of hot water in the oven, used to cook food very slowly or to keep food hot.

*Reduce (réduire)*: to boil a sauce, bouillon or stock until its volume is diminished by evaporation.

*Refresh (rafraîchir)*: to pass food under cold running water directly after it cooks.

*Season (assaisonner)*: to add salt and pepper according to your taste. I have indicated in the recipes the amount of seasoning I prefer and also my own preference for white pepper (except in a few instances), but, ultimately, the seasoning should be your decision. I do not measure salt and pepper by teaspoon amounts but by a certain amount I can hold between my two fingers—what I call a pinch. Of course, my hands may be larger than yours, and also there is a wide divergence in the amount of salt and pepper people like. You will find your own taste level for seasoning these recipes as you cook. For bouillons and stocks, use sea salt instead of table salt.

*Skim (écumer)*: to take off the scum that forms on the surface of a bouillon during the boiling.

*Sweat (suer)*: to cook a food slowly in fat (usually sweet butter), stopping the cooking just before the food begins to color or turn brown.

*Zest (zeste):* the shavings of a lemon, lime or orange peel produced by grating the peel, or thin strips of peel cut off the citrus fruit with a vegetable peeler.

*A note on ingredients:* I am very happy with the high quality and variety of American food. You should be able to find most of the ingredients in these recipes at your local stores or supermarket.

*A note on timing:* For boiling or simmering, cooking times always start after the ingredients have come to a boil.

# CANAPÉS

SMOKED RED
  POTATOES
POTATOES FILLED
  WITH BLUE CHEESE
PASSION FRUIT

CANAPÉ PROVENÇAL
SPICY PECANS
LOBSTER
  MEDALLIONS

SHELLFISH OR
  VEGETABLE
  FRITTERS
LIGHT CANAPÉS WITH
  ARTICHOKE HEARTS

**H**ere is a small offering of canapés—*amuse-gueules*, we call them in France—that go nicely with drinks. You are probably most familiar with canapés made with smoked salmon, crab meat, ham, pâté, foie gras, etc. There are also many delicious possibilities with puff pastry, such as fillings of blue cheese or anchovies.

I hope you will try some of the following recipes for your next party. The amounts given here are small; multiply to obtain the numbers you need.

A word of warning, do not make your canapés too far ahead of time. No matter how delicious the ingredients, a plate of dry or limp canapés is unappealing and certainly not a welcome tidbit to offer your guests.

4 small red potatoes
1 tablespoon sour cream
1 teaspoon salmon caviar (red)
1 teaspoon chopped smoked
  salmon
½ teaspoon chopped basil
1 teaspoon chopped parsley
1 teaspoon chopped scallion
Salt, freshly ground black
  pepper
1 lemon
Garniture: fresh parsley

# SMOKED RED POTATOES
## Pommes de terre nouvelles au saumon fumé

Cook the potatoes but do not peel them. Cut them in half and cut a very small piece off the bottoms so the potato halves sit solidly. With a spoon, scoop out a hole in the center of each half.

Mix the sour cream with the caviar, smoked salmon, basil, parsley and scallion, and season the mixture with a little salt and some pepper. Cut the peel from a lemon and section out 3 lemon wedges. Chop these finely.

Fill the potatoes with the sour cream mixture and top each one with a small piece of lemon and a few parsley leaves. Spread fresh parsley on a plate and arrange the potato halves on top.

6 small red potatoes
6 ounces blue cheese
1½–2 tablespoons sour cream
1 teaspoon chopped fresh
  basil
1 teaspoon chopped parsley
1 tablespoon chopped scallion
Freshly ground black pepper

# POTATOES FILLED WITH BLUE CHEESE
## Pommes de terre au fromage bleu

Peel the potatoes and cook them for 10 minutes in unsalted boiling water. Drain and dry. Cut them in half and cut a very small piece off the bottoms so the potato halves sit solidly. With a spoon, scoop out a hole in the center of each half.

In a food processor, mix the blue cheese with the sour cream, basil, parsley, scallion and pepper. Fill the potatoes with the mixture and chill. Serve as an appetizer or as canapés.

# PASSION FRUIT
*Fruit de la passion*

Cut the passion fruit in half and scrape the yellow and green centers into a bowl. Cut a small piece off the bottom of each shell so it will sit firmly. (See illustration.)

Whip the cream until it is firm. Stir the remaining ingredients into the passion fruit in the bowl, and fold in the whipped cream. Spoon the mixture into a pastry bag and pipe it into the passion fruit shells in swirls. Serve on a plate lined with a paper doily adorned with fresh flowers, and accompany with demitasse spoons for easy eating.

*2 passion fruit*
*½ cup heavy cream*
*½ teaspoon finely chopped red pepper*
*½ teaspoon finely chopped green pepper*
*½ teaspoon finely chopped parsley*
*A pinch of ground cumin*
*A drop of Tabasco*

# CANAPÉ PROVENÇAL

Toast the bread; slice the hard-boiled egg and the tomato. Using a 1¼-inch round cookie cutter, cut out toast rounds, then egg and tomato rounds. (The egg slices should not be too thin; you will find the cutter will take in the yolk and a surrounding circle of white.) In a small bowl, mix together the lemon juice, garlic, thyme, olive oil and pepper to make a sauce.

Put a round of tomato on each toast round and spoon some of the sauce on them. Do not use all the sauce. Place an egg round on each tomato, then a rolled-up anchovy filet, standing upright. Put 2 small capers on each anchovy. Spoon the rest of the sauce on top and garnish with tiny sprigs of parsley. Push a toothpick through each canapé or serve them in small paper baking cups.

*2 slices white bread*
*1 hard-boiled egg*
*1 tomato*
*1 teaspoon lemon juice*
*⅛ teaspoon chopped garlic (optional)*
*⅛ teaspoon chopped fresh thyme*
*1 teaspoon olive oil*
*Freshly ground black pepper*
*4 anchovy filets*
*8 small capers*
*Garniture: very tiny parsley sprigs*

# SPICY PECANS
*Noix épicées*

Preheat oven to 350°–400°. Heat the oil in a frying pan and agitate the pecans in it. Season the pecans with a very small pinch of salt and with ground cumin and cumin seed. Place in oven for 5–6 minutes.

Pat pecans with paper towels to remove any remaining oil and, while still warm, dip half of each pecan into honey mustard. Serve warm.

*1 teaspoon oil*
*A handful of pecans*
*Salt*
*Ground cumin and cumin seed*
*Honey mustard*

*2 slices white bread*
*1 cooked lobster tail (whole,*
  *not split in half)*
*2 tablespoons mayonnaise*
*1 teaspoon cognac or*
  *Armagnac*
*A pinch of chopped basil*
*Curry powder*
*Salt*
*Garniture: finely chopped*
  *parsley, ground cumin*

# LOBSTER MEDALLIONS
*Médaillons de homard*

Toast the bread and cut out 6 rounds with a 1¼-inch cookie cutter. Slice the lobster tail across so that you have 6 well-formed slices and little bits left over from each end. Chop the lobster scraps (there will be about 1 tablespoon) and mix them with 1 tablespoon of the mayonnaise, the cognac, chopped basil, and curry powder and salt to taste.

Spread the lobster-mayonnaise mixture on the toast rounds and place the lobster slices on top. Spoon the remaining tablespoon of mayonnaise into a pastry bag and decorate each piece of lobster with a little swirl or rosette. Top with chopped parsley and a very small shake of cumin and serve in small paper baking cups.

*Shellfish to be used raw:*
  *shrimp, scallops*
*Shellfish to be used slightly*
  *precooked in the process of*
  *opening shells: clams,*
  *oysters, mussels*
*Vegetables: baby carrots,*
  *zucchini, broccoli,*
  *cauliflower, whole scallions*
*3 egg whites*
*¾ cup beer*
*1 cup flour*
*Salt*
*Oil for deep frying*
*Lemon wedges*

# SHELLFISH OR VEGETABLE FRITTERS
*Beignets de crustacés ou légumes*

*Use any of the suggested shellfish and vegetables. If they need precooking, be sure to pat them dry with a towel after blanching before you dip them in the batter.*

Prepare the shellfish: cut shrimp in half lengthwise; if you are using sea scallops, cut them in half also. Open clams, oysters or mussels according to directions on pp. 45, 103 and 105. This will give them a few minutes' precooking. Prepare the vegetables: peel carrots and blanch them briefly. Cut zucchini into pieces, separate broccoli or cauliflower into flowerets with a small stem left on. Trim the scallions and cut them into several pieces.

Whip the egg whites until they are white and creamy-looking. Make a batter with the beer, flour, egg whites and 2 pinches salt. Heat oil in a deep fryer or a heavy frying pan. Test the oil to see if it is hot enough by dropping a small blob of batter into it; it should spatter when the oil is ready.

Dip the shellfish and vegetables into the batter, then carefully into the oil. Cook them until they are nicely brown all over, turning with a fork to ensure even browning. Remove them to a paper towel, pat off any fat, sprinkle with salt and serve warm with lemon wedges.

If you wish to serve a spicy sauce with these fritters, add Tabasco and chopped pimiento or curry powder and cumin to Green Sauce (p. 236).

*Note:* You can reserve the oil for another time by straining it.

# LIGHT CANAPÉS WITH ARTICHOKE HEARTS

*Canapés légers aux coeurs d'artichauts*

3 artichokes
½ teaspoon finely chopped
   red pepper
½ tomato, peeled and finely
   chopped
¼ teaspoon chopped green
   peppercorns
1 teaspoon lemon juice
⅛ teaspoon finely chopped
   garlic
¼ teaspoon chopped basil
¼ teaspoon chopped parsley
2 drops olive oil
A pinch of ground cumin
Garniture: lettuce leaves,
   lemon wedges

Cook the artichokes according to directions on p. 154. Remove the leaves and chokes and trim the remaining hearts so that they are nicely shaped. Cut each heart horizontally into 2 slices. Using a 1¼-inch round cookie cutter, cut out rounds from the slices. (You will have 6 rounds.)

Mix the red pepper, tomato and peppercorns with the remaining ingredients, and place a small spoonful of the mixture on each artichoke round. Put a toothpick through each canapé, and arrange on a plate decorated with lettuce and several wedges of lemon.

# APPETIZERS

VEGETABLE TART
HEARTS OF SALAD
BRIE WITH CABBAGE
CHEESE TART
SEAFOOD PANCAKE
CRISPY TUNA
DUCK CONSERVE
  SALAD WITH SLICES
  OF PEAR

CHICKEN SAUSAGE
CHICKEN LIVER
  CUSTARD
LEAN PHEASANT AND
  VEAL PÂTÉ IN
  LETTUCE
LIGHT LAMB PÂTÉ
CLEAR VEGETABLE
  AND LOBSTER PÂTÉ

EGGPLANT CAVIAR MY
  WAY
EGGPLANT CAVIAR IN
  THE STEAMER

COLD STUFFED
  VEGETABLES

BRANDADE OF COD
  MY WAY (p. 86)
MACKEREL RILLETTES
  (p. 88)
MUSSELS GRATIN
  (p. 103)
MUSSEL SALAD (p. 104)
OYSTERS GRATIN
  WITH TRUFFLES
  (p. 105)
SHELLFISH OR
  VEGETABLE
  FRITTERS (p. 18)
OYSTER AND
  VEGETABLE SALAD
  (p. 105)
WARM LOBSTER AND
  ASPARAGUS SALAD
  (p. 96)
CHICKEN SALAD
  (p. 120)

TOMATO TARTS
  (p. 239, Note)
ASPARAGUS CRÊPE
  (p. 156)
ASPARAGUS TART
  (p. 155)


TURNOVER WITH
  TRUFFLES (p. 32)
A LIGHT RAGOÛT OF
  POTATOES AND
  TRUFFLES (p. 33)
POTATOES FILLED
  WITH BLUE CHEESE
  (p. 16)
CAVIAR WRAPPED IN
  LETTUCE (p. 34)
CAVIAR CRÊPES (p. 34)
HOT FOIE GRAS (p. 35)
FOIE GRAS AND
  CABBAGE (p. 36)
HOT FOIE GRAS SALAD
  (p. 36)

Appetizers, the first course of lunch or dinner, are meant to excite your appetite. They should be light, easy to digest, fresh and served in delicate portions.

The originality and ingredients of an appetizer or hors d'oeuvre give a tantalizing hint of the meal to follow. If you are serving a main course of meat or chicken, you will create a balance with an appetizer of fish or shellfish. However, nothing prevents you from preparing a meal entirely of fish or game.

My own preference is for hot soup in wintertime, an hors d'oeuvre full of the freshness of fruits and vegetables in spring, in summer a cold dish or a composed salad and in autumn a hot fish, game or chicken pâté.

Any of the following appetizers or the suggested ones in other chapters would make a satisfying light lunch or supper.

# VEGETABLE TART
### Tarte aux légumes

1 cup julienne-cut leeks
1 cup julienne-cut carrots
1 cup julienne-cut zucchini
1 tomato, peeled and
    chopped (optional)
Puff pastry or Short Pastry
    (p. 185)
3 eggs
Salt, white pepper
2 cups heavy cream
Freshly ground nutmeg
1 tablespoon chopped parsley
1 teaspoon chopped basil
Sauce suggestion: Lemon
    Butter Sauce (p. 228)

SERVES 6

Preheat oven to 350°–400°. Mix the leeks, carrots and zucchini together, and add the tomato, if desired. Roll out the pastry very thin and place it in a 9-inch buttered tart pan; prick the bottom of the pastry with a fork. Distribute the vegetables over the pastry.

Beat the eggs in a bowl with the salt and pepper. Add the cream, nutmeg, parsley and basil, and mix well. Pour the eggs and cream over the vegetables. Cook the tart about 30 minutes in oven. Serve plain or with Lemon Butter Sauce.

# HEARTS OF SALAD
### Coeurs de salade

1 head Boston lettuce
1 head radicchio
1 endive
6 clumps mache or 2 heads
    arugula
Juice of ½ lemon (about 1
    teaspoon)
2 tablespoons oil
Salt, black pepper

SERVES 2

Remove the outer leaves from the Boston lettuce and radicchio, leaving just the inner hearts; cut these into pieces. Remove the small, bitter core of the endive and cut the endive into bite-size pieces. Separate the leaves from 2 clumps of mache. In a bowl, make a vinaigrette of the lemon juice, oil, 2 pinches salt and 1 pinch pepper. Add the cut-up lettuce, radicchio, endive and the separated mache leaves to the vinaigrette. Toss lightly.

Arrange the leaves from the remaining 4 clumps of mache on 2 plates so that they are in a circle with the stems pointing in. Pile the salad in the middle and serve.

# BRIE WITH CABBAGE
Brie au chou

Preheat oven to 350°–400°. Steam large outer leaves of a head of cabbage for about 5 minutes. Cut out a small triangle at the base of the leaves to remove the hard core. Sprinkle a pinch of cumin over each cabbage leaf. Cut the Brie into 4 wedges. Wrap each Brie piece in a cabbage leaf, trimming off the ends with a knife. Bake the cabbage leaves on a buttered baking dish or metal plate for 5 minutes in oven.

*4 large cabbage leaves*
*12 ounces Brie*
*Ground cumin*

*SERVES 2*

# CHEESE TART
Tarte au fromage

Preheat oven to 350°. Roll out the pastry until it is thin and large enough to fit a buttered 10-inch tart pan. Fill the buttered pan with the pastry, trim off the edges and prick tart shell with a fork. Slice the cheese into thin julienne strips. Strew them onto the pastry. Beat the eggs and cream together briefly, and season with nutmeg and pepper. Pour over the vegetables. Bake for 25–30 minutes.

*Puff pastry or Short Pastry*
*(p. 185)*
*½ pound Swiss cheese*
*2 eggs*
*1 cup heavy cream*
*Freshly grated nutmeg*
*White pepper*

*SERVES 6*

# SEAFOOD PANCAKE
Pannequet de la mer

Preheat oven to 350°–400°. Drain the tuna and mix it in a bowl with the parsley and basil. In another bowl, beat the cream into the flour, then the whole egg, 2 pinches salt and 1 pinch pepper. Beat the egg whites until they are firm, and incorporate them into the batter with a whisk.

Heat a small amount of oil in a very small crêpe pan, about 4½ inches in diameter. When the oil is hot, spoon in ⅙ of the batter. Spread ⅓ of the tuna on top and cover it with a large spoonful of batter. Cook the pancake in oven for about 10 minutes. Transfer it to an oven-proof platter and keep warm while you make the other 2 pancakes. Serve with Lemon Butter Sauce.

*1 7-ounce can tuna fish*
*(packed in water) or ½ cup*
*cooked scallops, shrimp or*
*crab*
*2 teaspoons chopped parsley*
*½ teaspoon chopped fresh*
*basil (or dill or tarragon)*
*1 cup heavy cream*
*½ cup flour*
*1 whole egg*
*Salt, white pepper*
*2 egg whites*
*Oil*
*Sauce suggestion: Lemon*
*Butter Sauce (p. 228)*

*SERVES 3*

# CRISPY TUNA
*Thon frit*

1 7-ounce can white-meat
    tuna fish (packed in water)
1 cup flour
2 eggs
½ cup milk
Freshly grated nutmeg
¼ teaspoon ground cumin
⅛ teaspoon chopped garlic
2 tablespoons finely chopped
    scallion
1 tablespoon oil
Oil for frying
Salt
Lemon wedges
Garniture: lettuce leaves

SERVES 3–4

Drain tuna fish and separate the chunks into small pieces. Make a batter with the flour, eggs, milk, a little nutmeg, the cumin, garlic, scallion and 1 tablespoon oil.

Heat oil in a pan or a deep fryer. When it is very hot, dip the tuna pieces in the batter, then into the oil. Fry them until they are golden brown, about 5–6 minutes, turning them several times during the cooking. Serve with salt and lemon wedges on a plate decorated with lettuce leaves.

# DUCK CONSERVE SALAD WITH SLICES OF PEAR
*Salade de confit de canard aux émincés de poir*

1 breast piece of cold Duck
    Conserve (p. 125)
½ pear
Lettuce for salad: arugula,
    mache
Truffle Vinaigrette (very little)
    (p. 175)
1 lime, juice and grated rind
Olive oil
Freshly ground black pepper

SERVES 2

*This is an unusual combination that I think will please your eye and your palate.*

Remove the skin and fat from the duck conserve and dry off the meat. Slice it lengthwise into very thin slices. Peel the pear, remove the core and cut half of the pear into thin slices. Make a mixed salad of the greens, for 2 people, and dress it with just a soupçon of Truffle Vinaigrette, or any vinaigrette of your choice. Divide the salad between 2 plates and arrange the duck and pear slices on top of the greens. Squeeze lime juice over the slices and sprinkle them with grated lime rind. Finish with a few drops of olive oil and a few grindings of black pepper.

# CHICKEN SAUSAGE
## Boudin de poulet

*This quick sausage-type appetizer can also be made with fish, such as bass, sole or red snapper. Serve hot or cold.*

Remove the skin and bones from the chicken breast and cut it into pieces. Dice the shallot finely and sweat it in the butter briefly. Add the chicken. Remove the pan from the heat and add the parsley, scallion and coriander. Puree the chicken mixture in a food processor along with the eggs, cream, Tabasco, salt and pepper. Add cumin if desired.

Pull the sausage casing up over a wide pastry tip that you have inserted in a pastry bag. Tie other end of the casing tightly with a string. Spoon the chicken mixture into the bag. Squeeze the mixture into the casing and tie it tightly when the sausage is the size you wish.

Place the sausages in boiling, salted water or chicken stock. Bring liquid to a boil again, reduce the heat and cook slowly for 10 minutes. Or cook the sausages in a steamer for 15 minutes.

If you plan to serve the sausages cold, let them cool to room temperature before placing in the refrigerator, where they will keep for 2 days.

*Note:* Pork casings are available from most butcher shops. For two fish sausages, use half a pound of fish.

*1 whole chicken breast*
*1 shallot*
*1 tablespoon butter*
*1 tablespoon chopped parsley*
*1 tablespoon chopped scallion*
*A few coriander or basil leaves*
*2 eggs*
*4 tablespoons heavy cream*
*A few drops Tabasco*
*Salt, freshly ground black pepper*
*Ground cumin (optional)*
*Pork casing for sausages (see Note)*
*Water or chicken stock (p. 221)*

*YIELD 2 fat sausages*

# CHICKEN LIVER CUSTARD
## Flan de foies de volaille

Preheat oven to 350°–400°. Remove the fat and any green spots from the livers. In a sauté pan, heat the oil and sweat the garlic, 1 tablespoon of the parsley, the scallion and the fresh herb. Add the chicken livers and sauté them for a few minutes. Remove livers from the heat and wipe off with a paper towel. Butter 4 individual soufflé molds (3½ inches in diameter). Put a chicken liver in the bottom of each mold.

Beat the eggs energetically with a whisk, whisking in the cream, nutmeg, the remaining tablespoon of parsley, 2 pinches of salt and 1 pinch of pepper. Pour the egg mixture over the chicken livers. Place the molds in a bain-marie of very hot water that comes halfway up their sides. A page of newspaper laid flat in bottom of the pan will prevent the water from boiling up into the molds. Cook the custards in the oven for about 20 minutes.

Remove the molds from the water and let them rest for about 5 minutes for the custard to firm up. Run a knife around the edges to loosen the custards, then invert them onto individual plates. Serve plain or with Lemon Butter Sauce.

*4 chicken livers*
*1 tablespoon oil*
*⅛ teaspoon chopped garlic*
*2 tablespoons chopped parsley*
*1 tablespoon chopped scallion*
*½ teaspoon chopped fresh herb, such as basil*
*Butter*
*2 eggs*
*1 cup heavy cream*
*Freshly grated nutmeg*
*Salt, white pepper*
*Sauce suggestion: Lemon Butter Sauce (p. 228)*

*SERVES 4*

4 pheasant legs
⅓ as much boneless veal as
   pheasant meat
1 tablespoon oil
⅛ teaspoon chopped garlic
1 tablespoon chopped parsley
1 tablespoon chopped scallion
1 teaspoon fresh basil or ½
   teaspoon fresh thyme or
   tarragon
2 tablespoons chopped
   shallots
Salt, white pepper
2 slices white bread
3 tablespoons heavy cream
1 egg
3–6 large outer leaves Boston
   lettuce
A few drops olive oil
Butter
Egg wash (see p. 13)
3 tablespoons white wine

*SERVES 3*

# LEAN PHEASANT AND VEAL PÂTÉ IN LETTUCE
*Caillettes maigres en laitue au faisan et veau*

*Here is what to do with pheasant legs after making Filet of Pheasant (p. 145) for dinner.*

Preheat oven to 350°–400°. Cut the pheasant meat from the bones and remove the skin. Cut the pheasant and the veal into small cubes. Heat 1 tablespoon oil in a pan and quickly sauté the pheasant and veal cubes along with the garlic, parsley, scallion, fresh herb and 1 tablespoon of the chopped shallots. Season with salt and pepper. Move the meat about with a wooden spoon while it cooks, about 1½ minutes. Remove the crusts and cut bread into cubes. Put the bread in a bowl with the cream and egg, and mash it all together with a fork. Add the pheasant and veal, and mix well.

Sprinkle the lettuce leaves with olive oil and cook them very briefly in a steamer, just to soften them. Refresh them under cold water. Butter a gratin dish. Spoon the pheasant-veal mixture onto the lettuce leaves and fold the lettuce around the pâté to make an envelope. (You may need 2 leaves for each package.) Put the lettuce packages in the gratin dish, paint them with egg wash and sprinkle them with the remaining 1 tablespoon of diced shallots and the white wine. Cook for 20 minutes in the oven.

6 thin small lamb chops
1 tomato
½ teaspoon chopped garlic
1 tablespoon chopped fresh
   basil
Salt, freshly ground black
   pepper
Butter
1 tablespoon Knorr Swiss
   aspic jelly powder
½ teaspoon olive oil
2 tablespoons white wine
Sauce suggestion: *Fresh
   Tomato Sauce (p. 239)*

*SERVES 2*

# LIGHT LAMB PÂTÉ
*Pâté d'agneau léger*

Preheat oven to 350°–400°. Cut the lamb off the bones and remove all the fat. Slice the lamb diagonally into very thin slices. Peel the tomato, squeeze out the water and seeds, and chop it. Mix the chopped garlic, basil, salt and pepper with the tomato.

Butter an individual soufflé mold (4½ inches in diameter) and put 2 slices of lamb in the bottom of the mold. Spoon ⅓ of the tomato mixture over the lamb slices, then 1 teaspoon of the aspic powder. Repeat with 2 more layers. sprinkle the olive oil and white wine on top. Butter a piece of aluminum foil and entirely cover the mold with it. Place the mold in a bain-marie of boiling water that reaches halfway up the mold's sides, and cook in the oven for about 40 minutes.

Allow pâté to cool to room temperature, then put in refrigerator, where it will keep for 2–3 days. Remove from the mold just before serving, slice pâté and serve cold with Fresh Tomato Sauce.

# CLEAR VEGETABLE AND LOBSTER PÂTÉ
### Pâté de légumes et homard

*You can make this recipe without the lobster (or you can substitute cooked chicken for the lobster), but you cannot do without the aspic to give the pâté the shiny look. A tablespoon of Knorr Swiss aspic jelly powder mixed with 1 cup boiling water makes 1 cup aspic.*

Peel and cook the carrot; cut it into little sticks and cut the zucchini into the same size pieces. (Use only the outer zucchini pieces so that you have the skin color.) Wash the leek, trim off the bottom and cut the leaves crosswise; cut the red pepper into small strips. Steam the vegetables for 8 minutes. Remove the lobster meat from the shell and cut it into bite-size pieces. Add the port to the melted aspic and season with salt and pepper.

Lay some of the vegetables in the bottom of each of 3 small soufflé molds (3½ inches in diameter); top with a piece of the lobster. Pour in some of the aspic. Continue layering the vegetables, lobster and aspic into the molds.

Refrigerate the molds for 6 hours, or overnight. This pâté will keep in the refrigerator (unsliced in the molds) for up to 3 days. When ready to serve, remove the pâté from the mold and cut it into slices. Serve with Fresh Tomato Sauce or with Truffle Vinaigrette.

*½ carrot*
*½ zucchini*
*½ leek*
*A small piece of red pepper*
*1 cooked lobster*
*1 tablespoon port*
*Scant ¾ cup melted aspic*
*Salt, white pepper*
*Sauce suggestions: Fresh Tomato Sauce (p. 239) or Truffle Vinaigrette (p. 175)*

*SERVES 3*

# EGGPLANT CAVIAR MY WAY
### Caviar d'aubergine à ma façon

Peel the eggplants and cut them into small cubes. Blanch them in boiling, salted water for 3 minutes. Drain and dry. Peel the onion, cut into thin slices and sweat it in a sauté pan in the 2 tablespoons oil; it should be soft but not brown. Peel and smash the garlic cloves and cut them into very fine dice. Add the eggplant, garlic and olive oil to the pan with the onion, season with salt and pepper, and turn down the heat. Cook very slowly for 30 minutes. The eggplant should not brown.

Pour off the oil and mash the eggplant in a bowl with a fork. Mix in the paprika and chill the eggplant in the refrigerator, where it will keep for 6 days. Serve on toast or crackers or spooned into warmed pita bread.

*2 eggplants (about 1 pound each)*
*½ large onion*
*2 tablespoons oil*
*3 cloves garlic*
*1 cup olive oil*
*Salt, white pepper*
*1 cup olive oil*
*¼ teaspoon paprika*

*SERVES 4*

2 eggplants (about 1 pound
    each)
Juice of 1 lemon
3 tablespoons olive oil
Salt, white pepper
2 cloves garlic
Leaves of a few stalks of fresh
    thyme or chopped fresh
    parsley (see Note)
A pinch of saffron threads

*SERVES 4*

# EGGPLANT CAVIAR IN THE STEAMER

*Caviar d'aubergine à la vapeur*

Peel the eggplants and cut them into small cubes. Sprinkle with the lemon juice, 1 tablespoon of the olive oil, salt and pepper. Peel, smash and finely dice the garlic. Perfume boiling water in the bottom of a steamer with the remaining 2 tablespoons olive oil. Steam the eggplant, garlic and thyme leaves for 30 minutes.

Pour the eggplant into a bowl and mash it with a fork. Season it with saffron and refrigerate. It will keep for 6 days. Serve on toast or crackers or spooned into warmed pita bread.

*Note:* If you do not have fresh thyme, substitute chopped fresh parsley or omit the herb.

# COLD STUFFED VEGETABLES
## Légumes farcis

*These poached vegetables, filled with a seasoned vegetable puree and served cold, are colorful and refreshing.*

First prepare the vegetables that will hold the stuffing. Peel the new potatoes and cut them in half; take a small slice off the bottom of each half so they will sit upright. Peel the carrots, cut them into big pieces and cook them in boiling, salted water for 6–8 minutes. Cut 1 zucchini crosswise into 4 large pieces and cut the eggplants in half crosswise; cut a small slice off the bottom of the eggplant halves so they will not roll. Cut the tomato in half; remove any seeds and white part from the bottoms of the peppers. Preheat oven to 250°.

With a spoon or a melon-ball cutter, scoop out and reserve the centers of the potatoes, carrots, zucchini, eggplant halves and tomato, being careful not to cut through the bottoms. Sprinkle the eggplant halves with lemon juice.

Chop the remaining zucchini and peel and slice the onion. In a sauté pan, heat the oil and cook the scooped-out centers, the chopped zucchini, the onion, parsley, basil, scallion, garlic, 1 teaspoon shallots, the peppercorns, salt and pepper over medium-high heat for about 10 minutes.

Blanch the vegetable pieces that will be stuffed (except for the tomato and carrots) in boiling, salted water for 5–6 minutes; you will have to push the eggplant down while it cooks. Drain and dry the vegetables, which are now ready to receive the stuffing. Butter a baking pan and sprinkle the remaining tablespoon of chopped shallots in it. Place the vegetable cases in the pan.

Turn the sautéed vegetables and the eggs into a food processor bowl and puree. Fill the cases with the puree. Pour the stock and ½ cup water around the vegetables and cover the pan with buttered aluminum foil. Bring to a boil on top of the stove and bake for 30 minutes in a slow oven. Cool and chill.

*4 small new potatoes*
*2 carrots*
*2 zucchini*
*2 small eggplants*
*1 large tomato*
*Bottom slice (about 1 inch) of 1 red pepper*
*Bottom slice (about 1 inch) of 1 green pepper*
*1 tablespoon lemon juice*
*½ large onion*
*1 tablespoon oil*
*2 tablespoons chopped parsley*
*3 fresh basil leaves*
*1 tablespoon chopped scallion*
*½ teaspoon chopped garlic*
*4 teaspoons chopped shallots*
*1 teaspoon green peppercorns*
*Salt, white pepper*
*Butter*
*1 egg*
*1 cup light brown stock (see Note p. 219), light chicken stock (p. 221) or vegetable stock (p. 223) and ½ cup water or 1 cup water, ½ cup white wine, a small piece of a chicken bouillon cube and a chopped shallot*

**SERVES 4**

# TRUFFLES, CAVIAR AND FOIE GRAS

TURNOVER WITH
  TRUFFLES
A LIGHT RAGOÛT OF
  POTATOES AND
  TRUFFLES

CAVIAR WRAPPED IN
  LETTUCE
CAVIAR CRÊPES
HOT FOIE GRAS
FOIE GRAS AND
  CABBAGE
HOT FOIE GRAS SALAD

CAVIAR SAUCE (*p.* 235)
OYSTERS GRATIN
  WITH TRUFFLES
  (*p.* 105)
RAGOÛT OF LEEKS
  AND TRUFFLES
  (*p.* 162)

coupée

entiéra

### The Truffle

**I**n spite of the high price and scarcity of truffles, I want to discuss them with you and give you a few recipes for special occasions. These "black diamonds" or "black pearls," as they are often called, are one of the noblest foods in cooking.

There are two sorts of truffles, black and white. Black truffles usually come from the Périgord or Haute-Provence in France. Their size varies from that of a small walnut to as big as a fist. They are harvested from November to March; the most savory are found during the first frosts. These truffles grow underground around the roots of oak trees, and the trick is to find them. In the Périgord some people hunt for truffles with the aid of a sow to sniff them out, others look for swarms of a particular type of fly that likes to lay its eggs in truffles.

White truffles come from the Piedmont region in the north of Italy. They are usually eaten raw, grated in thin flakes on fresh pasta or into a risotto. Eaten in this manner, they are one of the true marvels of gastronomy.

If you have the good fortune to have fresh truffles, the best way to store them is to place them in a napkin (or other piece of linen), then in a hermetically sealed box that you put in the refrigerator. You can also put them in a jar and cover them with peanut oil before refrigerating: the oil will become fragrant and perfect for a vinaigrette.

Either of these methods of conservation is good only for a maximum of 3 weeks; after that, the truffles must be sterilized. But let me assure you, there are many very good canned truffles on the market.

1 shallot
1 leek
1 tablespoon butter
Salt, white pepper
Puff pastry sufficient to roll
    out to a 12 × 12-inch thin
    square (see Note p. 185)
Egg wash (p. 12)
2 tablespoons sliced truffles

**SERVES 2**

# TURNOVER WITH TRUFFLES
### Chausson aux truffes

Preheat oven to 350°. Cut the shallot into small dice; wash the leek and quarter lengthwise, then cut it into medium-size pieces. Melt the butter in a medium-size frying pan; sweat the diced shallot for a minute, then add the leek and a pinch of salt and pepper. Sauté the vegetables very briefly, agitating the pan during this time. Remove from heat and turn the leek and shallot onto a plate to cool. (It is extremely important that you do not put the vegetables into the pastry while they are still hot.)

Roll out a piece of puff pastry to a square large enough to accommodate 2 circles about 6 inches in diameter; cut out the circles. (Use a small plate or saucer as a guide.) From the remaining puff pastry, cut 10 thin strips about 4 inches long (from a rectangular piece about 2 × 4 inches). A pastry wheel is the best tool for this; if you do not have one, use a sharp knife.

Brush the pastry circles with egg wash. Spoon the cooled leek and shallot onto the circles, and add 1 tablespoon of truffles to each circle. Fold them over to a crescent shape and, use the tines of a fork to press the edges together. With the tip of a sharp knife, make a small hole in the top of each crescent. Butter a metal plate lightly and put the crescents on it. Lay 5 strips of pastry across each crescent in a latticework pattern and brush them with egg wash. Bake the turnovers in the oven for 15–20 minutes, or until they are nicely browned.

# A LIGHT RAGOÛT OF POTATOES AND TRUFFLES

*Petit ragoût de pommes de terre aux truffes*

6 small red potatoes
Salt, white pepper
2 shallots
1 tablespoon butter
1 cup heavy cream
2 tablespoons port
3 tablespoons sliced truffles
Garniture: *chopped parsley*

**SERVES 2**

Peel the potatoes and cut them into medium-thick slices (about 4 from each potato). Sprinkle lightly with salt and steam for about 6–7 minutes. Dice the shallots and sweat them in the butter for just 1 minute; do not let them brown. Add the cream and reduce by half. Add the port to the cream and let cook briefly, about 2–3 minutes. Strain the sauce through a fine-meshed sieve into a clean pot.

Dump in the steamed potatoes and the truffles, and season with a pinch of salt and pepper. Let the sauce come just to a boil, about 1 minute, then serve the ragoût garnished with chopped parsley.

### Caviar

Caviar is made from the eggs of a large fish, the sturgeon. The salted, processed eggs are imported from Russia (previously from Iran). Caviar has been a luxury food for many years; the celebrated sixteenth-century French writer, Rabelais, spoke of it in his *Pantagruel*.

Caviar should be eaten as nearly "natural" as possible, with lemon juice and buttered toast. It seems a pity to spoil the noble taste of caviar with onions, capers, chopped eggs and parsley.

Beluga caviar has large grains and is brownish gray in color. Sevruga eggs are smaller and more black in color.

I do not want to ignore American caviar, but sadly I do not know enough about it yet to describe it. When you can find it, the price is considerably less than for imported beluga and sevruga.

Caviar is usually eaten as an appetizer, served in a bowl of crushed ice, or on little canapés with cocktails. You can use caviar in recipes such as the two suggested here; or you might like to try Caviar Sauce, p. 235.

# CAVIAR WRAPPED IN LETTUCE
## *Paupiettes de caviar*

*6 outer, green leaves of*
*  Boston lettuce*
*2 tablespoons sour cream*
*2 tablespoons caviar*
*1 teaspoon oil*
*Garniture: 4 leaves radicchio,*
*  2 leaves Boston lettuce*

*SERVES 2*

Choose 6 large lettuce leaves and steam them quickly, for half a minute or less. Refresh them under cold water, shake off excess water and lay them flat on your work surface. Put 1 teaspoon sour cream onto each leaf, then 1 teaspoon caviar. Fold the lettuce into little packets so the sour cream and caviar are securely inside.

Heat the oil in a small frying pan. When it is very hot, add the lettuce packets, seam side down, and sauté them over medium-high heat for about 2 minutes on each side. Shake the pan occasionally. Place 3 packets on each plate and surround them with sliced radicchio and Boston lettuce leaves.

# CAVIAR CRÊPES
## *Crêpes de caviar*

*2 eggs*
*1 cup flour*
*2 cups heavy cream*
*½ teaspoon oil*
*3 tablespoons caviar*
*2 lemon slices*

*SERVES 2*

To make the crêpes, put the eggs, flour and heavy cream in a food processor and mix until blended. Heat the oil in a crêpe pan about 9 inches in diameter. When it is hot, ladle in just enough crêpe batter so that it runs out to the edges of the pan, yet remains thin. Cook 4 crêpes so that they are lightly browned on both sides.

Put about 2 teaspoons caviar on each crêpe and roll them up. Serve immediately with a slice of lemon on each plate.

### *Foie Gras*

Fresh foie gras of duck produced in the United States is becoming readily available; in my experience, the quality is excellent.

A good foie gras should have a light pink color and its texture should be firm and smooth. Before cooking, it must be cleansed to eliminate the impurities and any blood. To do this soak it in milk or in cold, salted water for 24 hours. After this necessary procedure is finished, fresh foie gras lends itself to a number of hot recipes in which the taste and satiny texture of the flesh is sublime.

French chefs like to use goose foie gras from the southwest of France (le Périgord, la Dordogne, les Landes) and from Alsace, regions famed for the foie gras that is produced by force-feeding. I prefer duck foie gras because it is slightly more acid than that of the goose.

In general, fresh foie gras is sold to the consumer in a vacuum pack. It is possible to keep it, in the pack in the refrigerator, for 1 or 2 weeks.

Once opened, however, it must be used immediately. Be careful to thoroughly cook the foie gras before you eat it because raw foie gras is very dangerous. You can also buy canned foie gras that is half-cooked or fully cooked.

# *HOT FOIE GRAS*
## *Foie gras chaud*

*1 tart apple (Granny Smith)*
*2 slices fresh foie gras (about*
  *½ inch thick)*
*Salt, white pepper*
*1 teaspoon oil*
*½ cup duck stock (p. 220)*
*1 teaspoon capers*
*1 teaspoon cognac or*
  *Armagnac*
*2 teaspoons port or marsala*

*SERVES 2 as an appetizer*
*1 as a main course*

First prepare the apple. The foie gras will turn dark when it is exposed to air, so you do not want to slice it until you are absolutely ready to start cooking it. Take 2 thick slices from the center of the apple; remove the core but not the skin. Reserve. Now slice the foie gras and place the slices on a plate on which you have placed a paper or linen towel. Season them with a bare pinch of salt and pepper.

Heat the oil in a frying pan, and when it is very hot, add the foie gras and apple slices. Using a pair of tongs, turn the slices over after 1 minute. The foie gras will cook very quickly, it only needs about 2–3 minutes over high heat; it is done when it is soft to the touch of your finger. Fat will accumulate in the pan during the cooking; pour it off once halfway through the cooking time.

Remove the foie gras to the paper towel and continue cooking the apple slices until they get very brown. In a small pot, reduce the duck stock, capers, cognac and port for about 2 minutes after it boils, to allow the caper taste to appear. Put the apple slices on the towel with the foie gras and pat the foie gras and apple with the towel to pick up any extra fat.

Place an apple slice on each plate, then a foie gras slice on top of it. Spoon 1 tablespoon of the sauce over the top and serve immediately.

2 large outer leaves green
    cabbage
1 medium-size potato
2 slices fresh foie gras
Salt, white pepper

*SERVES 2 as an appetizer*
*1 as a main course*

# FOIE GRAS AND CABBAGE
*Foie gras au chou*

Steam the cabbage leaves until they are tender, about 4 minutes. Refresh them in cold water and trim them into approximate rectangles. Boil or steam the potato and cut it into 4 slices, 2 for each serving. Keep warm. Season the foie gras slices with salt and pepper, and place them in the cabbage leaves; fold the leaves around them to make packages. Steam the packages seam side down for about 6–8 minutes. Place the folded cabbage leaves and the potato slices on plates and serve immediately.

2 slices fresh foie gras
Salt, white pepper
1 teaspoon oil
1 teaspoon cognac
2 tablespoons red wine
    vinegar
1 tablespoon honey
Lettuce for the salad: mache,
    Boston, radicchio, endive

*SERVES 2 as an appetizer*

# HOT FOIE GRAS SALAD
*Salade de foie gras chaud*

Season the foie gras slices with a pinch of salt and pepper, and cook them quickly in the hot oil until they are soft to the touch of your finger, pouring off the fat halfway through the cooking process. Place the slices on a plate lined with a napkin or paper towel and pat to remove the fat.

Pour off any fat remaining in the pan and deglaze the pan with the cognac and vinegar. Add the honey. Shake the pan over a high heat; the sauce will froth and bubble. This whole process should only take about 1 minute.

Arrange a plate with about 20 mache leaves, 4–5 Boston, 4 radicchio and 3 endive leaves. Place the foie gras slices on the lettuce and pour the sauce over them.

# SOUPS

## HOT SOUPS

GARLIC
CAULIFLOWER AND CURRY
FARM SOUP
PISTOU
ASPARAGUS
SISTO'S CONSOMMÉ
MUSSEL SOUP WITH SAFFRON
SHRIMP
CLAM

## COLD SOUPS

MELON AND GRAPEFRUIT
EGGPLANT
ZUCCHINI SOUP WITH NUTMEG
POTATO AND LEEK BASE
VICHYSSOISE
PINK RADISH
CUCUMBER
GAZPACHO
STRAWBERRY
CHILLED BOUILLABAISSE

In times of trouble and misery, wars and revolutions, in practically all the countries of the world, people have saved their lives with soup. It has played a large role in the survival of the human race, but soup also has always had a place on the tables of kings, princes and grand seigneurs. In the great days of the grand restaurants, there was one chef who prepared only soups and consommés. Apicius, celebrated gourmet of ancient Rome, spoke often of soup recipes, usually based on cereals.

There are three words for soup in French. *Potage* usually means a cream of vegetable soup, for the most part elegant and refined, *soupe* is now more common. *Consommé* is a bouillon of meat or poultry, rich, light, concentrated and clarified of all impurities.

Some of the famous soups of France are onion, potage St-Germain and consommé madrilène. Equally well known are American clam chowder, black bean soup and Philadelphia hot pot, Italy's minestrone, Spain's gazpacho, turtle soup from Great Britain and the exotic swallows'-nest soup of China.

In French farm country soup is the most appreciated part of the meal, often "fortified" with a few tablespoons of red wine.

# GARLIC SOUP
## Eau d'ail

*Garlic soup is very popular in Provence, perhaps because of the sweet smell of garlic blending with sage and olive oil. We call this soup "boiled water," and say it is a soup that can save your life.*

1 whole head garlic
2 end pieces bread
6 cups water
¼ teaspoon sea salt
6 whole fresh sage leaves or 1
   tablespoon dried whole
   sage (see Note)
2 tablespoons olive oil (see
   Note)
4 tablespoons grated Gruyère
   or Swiss cheese
Garniture: fresh sage leaves
   (optional)

*SERVES 4*

Separate the garlic head into cloves. Peel the cloves. Cut 1 garlic clove in half and rub the cut garlic all over the bread. Cut the bread into pieces somewhat larger than dice; you should have about 16–20 pieces. Reserve.

Put the garlic cloves, water and salt into a large pot and bring to a boil over high heat. Let boil, uncovered, for 15 minutes, then add the sage and olive oil. Let boil for another 15 minutes.

Pour the soup through a sieve and ladle it into soup plates. Float the bread pieces in the soup; add 1 tablespoon grated cheese to each serving. If you have fresh sage, garnish each soup plate with 2 leaves of sage.

*Note:* Fresh sage is the best for this; dried whole sage is a second choice. Do not use dried powdered sage. Olive oil in Provence is very aromatic, so I recommend you use a good imported olive oil to give a strong flavor to your soup.

# CAULIFLOWER AND CURRY SOUP

*Potage de chou-fleur au curry*

*This soup is very simple. The marriage of cauliflower and curry is a happy one. If you like spiciness, a pinch of cumin would be welcome.*

1 head cauliflower
4 shallots
1 tablespoon butter
7 cups water
½ teaspoon curry powder
Salt
Garniture: *parsley*

**SERVES 4**

Separate the cauliflower head into flowerets; cut off and discard the thick white stem. Peel the shallots and slice them. In a medium-size saucepan, sweat the shallots in the butter until they are soft but not brown. Add the cauliflower and the water; cook, uncovered, over medium-high heat for 30 minutes.

Remove the pan from the heat and put the cauliflower, curry powder and 2 generous pinches of salt into a food processor. You will probably need to do this in 2 batches, but it is not necessary to put all the liquid in the processor. Process for about 1 minute, or until the soup is smooth.

Return the processed soup to the saucepan with enough of the leftover liquid to achieve the consistency you wish. Mix and reheat. Serve immediately, garnished with chopped parsley.

*Note:* You can make this soup up to 1 hour before serving and keep it hot in a double boiler. If you wish to keep it longer, let it cool to room temperature, then put it in the refrigerator in a covered bowl, where it will keep for 3 days; when you reheat the soup, you will need to add a few tablespoons of water.

*Variation:* Add 10–12 chicken wing tips. Cook the chicken with the cauliflower, but remove them before the soup goes into the processor. Save a few wing tips as a garnish for the soup. To save time, you can wrap the chicken pieces together in a cheesecloth square before cooking; this will make it easier to pull them out at the end.

# FARM SOUP
*Soupe de la ferme*

*It is very good to come home to a cup of soup after a long day's hard work on the farm, especially when the soup is fragrant with beautiful vegetables.*

1 large turnip
2 large carrots
2 Long Island–type potatoes
   (baking potatoes)
2 leeks
1 stalk celery
1 large onion
1 head Boston lettuce
1 tomato
1 tablespoon butter
8 cups water
Salt
A ham bone (optional)

**SERVES 4**

Prepare the vegetables: peel the turnips and carrots, slice them and cut them into large dice. Peel and slice the potatoes; clean the leeks and celery stalk and cut them crosswise into medium-size pieces. Peel the onion and chop coarsely. Cut out the hard center of the lettuce and slice the head crosswise. Cut out the small stem part of the tomato and cut it into large pieces. (It is not necessary to peel the tomato.)

Sweat the onion in the butter in a large heavy saucepan over medium-high heat until the onion is soft but not brown. Dump in the carrots and lettuce and let cook for 5 minutes, turning occasionally with a wooden spoon. Add the turnip and the ham bone if you have one, and the water. Season with salt, bring to a boil and let cook, uncovered, over medium-high heat for 25 minutes. Add the remaining vegetables—the leeks, celery, potatoes and tomato—and cook for another 20 minutes from the time the soup comes to a boil again after the addition of the vegetables.

Remove the pan from the heat, add 2 pinches salt and ladle the soup into a food processor. If you have used a ham bone, discard it. Process the soup in 2 batches until it is nearly smooth. (I like little pieces of carrot in my soup to give it texture, so I do not let the processor run too long.) Serve hot.

This soup will keep in the refrigerator for 1 week; it also freezes well.

*Variation:* For a somewhat richer soup, mix 1 beaten egg and 1 tablespoon butter into the hot soup before you serve it.

You could also add other vegetables to the soup: a zucchini, 3 ounces green beans or a handful of snow peas. Cut these vegetables into pieces and add to the soup at the same time as the potatoes.

# *PISTOU SOUP*
### *Soupe au pistou*

*Pistou is a traditional Provençal soup that is generally served as a main course. Pistou usually means a puree of basil with pine nuts and olive oil, but in the south of France, it is also another word for basil. Let me tell you a little story:*

*I was about six years old, and of course what I knew about cooking was quite limited; pistou to me simply meant the good soup of my maternal grandmother, Marguerite. One day my other grandmother told me to get her some pistou.*

*I did not know what I was supposed to do.*

*At that time my uncle Jacques had a dog named Pistou. So I decided I should bring her my uncle's dog. My grandmother was very astonished to see me arrive with Pistou, his tail wagging, surely thinking it was time for his soup.*

*This is a hearty soup, almost like my grandmother's. To lighten it, reduce the quantity of vegetables.*

4 baking potatoes
2 white turnips
2 large carrots or 3–4 medium ones
1 large onion
2 large leeks
1 medium zucchini
2 handfuls green beans (about ¾ cup cut up)
2 tablespoons oil (not olive oil)
8 cups water plus 4 cups chicken stock or 12 cups water plus ½ a chicken bouillon cube
3–4 large tomatoes
1½ teaspoons chopped garlic
2 tablespoons olive oil
½ cup finely chopped Italian parsley and basil, mixed together
Salt, white pepper
1 cup canned flageolets (white or green flat beans)
A handful of very thin spaghetti (about ⅙ pound)

*SERVES 8 as a soup course*
*6 as a main course*

Prepare the first 7 vegetables listed above so that they are all cut into baby dice or pieces of approximately the same size: peel and dice the potatoes, turnips, carrots and onion. Wash the leeks, trim off ends and cut leeks into baby dice. Cut the zucchini and green beans into small pieces.

Place the diced onion and the 2 tablespoons cooking oil in a large, heavy pot and cook for 2–3 minutes over medium heat until the onion just starts to brown. Add the carrots and turnips, and cook for another minute. Add the water and stock, or water and ½ a bouillon cube (a total of 12 cups liquid), and bring to a boil. Cook another 10 minutes over medium heat. Add the zucchini, green beans, leeks and potatoes. Cook for about 30 minutes.

Meanwhile, peel, squeeze out seeds and water, and chop the tomatoes. (You should have about 2 cups.) Put the tomatoes in a bowl and add the garlic, olive oil, parsley and basil. Mix these ingredients together.

Season the soup with 3 generous pinches salt, 2 pinches pepper. Add the flageolets to the soup; it is not necessary to drain them. Break the spaghetti into halves or thirds and add it to the soup. Cook another 15 minutes. About 2 minutes before serving, add the seasoned tomatoes to the soup.

This soup may be served at room temperature during the summer (not chilled from the refrigerator). It will keep for 2–3 days in the refrigerator, but you must add some water to it when you reheat it, because the vegetables absorb liquid.

4 stalks asparagus (raw or
    cooked)
1 tablespoon butter
1 tablespoon chopped shallots
1½ cups chicken stock
    (p. 221)
2 cups heavy cream
Salt

*SERVES 4*

# ASPARAGUS SOUP
*Soupe d'asperges*

We can now buy asparagus most of the year, so it is easy to prepare
this soup no matter what the season. The texture is velvety and
smooth, and the taste is exquisite. It is not necessary to buy
asparagus all the same size or of the best quality, because only the
taste is important.

Cut the asparagus stalks into large pieces. In a large pot over medium
heat, melt the butter, then add the chopped shallots and cook until just
translucent. Add the asparagus pieces, chicken stock, cream and several
pinches of salt. If you are using cooked asparagus, cook for 10–15
minutes after the liquid comes to a boil; raw asparagus needs longer,
about 20–30 minutes.

Pour the soup into a food processor and process until very smooth, a
little over 1 minute. Serve hot or cold. This soup will keep up to 1 week
in the refrigerator.

1 beef shank (about 3 pounds;
    see Note)
1 whole chicken (at least 3½
    pounds) plus any uncooked
    chicken bones you have;
    necks are particularly good
    (see Note)
2 large onions
½ a whole head of garlic
2 carrots
1 leek
½ stalk of celery with top
2 large onions
A small handful of mushroom
    stems
Green tops of celery root
Parsley stems from a bunch of
    parsley
A few branches of fresh thyme
    or ½ teaspoon dried thyme
2 bay leaves
1 teaspoon salt
6–7 peppercorns
1 whole clove

*YIELD ½ gallon*

# SISTO'S CONSOMMÉ

Consommé is the Rolls-Royce of soups. It is undoubtedly somewhat
complicated to prepare, but I am sure you can make it at home.
Sisto, one of my closest colleagues, wanted to give you this recipe.
By following this procedure carefully you will attain a good result
without too much pain, but you must pay attention to the
clarification.

It is practically impossible to make good consommé in small
quantities. But it keeps well: either a week in the refrigerator or
several weeks in the freezer. You should take the precaution of
bringing it to a boil each time you reheat it.

Wash and rinse the beef shank and chicken 2–3 times to remove any
blood. Place in a large stock pot with cold water to cover the meat by
about 1½ inches, approximately 1 gallon water. Bring to a boil, skimming off the scum that rises to the surface.

Peel the onions, cut in half and sear them on the cut sides so that
they brown. Cut a shallow incision across the half head of garlic cloves
(you do not have to peel them). Peel the carrots. While you are preparing the vegetables, keep an eye on the pot and remove any scum that
comes to the surface. Do this several times and again before you add the
vegetables.

Add all the vegetables, herbs and seasonings to the stock. Let it come to an easy boil over high heat, then cook over low heat for about 4 hours. As fat rises to the top, remove it with a ladle or flat spoon. If the liquid is reduced too much during the cooking, add water to the pot; you should have 1 gallon of stock at the end.

*Note:* Shank is particularly good because it contains marrow. Beef shank cooked in this way is delicious for a winter dinner; eat it boiled, just as it comes from the stock, or sautéed with cornichons and capers. Do *not* use any lamb, pork or game bones, or any liver or kidneys for the stock. Uncooked duck or squab bones or veal bones or scraps, on the other hand, are tasty additions. Do *not* use bones from a cooked chicken, or any cooked chicken remnants; these will diminish the quality of the stock. If you wish poached chicken, the breasts and thighs can be removed from the pot after 30 minutes of cooking.

Strain off ½ gallon of the stock into a large, heavy pot. (Do not use a stainless-steel pot because the egg whites will stick to it. A heavy aluminum pot is fine.) Stock should be warm, but not so hot it will burn your fingers.

Peel the onion, cut in half and sear it on the cut sides. Peel the tomato, squeeze out water and seeds, and chop coarsely. Peel the carrots. Chop or grind together coarsely the carrots, celery and leek leaves. (Do *not* use a food processor for this; you do not want pureed vegetables.) Mix the chopped vegetables with the ground beef and the egg whites. Add the onion halves, the vegetable, meat and egg white mixture, and the bay leaf, parsley and garlic to the stock; bring to just under a boil. Lower the flame and cook over the lowest possible heat. The top will begin to harden, creating a crust. When you see this begin to happen, make a hole in the center of the crust large enough for a small ladle. Using this ladle, dip down and bring up some liquid to pour over the crust. Continue bringing the liquid up and wetting the top of the crust during the cooking period of about 50 minutes.

When the consommé looks clear to you, place a cone-shaped sieve (a chinois) into the hole in the center. (See illustration.) Ladle the liquid that comes into the chinois into a sieve lined with cheesecloth over a bowl or clean pot. Take as much as you can without in any way pressing the solid matter or squeezing it out.

Serve the consommé hot. You may wish to float blanched, julienne carrots or celery, or julienne strips of zucchini in the soup. The consommé and the stock will keep 5–6 days in the refrigerator and may be frozen.

## THE CLARIFICATION

*½ gallon stock*
*1 onion*
*1 large tomato*
*2 carrots*
*2 stalks celery*
*4–5 leek leaves*
*1 pound very lean ground beef*
*8 egg whites*
*1 bay leaf*
*Parsley sprigs*
*1 clove garlic*

*The following three shellfish soups are all based on the same principle. If you are planning a meal with fish, one of these soups would be a good appetizer and easy to prepare.*

# MUSSEL SOUP WITH SAFFRON
*Soupe de moules au safran*

*16 mussels*
*Juice from the cooked mussels*
*½ cup heavy cream*
*1 pinch saffron threads*
*Salt, white pepper*
*Garniture: 2 mussels in their*
  *shells (from above); 2*
  *parsley sprigs; green top of*
  *1 scallion, chopped*

*SERVES 2*

Cook the mussels briefly to open them (see directions p. 103). Open the mussels. Reserve 2 of the shells, with the mussels still attached, for the garniture; discard the remaining shells. Strain the juice from the mussels through a fine sieve or cheesecloth into a saucepan. Add the cream to the pan and bring to a boil over medium heat. Add the saffron, a pinch each of salt and pepper, and let the soup cook, still over medium heat, for about 5 minutes. Add the mussels and cook another 2 minutes.

Ladle the soup into soup plates and garnish with the chopped green scallion top and the 2 reserved mussels in their shells, decorated with the parsley sprigs.

*16 large raw shrimp (and their*
  *shells)*
*4 shallots*
*1 carrot (optional)*
*1 leek (optional)*
*3 tablespoons chopped*
  *scallion (optional)*
*1 tablespoon butter*
*1 tablespoon flour*
*1½ cups white wine*
*4 cups water or light fish stock*
  *(p. 222)*
*Salt, white pepper*
*2 cups heavy cream*
*1 teaspoon oil*

*SERVES 4*

# SHRIMP SOUP
*Soupe de crevettes*

Remove the shrimp from their shells and slice them in half lengthwise (so that you have 2 even curled halves for each shrimp); discard any intestine you may find. Reserve the shells.

Peel and slice the shallots. If you wish to add vegetables, peel and blanch the carrot briefly, then slice it thinly. Wash the leek well and cut it into thin julienne strips, and chop the scallion.

In a medium-size saucepan, sweat the shallots and shrimp shells in the butter for about 1 minute. Add the flour and mix well, but do not let it brown. Add the white wine and water or fish stock, stir two or three times, season lightly with salt and pepper, and bring to a boil. Cook soup, uncovered, over medium-high heat for 30 minutes.

Strain the soup into a clean pot, pressing the shrimp shells and shallots against the strainer with a wooden spoon as you do so; discard shells and shallots. Return soup to heat, add the cream and stir 2 or 3 times with a wooden spoon. Let come to a boil, and cook for another 20–30 minutes, uncovered, over medium-high heat. Several times during the cooking process, spoon off any light film or scum that may form.

Add the vegetables, if desired, 5 minutes or more before the soup is finished.

Brown the shrimp briefly (about 30 seconds on each side), either on a griddle or in a pan with a little oil or under the broiler on a lightly oiled plate.

Add the shrimp to the soup (2 minutes after the vegetables) and cook for another 3 minutes. Season lightly to taste with salt and pepper. Serve immediately.

*Note:* If you wish, you can make this soup up to 2 hours ahead of time, to the point 5 minutes before serving. Add 1–2 tablespoons water or white wine, and reheat over medium heat. Add the vegetables and shrimp as directed above.

# CLAM SOUP
## Soupe de palourdes

Rinse the clams under running water. Put them in a medium-size saucepan with the 1 cup white wine, the water and 2 generous pinches salt. Bring to a boil, cover the pan and cook over high heat for 10 minutes. Peel the garlic cloves and smash them. In a small saucepan, reduce the garlic and cream by ¼ over medium-high heat. Meanwhile, remove the clams from the heat and, as soon as you can handle them, put the clams in a bowl and discard the shells. Some juice will come out of the shells with the clams. Strain this juice through cheesecloth or a coffee filter into the cream while it is cooking. Pour a small amount of white wine onto the clams and mix them around to clean them; discard the wine. Add the leaves stripped from the thyme branches to the clams.

Cut the half zucchini in half lengthwise and slice it finely. Slice the leek leaves diagonally and chop the scallions. Strain the cream into a clean pot (to remove the garlic); add the leek leaves, scallions and cumin. Cook only half a minute longer, then add the clams and thyme. Cook another 20–30 seconds. (If the clams cook too long they will toughen up.) Season with a pinch of white pepper.

Place the zucchini slices in soup plates and pour the soup over them.

*12 hard-shell clams*
*(littlenecks)*
*1 cup white wine plus a little*
*extra*
*1 cup water*
*Salt*
*2 cloves garlic*
*2 cups heavy cream*
*2 branches fresh thyme* or *½*
*tablespoon freshly*
*chopped parsley*
*½ zucchini*
*2 green leek leaves (optional)*
*3 scallions*
*1 generous pinch cumin*
*powder*
*White pepper*

*SERVES 3*

1 Cranshaw melon
2 grapefruit
Grated rind of 1 lime

SERVES 4

# MELON AND GRAPEFRUIT SOUP

*Soupe de melon et pamplemousse*

*This is a beautiful, easy soup for a hot day.*

Cut the melon in half and scoop out the seeds. Peel the melon, quarter it, cut the quarters into pieces and process in a food processor for about 1 minute, until smooth. Peel the grapefruit and cut out thin slices from between the white membranes. Pour the soup into bowls and place the grapefruit slices on top. Sprinkle with grated lime rind.

This soup must be served immediately or it will separate. It should not be kept in the refrigerator because it will absorb flavors.

*Variations:* Sprinkle with a melon liqueur, such as Midori; or grind black pepper on the soup for a completely different taste; or use grated lemon rind instead of the lime. You can also make the soup with cantaloupe or other melons.

2 eggplants
2 teaspoons chopped shallots
1 tablespoon butter
5 cups milk
Salt
1 saffron thread
1 cup heavy cream
Garniture: 5–6 coriander
    leaves, 6–8 saffron threads

SERVES 4

# EGGPLANT SOUP

*Soupe d'aubergine*

*The saffron gives this soup a rich yellow color.*

Peel the eggplants, quarter and cut them into pieces. In a medium-size saucepan, sweat the shallots in the butter until soft but not brown. Add the eggplant pieces and 4 cups of milk. Cook slowly for 20–30 minutes.

Drain the eggplant and milk through a sieve; discard the milk. Put the eggplant in a food processor along with a small pinch of salt and the saffron thread. Process for half a minute or less. Add the remaining cup of milk and the cream, and process until well blended.

Cool to room temperature, then chill in the refrigerator. The flavors will intensify. This soup can be made successfully the day before serving. Garnish with coriander leaves and saffron threads.

# ZUCCHINI SOUP WITH NUTMEG

### Soupe de courgette et noix muscade

*Here is a nice light summer soup that is particularly good if you are on a diet.*

Slice ends off the zucchini and quarter it lengthwise; cut the quarters into pieces, into a saucepan. Add the water and herb of your choice, bring to a boil and cook over medium heat for 10–15 minutes.

Pour the soup into a food processor and season with the nutmeg and a pinch of salt and pepper. Process briefly until you have the consistency you like. The soup is more interesting if it is not absolutely smooth. Chill in the refrigerator, where the soup will keep for 2 days.

Serve soup cold in large, flat soup plates. Place 1 tablespoon cottage cheese or yogurt in the middle of the soup and sprinkle with chopped parsley or chives.

1 medium-size zucchini
2 cups water
4 basil leaves or 4 sprigs of dill or tarragon
¼ teaspoon freshly grated nutmeg or ground nutmeg
Salt, white pepper
2 tablespoons low-fat cottage cheese or plain yogurt
Garniture: *parsley or chives*

**SERVES 2**

# POTATO AND LEEK BASE

### Vichyssoise base

*In France potato and leek soup is called* Potage Parmentier *in honor of the late eighteenth-century French pharmacist who devoted much of his research to agronomy, and especially to the potato. This recipe for the soup is a little more concentrated than usual and can serve as the base for many cold soups. It keeps well—up to 2 weeks in the refrigerator, or you can save it in the freezer in small portions.*

Peel the onion and slice thinly, wash the leeks and cut them into julienne strips. Peel the potatoes and chop them coarsely into large pieces.

In a large pot over medium heat, sweat the onion in the butter until soft but not brown. Add the leeks and potatoes, cook 1 minute, stirring, then add the water and bouillon cubes or the chicken stock. Bring to a boil and cook over medium heat, uncovered, for 30 minutes.

Pour the soup into a food processor and process for about 1 minute, until smooth and well blended. Cool to room temperature, then refrigerate in a covered container.

1 large onion
3 leeks
3 Idaho potatoes (baking potatoes)
1½ tablespoons butter
2 chicken bouillon cubes or 1 tablespoon chicken flavor base
4 cups water (or use chicken stock, p. 221, instead and eliminate the bouillon cubes)

**YIELDS 3½ cups**

3½ cups Potato and Leek
 Base (p. 47)
1 cup heavy cream
1 cup milk
Garniture: chopped chives or
 parsley; or ½ scallion,
 chopped crosswise; or 4
 shrimp

SERVES 4

# VICHYSSOISE

Mix all ingredients except garniture in a food processor until well blended. Strain the soup through a sieve, beating with a whisk to help it along. Chill 4–24 hours.

Before serving, stir the soup with a spoon. Garnish with chopped chives or parsley or scallion.

Shrimp makes a very nice addition to vichyssoise. Remove the shrimp from their shells and cut them in half lengthwise. Grill or sauté them briefly on a griddle or in a frying pan so that they brown a little. Finish cooking in a 400° oven, about 3 minutes.

20–22 red radishes
5 basil leaves
¾ cup Potato and Leek Base
 (p. 47)
2 cups heavy cream
2 cups milk
Salt
A small pinch ground cumin
 (less than ¼ teaspoon)
Garniture: 3 radishes, very
 thinly sliced; parsley

SERVES 6

# PINK RADISH SOUP
### Soupe de radis roses

Trim tops and bottoms off the radishes and remove any brown spots. Chop the basil leaves. Process the radishes in a food processor for about half a minute, until they are finely chopped. Add Potato and Leek Base, basil, cream, milk, a large pinch of salt and the cumin. Blend well together.

Refrigerate soup for at least 2–3 hours. This can be done in the morning for the evening, but not the day before because the radishes, being uncooked, may start to ferment. When it is first made, this soup seems thick, but it thins out as it sits.

Stir the soup before serving. Garnish with very thin slices of radish and chopped parsley sprigs.

2 cucumbers
1½ cups Potato and Leek
 Base (p. 47)
1 cup milk
1 cup heavy cream
Salt
Garniture: ½ slice smoked
 salmon, diced; ½ scallion,
 chopped; cumin

SERVES 4

# CUCUMBER SOUP
### Soupe de concombres

Peel and seed the cucumbers. Process them in a food processor for half a minute, until chopped. Add the Potato and Leek Base, milk, cream and 2 pinches salt, and process until smooth. Chill at least 2–3 hours. Stir with a spoon before serving. Garnish with diced smoked salmon and/or chopped scallion, and a pinch of cumin. This soup may be made up to 2 days before needed.

# *GAZPACHO*
## *Gaspacho*

*This cold soup should be made in the summer when tomatoes have real flavor. It can be done with winter tomatoes, but the color and taste will not be as intense.*

Peel the tomatoes (see illustration on p. 11), reserving peel for tomato-peel roses, if desired. Remove the hard core under the stem and squeeze out the seeds and water. Cut tomatoes into large pieces. Core and seed both green pepper halves, and cut one of them into large pieces. Reserve the other half for the garniture. Peel and seed the cucumber and cut it into thin slices. Peel the shallots and garlic cloves and cut them into large pieces. Cut the scallions into large pieces. Chop the basil and parsley coarsely. Remove the crusts from the bread and cut it into large pieces.

Process the vegetables, basil, parsley and bread in a food processor for about half a minute. Add the remaining ingredients, except garniture, 2 at a time, whirring the blades briefly after each addition.

This soup needs to chill before serving to marry the flavors together. Let it rest in the refrigerator at least 2–3 hours; it can be made the day before serving and will keep for 2 days.

Garnish with very thin slices of green pepper that have been briefly blanched, then rinsed immediately in cold water. If you wish, you might add a tomato-peel rose (p. 11) with a basil leaf tucked under it to each serving.

6 tomatoes
½ green pepper (see
   Garniture)
½ cucumber
2 shallots
2 cloves garlic
2 scallions
6 large basil leaves
2–3 parsley sprigs
2 slices white bread
1 tablespoon red wine vinegar
5 drops Tabasco
¼ generous teaspoon ground
   cumin
1 tablespoon white wine
Grated rind of 1 lime
Salt to taste
3 tablespoons tomato juice
¼ teaspoon Worcestershire
   sauce
⅛ teaspoon curry powder
Garniture: ½ green pepper, 4
   tomato-peel roses, 4 basil
   leaves or parsley

**SERVES 4**

# *STRAWBERRY SOUP*
## *Soupe de fraises*

Clean the strawberries and put them in a food processor with the lemon juice and water. Process briefly, about half a minute. Pass mixture through a fine sieve, but do not press hard against the sieve as you do so. Ladle into large flat soup plates and garnish with one of the following: grated lime or lemon rind; a few cherries or grapes; very thin slices of purple plum or apple or kiwi fruit; rhubarb, peeled and thinly sliced crosswise.

Do not garnish with sweet fruits, such as bananas, peaches, raspberries or blueberries; the soup needs the acidity of the fruits in the list above.

1 pint strawberries
Juice of 1 lemon
¾ cup water
Garniture: *grated lime or
   lemon rind; or cherries or
   grapes; or plum, apple,
   kiwi or rhubarb slices*

**SERVES 4**

2½ pounds fish (sole is good,
   but expensive; monkfish,
   flounder or halibut are all
   good choices; see Note)
2 large onions
5–8 cloves garlic
9 scallions
2 tablespoons oil
A fresh bouquet garni (2
   carrots, 1 stalk celery, a
   handful of parsley, 2
   branches basil, p. 182)
2 tablespoons flour
3 tablespoons tomato paste
2 cups white wine
10 cups fish stock (p. 222)
3 dried bay leaves
Salt, white pepper
6 pieces red snapper (about ¾
   pound)
6 pieces bass (about ¾
   pound)
6 shrimp
1 carrot
1 teaspoon Pastis (anise
   liqueur)
Garniture: saffron threads,
   parsley

**SERVES 6**

# CHILLED BOUILLABAISSE
## Bouillabaisse en gelée

*My adaptation of this classic French soup uses fish that is easily available in the United States. The fish is not poached in the soup, but is steamed separately and then added to the soup. This way the fish is fresher and stays white, which gives a nice contrast to the soup color. There are several different types of fish needed: first the sole or monkfish required for the soup base, then the separately steamed pieces of bass, red snapper, etc. I have given you this recipe as a cold soup, but it is just as good hot.*

*Here is a little story about how bouillabaisse got its name: A long time ago in Marseilles fishermen made fish soup on their boats. They knew that fish must not boil too hard in soup, or it will fall apart. So they taught each other this little phrase, "quand ça bout, tu baisses" (when it boils, turn down the heat), and that is how the name* bouillabaisse *was born.*

Prepare the 2½ pounds fish for the soup base, cutting it into large pieces. Peel the onions and slice thinly, peel the garlic cloves and flatten them. Trim the ends of 3 of the scallions.

In a large, heavy saucepan, cook the onions in the oil over medium-high heat until they just begin to brown. Add the fish pieces and stir vigorously with a wooden spoon. Add the bouquet garni and the 3 scallions, and stir again. Turn up the heat to high, and stir the flour and tomato paste into the pot. The mixture will get dry, and a crust will form on the bottom of the pot. Add the white wine and cook for 2 minutes, stirring continuously. Add the fish stock, bay leaves, 2 generous pinches salt and a generous pinch pepper. Cook over high heat for 30–45 minutes.

Remove the pot from the fire, pull out the bouquet garni and discard it. Scoop the fish and vegetables from the soup with a shallow ladle with holes or with a wire strainer and put them into a food processor. Include all fish bones. Process very briefly, about half a minute. Return the chopped fish and vegetables to the pot, and cook the soup for 5 minutes more over high heat. Put through a fine-meshed sieve into a bowl, pressing with a wooden spoon to help it along.

Cut the red snapper and bass into large pieces. Clean the shrimp and discard the shells. Discard the green tops of the remaining 6 scallions and cut them in half lengthwise. Peel the carrot and cut it into thick slices.

Steam the scallions and carrot briefly, about 5 minutes. Refresh them in cold water. Steam the fish and shrimp for about 10–15 minutes, or until they are cooked through.

Place 4 scallion halves and 2 carrot slices in the bottom of each of 3 large soup plates. Mix a small amount of Pastis into the soup and pour it into the plates. Add the steamed fish and shrimp to the soup, and sprinkle a few threads of saffron and a bit of chopped parsley over each plate. Let the soup cool, then cover with aluminum foil and chill in the refrigerator 6 hours or overnight. Serve cold as a gelée or, if you wish, hot.

*Note:* If you are using monkfish, include tail pieces, bones and the shoulder just below the head. Remove the skin.

# *EGGS*

POACHED IN WHITE WINE
BAKED WITH LETTUCE
CRISPY
STUFFED
ONION OMELETTE

$H$ere are six easy recipes that are good made with duck eggs, pheasant eggs, quail eggs or goose eggs, to name but a few, as well as with the chicken eggs that we can buy easily at the store.

Be careful, however, if you are working with quail eggs; their shell is very hard. If you put too much pressure on the shell in order to crack it, the egg will separate and the yolk may break. Crack the shell by rapping it briskly on a sharp edge.

*About 20–24 snow peas*
*A scant teaspoon oil*
*2 cups white wine*
*½ orange, cut into 3 wedges*
*2 eggs*
*Salt, white pepper (optional)*

**SERVES 2**

# EGGS POACHED IN WHITE WINE
*Oeufs pochés au vin blanc*

Sprinkle the snow peas with a little oil and steam them for about 2 minutes. Put the wine and orange wedges into a saucepan and bring to a boil. Break the eggs into the wine and poach them for about 1½ minutes. The yolk should be soft and runny.

On each plate, arrange about 10–12 snow peas in a circle, like the petals of a flower. Place a poached egg in the middle of each circle and garnish with half of one of the orange wedges. Season with salt and pepper if desired (but not while the eggs are cooking in the wine).

*Note:* If you like your eggs a little better done, cook a half minute or so longer. If you are cooking 4 eggs, you do not need to increase the amount of wine.

*1 full head Boston lettuce or 2*
*    heads Bibb lettuce*
*Salt, herbed pepper*
*1 teaspoon olive oil*
*3½ teaspoons butter*
*2 eggs*
*Pinch nutmeg*
*1 teaspoon butter (optional)*

**SERVES 2**

# BAKED EGGS WITH LETTUCE
*Oeufs aux laitues*

Preheat oven to 350°–400°. Tear the lettuce head or heads apart, and reserve 6 large outer leaves. Season the remaining lettuce with a pinch of salt, herbed pepper and ½ teaspoon olive oil. Cook in a steamer for about 6–8 minutes. Dry the lettuce and puree it in a food processor, along with 3 teaspoons butter, for less than 1 minute.

Season the 6 outer lettuce leaves with salt, herbed pepper and the remaining olive oil, and steam them briefly, for only 10 seconds. Rinse them with cold water, then dry on paper towels. (The oil is important to make the leaves shiny.)

Butter 2 individual soufflé molds. Using 2 of the outer leaves, cover the bottom and sides of one mold so that part of the lettuce overlaps the edges. Spoon half of the pureed lettuce into the mold, and break an egg on top of it. Season the egg to taste with nutmeg, salt and pepper. Cover the egg with a third lettuce leaf and fold the overlapping leaves onto the top. Dot with ½ teaspoon butter, if desired. Repeat with the other mold.

Bake in the oven in a bain-marie containing very hot or boiling water. The water level should reach ⅔ of the way up the molds. Cook for 10–15 minutes to produce very soft-boiled eggs; cook longer if a firmer egg is desired. Serve with toast.

# CRISPY EGGS
## Oeufs croustillants

*2 thin crêpes (p. 184)*
*2 eggs*
*Salt, herbed pepper, white pepper*
*1 tablespoon oil*
*2 thin lemon wedges*

**SERVES 2**

Spread a crêpe out on a plate and break an egg into it. Sprinkle the egg with salt and herbed pepper, and fold up the crêpe around the egg as if you were wrapping a package. (See illustration.) Repeat with the other crêpe and egg.

Heat the oil in a small frying pan. When it is hot, add the crêpes, folded side up; season with salt and white pepper and sauté briefly over medium-high heat, first on one side, then on the other. In order to have the yolks runny, you should only cook the eggs about 2 minutes. Serve each with a thin lemon wedge.

*Note:* If the crêpes have been made some time before, they may be stiff; if so, heat them in the oven for about 1 minute before using.

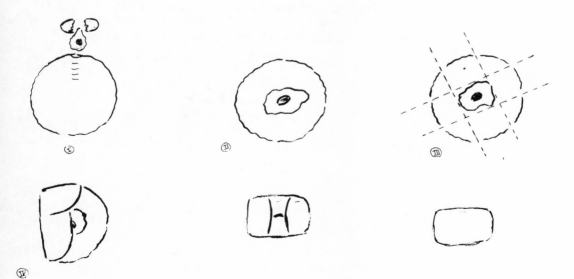

2 hard-boiled eggs
1 shallot
2 teaspoons chopped tomato
½ teaspoon chopped basil
1 large, thin slice smoked
   salmon
2 generous tablespoons
   mayonnaise
Salt, white pepper
8 radicchio leaves
8 endive leaves
Garniture: grated rind of 1
   lime

SERVES 2

# STUFFED EGGS
## Oeufs farcis

Slice the hard-boiled eggs in half lengthwise, remove the yolks and mash them in a bowl with a fork. Chop the shallot very finely and add it to the egg yolks along with the tomato and basil. Cut the smoked salmon into very thin strips. Chop about ⅓ of the salmon strips into very small dice and add to the egg yolk mixture. Add the mayonnaise, and salt and pepper to taste.

Fill the egg white halves with the yolk mixture and decorate each egg half with 2 thin strips of smoked salmon in the shape of a cross. Serve on a salad of 4 radicchio leaves alternating with 4 endive leaves for each serving. Sprinkle grated lime rind over all.

1 large onion
1 tablespoon oil
½ teaspoon sugar
4 eggs
A few drops Worcestershire
   sauce
Salt, white pepper

SERVES 2

# ONION OMELETTE
## Omelette aux oignons

*This very thin omelette is delicious cold, a perfect picnic dish.*

Peel the onion and cut into very thin slices. Heat the oil in an omelette pan, or any similar pan with sloping sides. Cook the onion over medium-high heat in the hot oil until brown, turning occasionally. Toward the end of cooking, add the sugar.

Beat the eggs and season them with the Worcestershire sauce, salt and pepper. Pour the eggs onto the onion, and cook the omelette on both sides. Remove it to a plate, roll it up and serve hot or cold.

# FISH

POACHED FILETS OF
  SOLE
SOLE SOUFFLÉ
FILETS OF SOLE IN
  THE STEAMER
FILETS OF SOLE AND
  SMOKED SALMON

FLOUNDER WITH
  CAPERS AND LEMON
FLOUNDER IN THE
  STEAMER WITH
  CINNAMON
FLOUNDER AND
  POTATOES
FLOUNDER WITH
  SWEET GARLIC

BASS WITH PEPPERS
BASS WITH PASSION
  FRUIT
BASS WITH FRESH
  TOMATOES
BASS IN PUFF PASTRY
BASS COOKED IN TEA
TO COOK A WHOLE
  FISH

SALMON WITH
  HEARTS OF
  ARTICHOKE

SALMON WITH
  ASPARAGUS
RED SNAPPER WITH
  CARROTS
QUICK QUENELLES OF
  RED SNAPPER
OLD-FASHIONED RED
  SNAPPER IN THE
  OVEN
RED SNAPPER WITH
  ANCHOVIES
RED SNAPPER
  RISOTTO

TROUT POACHED IN
  VINEGAR
TROUT STUFFED WITH
  VEGETABLES
SMOKED TROUT
  SALAD

STEAMED SKATE WITH
  ORANGE
SKATE WITH RED
  CABBAGE
SKATE WITH ONIONS

MONKFISH STEW
  WITH ANISE

MONKFISH
  BROCHETTES
MONKFISH
  MASQUERADING AS
  A LITTLE LEG OF
  LAMB

MOLDED RED
  MULLET
RED MULLET COOKED
  IN AN ENVELOPE
RED MULLET
  MEUNIÈRE WITH
  BASIL

BRANDADE OF COD
  MY WAY
COD WITH
  VEGETABLES
COD IN COURT
  BOUILLON WITH
  GARLIC MAYONNAISE

MACKEREL RILLETTES
STEAMED MACKEREL
  ROLLS

BLUEFISH WITH
  PINEAPPLE
BRAISED BLUEFISH

During the years of my early apprenticeship in restaurant kitchens, when I was carefully watching the many activities going on around me, I very quickly found I had a preference for fish.

My two seasons with Charles Berot at L'Escale confirmed and strengthened this feeling. In his cheerful restaurant, designed like the interior of a ship and open to the sparkling Mediterranean, I learned to work with many kinds of fish and appreciate their variety of tastes and textures. Every morning I went down to the docks to help the fishermen bring in their boats, and I admired the fantastic colors of the fish jumping and wriggling in their baskets. I especially liked the wonderfully ugly pink and red scorpion fish with a head resembling a monster appearing out of the abyss.

Charles Berot taught me a great deal about the art of cooking and refined my understanding of fish, but he has been a major influence in my professional life for another reason. He was the first chef in my long years of apprenticeship who introduced me to the idea that a restaurant kitchen could be a happy place. This small, round man with a perpetually amused expression on his amiable face is a Maître Cuisinier of France, he was the head saucier on the *Normandie* and, at L'Escale, he has earned his two stars from the *Guide Michelin.* Yet he runs a kitchen where his staff works together in a cheerful atmosphere, something that at the time was entirely new to me. I have made his philosophy my own.

For me, fish are an invitation to creativity. Their fresh meat is often smooth and satiny with a delicate taste that marries well with almost all the comestibles of nature. I know many people disagree with me, and of course, some few fish are indeed too tough or too smelly, but for me they are the ultimate food that offers unlimited possibilities.

In the United States it is easy to buy fish filets already cleaned and weighed, fresh or frozen, in almost all big supermarkets. But the best way to buy fish is from a fish store known for its fresh fish, where you can look at the whole fish before you buy. Bright and well-formed eyes, shiny scales and bright red gills are all reliable signs of freshness.

### Seven Ways to Cook Fish

1. *Poached:* cooked in a delicate court bouillon that is perfumed with oil and herbs; a whole fish may be cooked in this manner.

If fish is poached in a fish stock *(fumet),* its flavor will be enhanced by the flavor of the stock; if fish is poached in water (with vegetables and seasonings added), the water then becomes stock.

2. *Steamed:* cooked over water that has been seasoned with a little oil and herbs; a good choice of method for those on a diet.

3. *Grilled:* cooked over a wood fire or in the broiler; also a good choice for dieters.

4. *Roasted:* cooked in a frying pan or on a metal plate, with just a little oil or butter.

5. *Baked in the oven:* suitable for cooking fatty fish or fish that are stuffed.

6. *Fried:* cooked in oil, either in a deep-fat fryer or in a frying pan.

7. *Braised:* cooked in a stock, accompanied by vegetables, and finished in the oven.

### *Three Cuts of Fish I Use Most Often* (See illustration)

1. *Steak:* a piece of fish about 3½ inches in diameter and 1 inch thick; bass, salmon and red snapper are most often cut in this way.

2. *Filet:* a boneless piece of fish, more or less the size of the whole fish, that has been removed from the backbone and ribs with a flexible knife.

3. *Escalope:* a thin piece cut from the filet at an angle.

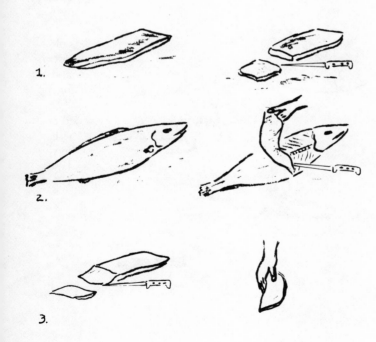

To filet a sole: with scissors trim off the head and half the tail; cut off the bony edges on both sides of the fish. Place the fish on your work surface with the tail toward you. With the point of a flexible knife, scrape the skin from the tail away from you until you have enough skin to hold in your fingers; pull the skin off one side of the fish; turn the fish over and repeat on the other side. With the tail of the fish still toward you, make a vertical cut down the middle of the fish until you come to the horizontal bones. Glide the knife along the top of the bones toward the left side of the fish; cut the filet away from the edge of the fish. Turn the fish around so the tail is away from you and repeat. Turn the fish over and repeat the process on the other side. You will have 4 filets, 2 from each side. Save the bones for fish stock.

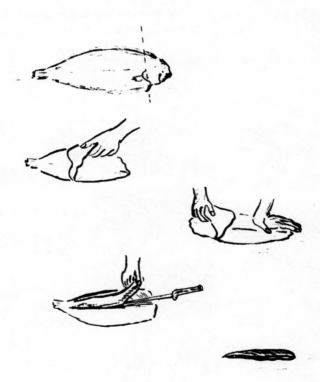

### *Three Ways to Prepare Filets for Cooking* (See illustration)

1. Roll them up and stand them on end. The side of the filet that was attached to the skin should be on the inside because the bone side is moister and more delicate.

2. Trim the long side of each filet so it is uniform, then make shallow, diagonal slashes on the top of each one. (This helps tenderize the fish.) Fold each filet in half end to end, with the dark side of the fish on the inside (for stuffing).

3. Cut each filet into diagonal strips (*gougonettes*).

I have chosen the following forty recipes for twelve different kinds of fish that should not be hard for you to obtain. At the end of most of the recipes you will find suggestions for other fish that will work well with that recipe. For example, I direct your attention to Red Mullet Cooked in an Envelope, p. 84. I know mullet may not always be available, but, as you see, the recipe is adaptable to many different kinds of fish, and it is so easy to prepare that I hope you will try it and want to make it part of your weekly menus.

# POACHED FILETS OF SOLE

*Filets de sole à la nage*

*¾ pound sole filets*
*Salt, herbed pepper*
*½ onion*
*½ carrot*
*¼ zucchini*
*½ leek*
*½ clove garlic*
*½ tomato*
*2 cups fish stock (p. 222)*
*1 cup white wine*
*A bouquet garni made with*
*fresh thyme and basil or ¼*
*teaspoon each dried thyme*
*and basil (p. 182)*
*1 teaspoon green peppercorns*

*SERVES 2*

*Sole, above all Dover sole, is a top-quality fish whose fineness and texture are remarkable. There are innumerable ways to cook sole; many recipes for filets of sole are among the most brilliant in French gastronomy.*

*Poaching in an aromatic mixture of fish stock, wine and herbs is a good way to preserve the delicate taste of many different kinds of fish.*

Lay out the fish filets and sprinkle them with salt and herbed pepper. Roll them up and fasten with toothpicks. Prepare the vegetables: peel the onion and slice very thinly, then separate the slices into rings. Peel the carrot (see *Note*). Slice carrot and zucchini very thinly. Cut the leek in half lengthwise, then cut it into pieces crosswise. Peel and smash the garlic. Cut the tomato into slices (not necessary to peel).

In a medium-size saucepan, put the stock, white wine, vegetables, bouquet garni, peppercorns and 2 pinches of salt. Bring to a boil. Add the rolled filets. Lower the heat to medium and cook for 8–10 minutes. Turn the filets once during the cooking.

Serve the filets in large shallow bowls (or deep plates) with several large spoonfuls of the bouillon and some of the vegetables.

*Note:* I like to shape the carrot and zucchini slices like the petals of a flower. To do this, use a lemon zester (a firm, nonflexible tool that is similar to a vegetable peeler but makes deeper grooves). After you have peeled the carrot, make 4 vertical strokes along it with the lemon zester. Repeat with the zucchini. Then slice the vegetables into very thin slices. (See illustration.)

Bass, red snapper, monkfish and salmon filets are also good choices for poaching.

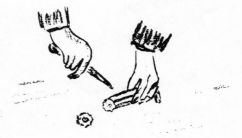

# *SOLE SOUFFLÉ*

*Here is a recipe that is perfect for entertaining. It can be assembled a little bit ahead of time (see* Note *below) and will impress your guests with your ability as a talented* cordon bleu.

Preheat oven to 350°–400°. Cut each sole filet in half lengthwise; you will have 16 pieces. Season with salt and pepper on both sides. Generously butter a metal platter or baking pan. Place 8 of the filets on the pan in pairs, each pair side by side to resemble the shape of the sole. The whiter side of the filets should be facing up. Reserve the other 8 filets. Sweat the shallots in 1 tablespoon butter.

Cut the fresh salmon into large pieces and put it in a food processor with the smoked salmon, scallops, scallion, shallots, basil and parsley. Process for several seconds. Add the whole eggs and cream; process for about 1 minute. (Halfway through, stop the processor and scrape down the sides of the bowl with a rubber spatula.) Turn the blended ingredients into a large bowl.

Whip the egg whites until they are firm, and fold them into the salmon mixture. Spread this preparation on the 4 pairs of filets; cover with the reserved filets. (See illustration.) Brush the egg wash on the filets with a pastry brush (or small flat brush) so that they are well gilded.

Bake in the oven for about 10–15 minutes, or until the soufflé is firm.

Serve with quarters of lemon or lime, or with a small amount of Madras Sauce and/or Lemon Butter Sauce.

*Note:* The sole and soufflé mixture may be prepared and assembled half an hour before cooking and kept in the refrigerator until needed. Flounder filets will also work in this recipe although the taste will not be as delicate.

*4 whole sole, yielding 8 filets*
*Salt, white pepper*
*1 tablespoon chopped shallots*
*1 tablespoon butter plus a*
*little extra*
*1 pound fresh salmon*
*1 thin slice smoked salmon*
*2 cups scallops*
*1 tablespoon chopped scallion*
*1 tablespoon chopped basil*
*1 tablespoon chopped parsley*
*2 whole eggs*
*⅓ cup heavy cream*
*3 egg whites*
*Egg wash (p. 13)*
*Lemon or lime quarters*
*Sauce suggestions: Madras*
*Sauce (p. 235) and/or*
*Lemon Butter Sauce*
*(p. 228)*

*SERVES 4*

# FILETS OF SOLE IN THE STEAMER

*Filets de sole à la vapeur*

¾ *pound sole filets*
*Salt, white pepper*
½ *leek*
½ *carrot*
½ *zucchini*
*1 scallion*
*1 tablespoon chopped tomato*
*1 tablespoon olive oil plus a*
    *few drops*
*4 basil leaves*
*Butter*
*Garniture: lemon slices*

*SERVES 2*

*If you are on a diet, steamed fish filets will give your regimen an air of gastronomy; the filets have very few calories, but the taste is elegant and satisfying.*

Season the filets with salt and white pepper. Wash the leek and slice it crosswise into pieces. Blanch the carrot briefly and slice it thinly. Cut the zucchini in half lengthwise and then slice it. Chop the scallion and the tomato.

Fill the bottom of a steamer with about 6 cups of very hot or boiling water. Bring the water to a boil and add the tablespoon of oil and 2 basil leaves. Lightly butter the perforated top section of the steamer so the fish will not stick. Place the filets on the buttered surface, arrange the vegetables on top of them, and sprinkle with salt, white pepper, the remaining 2 basil leaves chopped finely and a few drops of oil. Cover the steamer and cook for 10–15 minutes. Serve immediately with a few lemon slices on the side.

*Note:* Salmon, cod, bass, red snapper and halibut filets are all good choices for steaming. Red snapper filets will need to be steamed about 5 minutes longer than the sole.

# FILETS OF SOLE AND SMOKED SALMON

*Filets de sole au saumon fumé*

1½ *pounds sole filets*
*Salt, white pepper*
*3 large, thin slices smoked*
    *salmon*
*2 tablespoons white wine*
*1 cup fish stock (p. 222)*
½ *cup light fish velouté*
    *(p. 227)*
½ *cup heavy cream*
*2 tablespoons chopped*
    *scallion*
*1 teaspoon chopped basil*
*1 tablespoon butter, softened*

*SERVES 4*

*The combined flavors of sole and smoked salmon give a very subtle taste. Here is a recipe that offers you a choice of two preparations that will enable you to enjoy the marriage of tastes of these fish. In the first method the filets are baked and served with a wine and cream sauce; this is a perfect dish for entertaining. In the second the rolled filets are simply steamed and served with pieces of lemon.*

Preheat oven to 350°–400°. Cut the filets of sole in half lengthwise. Season them with salt and pepper. Cut the smoked salmon slices into long, thin strips equal in number to the pieces of sole. Reserve any smoked salmon ends or unused pieces. Lay a strip of smoked salmon on each sole filet and roll them up; secure each with a toothpick. Trim off any smoked salmon bits that protrude from the rolls, and reserve.

Pour the white wine and about ½ cup of the fish stock into a baking dish to just cover the bottom. Add the rolled filets and cover the dish with foil. Cook in the oven for 7–10 minutes.

Make the sauce: chop the reserved smoked salmon into small pieces. In a medium-size saucepan, bring the fish velouté, the remaining ½ cup fish stock and the cream to a boil; reduce for about 5–6 minutes. Add the scallion, basil, chopped smoked salmon pieces; season with a generous pinch of salt and white pepper. Drop pieces of the softened butter into the sauce; agitate the pan to incorporate the butter, then ladle the sauce onto plates and place 3 rolled filets on each plate.

*Alternate Method:* Perfume water in the bottom of a steamer with 1 tablespoon oil and 2 basil leaves. Lightly butter the perforated top section of the steamer and place the rolled fish filets in it. Sprinkle chopped smoked salmon pieces, chopped basil and 1 tablespoon olive oil over the fish. Cook for 7–10 minutes and serve with a few lemon slices.

Bass, red snapper, monkfish and even fresh salmon filets are other possibilities for preparation by one of these two methods.

# FLOUNDER WITH CAPERS AND LEMON
### Flounder à la grenobloise

*Flounder belongs to the same family as sole, but it cooks faster. It lends itself well to soufflés or to being stuffed.*

Season the filets with salt and white pepper. Cut the crusts off the bread and cut the slices into cubes. Peel the lemon, cut in half and slice thinly. Chop the basil leaves. Heat 4 tablespoons of the oil in a frying pan until it is very hot. Dump in the bread pieces and shake them over high heat until they are uniformly browned. Drain them in a sieve to remove excess fat. Reserve.

In a clean pan, heat the remaining 1 tablespoon of oil, and when it is hot, add the fish filets. Flounder filets do not take long to cook in hot oil, perhaps 3 minutes in all. Turn them once or twice during the cooking.

Remove the fish to plates or a platter, and discard the oil; wipe out the pan. Heat the lemon slices, capers, basil and vinegar in the pan; finish sauce with the butter and serve over the fish or on the side. Place the croutons in little piles on each plate.

*Note:* If you like more sauce, use 2 tablespoons butter.

You can also prepare this recipe with skate, bass or red snapper.

*¾ pound flounder filets*
*Salt, white pepper*
*2 slices white bread*
*1 lemon*
*3 large basil leaves*
*5 tablespoons oil*
*1 generous tablespoon capers*
*1 teaspoon red wine vinegar*
*1 tablespoon butter, softened*

**SERVES 2**

1 apple
1 lemon
2 cinnamon sticks
1 tablespoon butter plus a
    little extra
¾ pound flounder filets
Salt
Small pinch ground
    cinnamon
Garniture: *chopped parsley,*
    *lemon wedges*

SERVES 2

# FLOUNDER IN THE STEAMER WITH CINNAMON

*Flounder à la vapeur de cannelle*

Peel and core the apple, and cut it into thick slices. Grate the lemon rind and reserve. Fill the bottom of the steamer with hot water, add the cinnamon sticks and 1 tablespoon butter, and bring the water to a boil. Lightly butter the perforated top section of the steamer. Place the apple slices in the steamer and sprinkle them with the grated lemon rind and the juice of the lemon. Cook the apple for 6 minutes; remove from the steamer and keep warm.

Season the fish filets with a pinch of salt and the ground cinnamon. Steam for about 6 minutes.

With a spatula, carefully remove the filets from the steamer and put them on plates. Arrange the apple slices on top and garnish with chopped parsley. Serve with lemon wedges.

*Note:* If you wish a sauce, serve Lemon Butter Sauce (p. 228) on the side.

¾ pound flounder filets
Salt, white pepper
8 small red potatoes
1 large onion
2 cloves garlic
3 tablespoons oil
1 tablespoon butter
2 tablespoons chopped parsley
½ teaspoon paprika
1½ tablespoons sour cream

SERVES 2

# FLOUNDER AND POTATOES

*Flounder aux pommes de terre*

Preheat oven to 350°–400°. Season the fish filets with salt and white pepper. Peel the potatoes and slice them (not too thinly). Peel and slice the onion and garlic into thin slices. Heat the oil in a medium-size frying pan. Add the onion slices, and cook over medium-high heat until they are brown. Add the potatoes and the butter; after a minute or so, add the parsley and garlic, and continue cooking until done.

Meanwhile, brown the filets quickly, either on a griddle with a little oil or under the broiler in a highly oiled metal plate, then sprinkle with paprika and put them in the oven for about 5 minutes to finish cooking.

Remove the potatoes from the pan and pat off any extra oil. Spread them onto plates. Serve the flounder filets on top of the potatoes, garnished with the sour cream.

# FLOUNDER WITH SWEET GARLIC

## Flounder à l'ail doux

*I think you will like this interesting combination of flounder with garlic that has been poached in a light sugar syrup.*

Bring the sugar and water to a boil over medium heat, and add to it 4 unpeeled garlic cloves for each filet you plan to serve. Cook for about 10 minutes. You may do this up to 2 hours ahead of time, in which case simply reheat just before serving.

In a medium-size saucepan, reduce the fish stock and cream with 4 peeled and quartered garlic cloves, salt, white pepper and a few drops of Pastis. Reduce by half. Halfway through the reduction, add ¼ teaspoon of chopped garlic.

Fill the bottom of the steamer with hot water and 3 garlic cloves, crushed but not peeled. Lightly butter the perforated top section of the steamer, and bring the water to a boil. Season the flounder filets with salt and freshly ground black pepper. Spread the remaining 1 teaspoon of the chopped garlic and some chopped parsley on the fish; sprinkle with a few drops of olive oil. Cook the filets in the steamer for about 6 minutes and remove them to plates.

When the fish stock and cream mixture is reduced, finish the sauce with butter, if you wish, and strain it onto the fish. Place half the sweetened garlic cloves on each plate, and top the fish with very small parsley sprigs. Serve with steamed spinach or other green vegetable on a separate side dish.

Sole and monkfish are two other good choices for use in this recipe.

*6 tablespoons sugar*
*1 cup water*
*2 whole heads garlic*
*1 cup fish stock (p. 222)*
*1 cup cream*
*Salt, white pepper*
*2 drops Pastis (anise liqueur)*
*1¼ teaspoons chopped garlic*
*Butter, softened*
*¾ pound flounder filets*
*Freshly ground black pepper*
*Chopped parsley*
*Olive oil*
*Garniture: 2 small parsley sprigs*

***SERVES 2***

¾ pound bass filets
½ red pepper
½ green pepper
1 clove garlic
2 shallots
1 tablespoon oil plus a little
    extra
Salt, white pepper
3 tablespoons white wine
1 tablespoon chopped parsley
Sauce suggestions: ½ cup veal
    stock (p. 219) with 1½
    tablespoons butter and
    chopped fresh herb, or
    Lemon Butter Sauce
    (p. 228)
Garniture: 4 very thin slices of
    pepper (2 green, 2 red)

SERVES 2

# BASS WITH PEPPERS
## Bass aux poivrons

*Sea bass is the king of fish, so it is not surprising that it is expensive. Like red snapper, it should be used for the most delicate recipes.*

Preheat oven to 350°–400°. Cut the filets into large pieces and then in half horizontally so that you have thin slices. Remove the seeds and white sections of the peppers and slice them, then halve the slices. Smash the garlic clove and mince it; slice the shallots.

Heat 1 tablespoon oil in a small frying pan; when it is hot, add the shallots and cook for 1 minute over medium-high heat. Add the peppers, season lightly with salt and pepper, and cook for 2 minutes more, agitating the pan back and forth. Add the garlic and cook for 2 minutes longer. Add the white wine and the parsley, and stir it all around with a wooden spoon. Put the pan in the oven for about 5 minutes.

Season the fish with a generous pinch of salt and pepper, and brown quickly, either on a griddle or in a pan with a little oil or under the broiler on a lightly oiled metal plate. Add the fish pieces to the pan with the peppers and cook for 2 minutes.

Reduce the veal stock, incorporate the butter into it and season with any chopped fresh herb, or prepare Lemon Butter Sauce. Distribute the vegetables onto the plates and place the fish pieces on them. (If the garlic has burned, discard it.) Ladle the sauce over the fish, and garnish with slices of green and red peppers.

¾ pound bass filets
1 cup heavy cream
4 tablespoons white wine
2 passion fruit (see Note)
White pepper, salt
1 tablespoon butter, softened
Garniture: 1 passion fruit, a
    handful of parsley or
    mache

SERVES 2

# BASS WITH PASSION FRUIT
## Bass aux fruits de la passion

Cut the filets in half, and where they are thick, slice them horizontally to make thin pieces. Steam the fish briefly, about 3–4 minutes, until just cooked. Put the cream and white wine in a small pot and reduce it by half over medium heat. Cut the 2 passion fruit in half and scrape the greenish yellow seeds and pulp into a small bowl. Discard the shells and add the seeds and pulp to the cream and wine. Season the sauce with a generous pinch of pepper, very little salt. Drop pieces of the softened butter into the sauce; agitate the pan to incorporate the butter.

Place the bass slices on a plate, slightly overlapping each other, and spoon the sauce over them. Garnish with half a passion fruit, with parsley or mache beside it, and serve with steamed spinach, steamed carrots or potatoes.

Filets of red snapper, monkfish or halibut are also good choices for this recipe.

*Note:* If you cannot get passion fruit, you could substitute thin grapefruit slices or peeled white grapes.

# BASS WITH FRESH TOMATOES
*Bass aux tomates fraîches*

*¾ pound bass filets*
*4 tomatoes*
*1 medium to large onion*
*1 tablespoon butter*
*Salt, white pepper*
*6 tablespoons water*
*Juice of 1 lemon (2 tablespoons)*
*6 stalks fresh thyme or ¼ teaspoon dried thyme*
*¼ teaspoon chopped garlic*
*¼ teaspoon chopped parsley*
**Garniture:** *tomato-peel roses (p. 11)*

**SERVES 2**

Cut the bass filets into large pieces. Blanch or steam the tomatoes briefly; then peel, cut out the hard center, squeeze out the water and seeds. Cut the tomatoes into large slices. Peel the onion and slice thinly.

Let the butter just soften in a medium-size frying pan; add the onion slices, to sweat them, but do not let brown. Add the tomatoes and a generous pinch of salt, a very small pinch of pepper. Cook for about 1 minute over medium heat; pour in the water and lemon juice, and bring to a boil. Pull off the thyme leaves and add them to the pot. Reduce the heat, cover the pot and cook slowly for 5–6 minutes. Halfway through the cooking, add the garlic and parsley.

Salt and pepper the bass filets on both sides and drop them into the tomatoes. Continue to cook over low heat for another 6 minutes. Halfway through, turn the filet pieces over.

Spoon the bass onto plates and surround with the vegetables. Garnish with a tomato-peel rose.

You can also use red snapper, salmon, halibut or monkfish filets for this recipe.

# BASS IN PUFF PASTRY
*Bass en croûte*

¾ *pound bass filets*
*Puff pastry (see* Note *p. 185)*
*Egg wash (p. 13)*
½ *carrot*
½ *zucchini*
2 *basil leaves*
4 *leek leaves (green part only)*
1 *tablespoon oil*
*Salt, white pepper*
2 *tablespoons chopped*
  *scallion*
*Sauce suggestion:* Lemon
  Butter Sauce *(p. 228)*

*SERVES 2*

Preheat oven to 350°–400°. Cut the bass filets horizontally to make thin slices, then cut them on an angle into bite-size pieces. Roll out puff pastry into 2 rectangles, 3½ × 4½ inches. Draw a latticework pattern on the pastry by making diagonal lines with a knife; brush with egg wash. Bake the rectangles in the oven for 15–20 minutes.

Blanch the carrot briefly, then cut it in half lengthwise and slice into thin slices. Slice the zucchini the same way. Chop the basil leaves. Wash the leek leaves and slice them diagonally.

Heat the oil in a medium-size frying pan until it is very hot. Season the fish slices with a pinch of salt and pepper, and sauté them in the hot oil over medium-high heat. After the slices have browned on one side, turn them over and add the carrot, zucchini, leek leaves, scallion and basil. Agitate the pan while the fish and vegetables continue cooking, about 4 minutes in all.

Meanwhile, remove the pastry from the oven and slice the rectangles in half horizontally. Take out and discard the insides of the pastry, leaving only the crust. Return the 4 halves to the oven to dry for a minute or two.

Place the 2 bottom pastry halves on plates and heap the fish and vegetables on them. If desired, ladle 3 tablespoons Lemon Butter Sauce over each filled pastry half, and cover with the pastry lids.

Salmon, flounder and halibut are all good in pastry.

¾ *pound bass filets*
*Salt, white pepper*
4 *tea bags*
1 *cup white wine*
4 *cups hot water*
½ *carrot*
¼ *cucumber*
1 *leek leaf (green part only)*
1½ *lemons*
2 *tablespoons frozen peas*
4 *tablespoons butter, softened*
  *(optional)*

*SERVES 2*

# BASS COOKED IN TEA
*Bass au thé*

Cut each filet into 4 pieces, and season on both sides with salt and pepper. (Do this first so that the fish has time to absorb the salt and pepper.)

Put the tea bags in a medium-size saucepan with the white wine and hot water, and boil for a few minutes. Blanch the carrot, then cut it into thin slices lengthwise. Peel and seed the cucumber, cut it in half and then into slices. Wash the leek leaf and slice it crosswise.

Squeeze the juice of 1 lemon (about 2 tablespoons) over the fish pieces. Remove the tea bags from the saucepan and discard. Put in the ½ lemon, the fish pieces, the carrot, cucumber, leek leaf and peas. Cook over medium-high heat for 5–6 minutes, at just under the boil. The fish will take on a light brown color from the tea. It may be served with just the vegetables, a particularly good way if you are on a diet.

If you wish a sauce, ladle several spoonfuls of the tea into a small pot after you add the fish to the saucepan. Reduce this by half and drop in pieces of the softened butter to finish the sauce, agitating the pan to incorporate the butter. Season with 2 pinches white pepper. Place the vegetables around the fish on 2 plates, and ladle the sauce over the top.

Monkfish and turbot are also good cooked in tea.

# TO COOK A WHOLE FISH

*When you cook a large, whole fish such as bass or salmon in this way, its flesh remains moist and tasty. The same procedure is used for salmon, but the timing is slightly different (see Note).*

Into the body cavity of the bass, sprinkle 2 pinches salt, and add a few stalks of parsley, thyme or basil. Using 5 pieces of string, tie the fish closed in 5 places from below the head to the tail.

Peel the onions and cut into quarters, and cut the carrots into large pieces. It is not necessary to peel the carrots or the garlic cloves. Wash the leeks and cut them into large pieces; cut the white bottom parts in half lengthwise before chopping.

Put all the ingredients in a fish steamer or any pot large enough to hold the whole fish; add the sea salt last. Bring to a boil, then lower the heat to medium and cook slowly (just below the boil) for 10–12 minutes. Let fish rest in the bouillon until it is cold. Reserve in the refrigerator in the liquid until needed; it will keep this way for 5–6 days.

If you plan to eat the fish hot, cook it for 20–25 minutes after it comes to a boil. A smaller fish needs the same cooking time after the boil as a larger one. (The smaller fish will take a shorter time to come to the boil.) Once the fish has poached in the liquid, the liquid becomes a light stock. You can reduce it, strain it and reserve for another use.

*Note:* For cold salmon, cook 6–8 minutes after it comes to a boil, for hot salmon, 18 minutes.

*1 7-pound bass*
*Salt*
*A few sprigs of fresh parsley,*
   *basil or thyme*
*2 large onions*
*2 large carrots*
*6 cloves garlic*
*2 leeks*
*6 cups white wine*
*Water to cover the fish*
   *entirely*
*A handful of peppercorns*
*1 tablespoon wine vinegar*
*3 tablespoons sea salt*

**SERVES 8–10**

*Salmon is often poached whole for grand occasions. (See p. 71) for directions on how to cook a whole fish.) Here are two quick recipes for filets of salmon.*

# SALMON WITH HEARTS OF ARTICHOKE
*Saumon aux coeurs d'artichauts*

¾ pound salmon filets
3 artichokes
1 tomato
½ cup champagne (or white wine)
1 cup heavy cream
Salt, white pepper
2 tablespoons chopped scallion
1 teaspoon oil
2½ tablespoons chopped parsley
1 tablespoon butter, softened

SERVES 2

Preheat oven to 400°. Cut the salmon into 4 slices. Cook the artichokes according to directions on p. 154. Drain, and refresh them in cold water. Remove the leaves and cut out the chokes. Cut off the stem ends. Slice the artichoke bottoms into thin slices, 3 slices from each bottom. Using a small heart-shaped cookie cutter (2 inches across at the widest point, 2 inches long), cut each artichoke slice into a heart shape. Peel the tomato, squeeze out water and seeds, and chop into small pieces.

In a medium-size saucepan, reduce the champagne and cream by half over medium-high heat. Halfway through the reduction, add 2 pinches salt and 1 pinch pepper; add the chopped scallion and tomato.

Heat the oil in a small frying pan, and when it is hot, add the artichoke hearts. Sauté them for about 2–3 minutes, until they are brown on both sides. Remove them to a plate lined with a paper towel or a tea towel to draw out the fat. Pat the tops with the towel also.

Brown quickly, either on a griddle with a little oil or under the broiler on a lightly oiled metal plate. Finish cooking the salmon slices in the oven for 2 minutes.

Add 1 tablespoon of the chopped parsley to the sauce. Drop in pieces of the softened butter, agitating the pan to incorporate the butter. Spoon the sauce onto 2 large plates; add the salmon slices and the artichoke heart slices. Garnish each salmon slice with 1 teaspoon chopped parsley.

1½ pounds fresh salmon filets
16 cooked asparagus spears
1 carrot
½ cup fish velouté (p. 227)
1 cup heavy cream
2 tablespoons white wine
Oil
2½ tablespoons butter, softened
Salt, white pepper
Garniture: chopped parsley

SERVES 4

# SALMON WITH ASPARAGUS
*Saumon aux asperges*

Cut the salmon filets into 8 thin slices. Cut the tips off the asparagus (they should be about 2½–3 inches long) and reserve. Chop the remaining asparagus stalks into pieces. Peel the carrot, then with the peeler make 4 long strips. Put the chopped asparagus pieces, fish velouté, cream and wine into a medium-size saucepan, and bring to a boil. Reduce for 5–8 minutes over medium heat. Halfway through the cooking, add the carrot strips.

Brown them quickly, either on a griddle with a little oil or under the broiler on a lightly oiled metal plate. Turn them once; they should cook no more than 1½ minutes. Keep warm.

In a frying pan, quickly sauté the asparagus tips in 1 tablespoon of the butter. Remove the carrot strips from the sauce and pat them dry with a paper towel. Lay 4 asparagus tips together and wrap a carrot strip around them so that you make a little package. Repeat with the remaining asparagus and distribute the asparagus packages onto 4 plates.

Pour the velouté, cream and asparagus pieces into a food processor, and whirr briefly, about half a minute or less. Pour the sauce through a fine-meshed strainer back into the saucepan. Reheat. Season with a pinch of salt and pepper. Drop the remaining 1½ tablespoons softened butter into the sauce in pieces; agitate the pan to incorporate the butter. Put 2 salmon slices on each plate and ladle the sauce over them. Sprinkle with chopped parsley.

This spring recipe is also good made with filets of bass, red snapper, turbot, Dover sole, halibut or monkfish.

# RED SNAPPER WITH CARROTS
*Red snapper aux carottes*

*Red snapper is a delicate fish with a quality equal to that of bass. Its neutral taste makes it adaptable to many different sauces and preparations. Many cooks find it similar to red mullet, but I think the two fish are completely different.*

Cut the skin off the filets and cut them into several pieces. Season them on both sides with salt and pepper. Peel the carrots and cut them into thin slices on the bias (a mandoline is best for this). Cook them in boiling, salted water for 6 minutes, then refresh the slices under cold water. Drain. Cut off the lemon rind and section out thin lemon wedges from between the white membranes.

You will need 2 small- to medium-size frying pans. Heat the oil and 1 teaspoon butter in one pan, and when it is hot, put in the fish filets. Heat 1 tablespoon butter in the other pan. When the butter is melted, add the carrots and season them with a pinch of salt and pepper.

Turn the fish carefully after about 2 minutes' cooking over medium-high heat. The fish filets should cook for about 4–5 minutes; turn them several times. About 1 minute after the carrots begin to cook (over high heat), add the garlic and parsley; shake the pan well and let carrots cook another 2 minutes, approximately.

Remove the fish to a plate and wipe out the pan. Add about 1½ tablespoons butter to the pan, then the lemon juice and the lemon slices. Arrange the carrots on the plates and place the fish on top of them; pour the lemon sauce over the fish.

Other possible fish here are bass, monkfish or halibut.

*¾ pound red snapper filets*
*Salt, white pepper*
*2 carrots*
*1 whole lemon plus 2*
  *tablespoons lemon juice*
*1 tablespoon oil*
*3 tablespoons butter*
*¼ teaspoon chopped garlic*
*2 tablespoons chopped parsley*

**SERVES 2**

*¾ pound red snapper filets*
*2 shallots*
*1 teaspoon butter*
*1 whole egg*
*½ cup heavy cream*
*Salt, white pepper*
*3 cups fish stock (p. 222)*
*2 egg whites*
*Sauce suggestion: Lobster*
  *Sauce (p. 234)*

*SERVES 2*

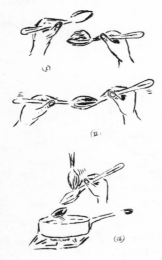

# QUICK QUENELLES OF RED SNAPPER
*Quenelles minutes de red snapper*

Remove the skin from the red snapper filets and cut them into chunks, about 14 pieces. Dice the shallots, then sweat them in the butter briefly. Put the fish and sweated shallots in a food processor and puree for about half a minute. Add the whole egg, cream, 2 pinches salt and 1 pinch pepper, briefly running the processor after each addition.

With a rubber spatula, remove the fish puree to a fine-meshed wire strainer. Rub it through the strainer with the spatula. Scrape it off the other side of the strainer into a bowl. (You will have about 1½ cups.)

In a medium-size saucepan, bring the fish stock to a boil, then lower the heat to just under the boil, so that the liquid is just quivering.

Beat the egg whites into the fish puree with a whisk, making sure they are fully incorporated. Bring the bowl of fish puree and 2 dessert spoons over to the stove. Scoop up a spoonful of the puree on one spoon, then place the other spoon on top to form the puree into a neat oval shape. Drop it gently into the stock. (See illustration.) Repeat until you have 8 quenelles.

Cook the quenelles gently. When they rise to the surface, one side is done; gently turn them over and cook another 4 minutes. When they are done, the quenelles will be soft but firm to the touch of your finger. Remove the quenelles to a platter lined with a paper towel or a tea towel. (You can strain the stock and save it for another time.) Serve with Lobster Sauce, accompanied by steamed spinach, snow peas or a puree of vegetables.

*1 whole red snapper (about*
  *1½ pounds, head and tail*
  *on)*
*Salt, white pepper*
*Fresh basil, thyme or parsley*
  *leaves*
*Flour*
*1 leek*
*Several parsley sprigs*
*3–4 shallots*
*½ carrot*
*1 tablespoon oil*
*1½ teaspoons butter*
*3 tablespoons white wine*
*1½ tablespoons butter,*
  *softened (optional)*

*SERVES 2*

# OLD-FASHIONED RED SNAPPER IN THE OVEN
*Red snapper à l'ancienne au four*

Preheat oven to 350°–400°. With a sharp knife, make 4 shallow diagonal slices (2 one way, 2 the other) on each side of the red snapper. Salt and pepper both sides of the fish and the body cavity. Place a few leaves of the fresh herb of your choice in the cavity. Flour the fish lightly. Wash the leek and cut it in half; tie it with the parsley sprigs to make a bouquet garni (p. 182). Peel the shallots and the carrot, and cut the carrot into large pieces.

Heat 1 tablespoon oil in a baking pan large enough in which to lay the fish flat. When oil is very hot, add the fish and cook it for about 1 minute over high heat, until it browns on one side. Add the shallots, carrot and bouquet garni, shake the pan vigorously and put in the oven for 20 minutes. Halfway through this cooking time, turn fish once and dot top of fish with the 1½ teaspoons butter.

When done, lift the fish onto a platter. Pour out any fat remaining in the pan (but keep the vegetables), and deglaze the pan with the white wine. If you wish, finish the sauce by dropping pieces of the softened butter into the wine; agitate the pan to incorporate the butter.

To serve, lift pieces of the snapper off the backbone from first one side of the fish, then the other, and place on plates. Discard the bouquet garni and pour the sauce and vegetables over and around the fish.

You can cook bass, monkfish and halibut in this manner.

# RED SNAPPER WITH ANCHOVIES
*Red snapper grillé aux anchois*

Preheat broiler. Brown the fish quickly, just enough to color, either on a griddle with a little oil or in a heavy frying pan. Transfer to a metal plate, season with salt and pepper, and dot with ½ teaspoon butter. Place filets under the broiler for 4–5 minutes.

Chop the anchovy filets very finely. Put them in a bowl with 2 tablespoons softened butter, a pinch of pepper and the garlic, if desired. Mash all together until well incorporated. A pestle is a good tool for this.

Remove the fish filets to plates and spread the anchovy butter over them. Serve with 2 small boiled potatoes or ½ a baked potato on each plate.

*Note:* Red snapper is not a very firm fish; therefore, it needs the brief browning on top of the stove before it goes into the broiler to prevent the flesh from falling apart.

You might like to decorate the filets just before serving, by heating the end of a metal rod in a flame for about 2 minutes, then laying it across the fish to form a lattice pattern.

Bass, salmon or halibut filets are good choices for use with this recipe.

*¾ pound red snapper filets*
*Oil*
*Salt, white pepper*
*2 tablespoons softened butter,*
*    plus ½ teaspoon*
*6 anchovy filets*
*¼ teaspoon garlic (optional)*
*Garniture: 4 small boiled*
*    potatoes in their skins*
*    or 1 baked potato*

**SERVES 2**

# RED SNAPPER RISOTTO

¾ pound red snapper filets
Salt, white pepper
2 shallots
1 clove garlic
½ cup white wine
1 cup heavy cream
½ zucchini
Fresh thyme leaves (from 2
    sprigs) or ¼ teaspoon dried
    thyme
Oil
1½ cups cooked white rice
Grated rind of 1 orange and 1
    lime

SERVES 2

Preheat oven to 400°. Cut the filets in half so there are 2 pieces for each person; season with salt on both sides. Dice the shallots and smash the garlic clove, then chop it very finely. Put shallots and garlic in a saucepan with the wine and cream, and reduce by ⅓. Halfway through the reduction, add the zucchini, very thinly sliced, the thyme, and a pinch of salt and pepper.

Oil the fish filets and brown them quickly, either on a griddle or under the broiler on a lightly oiled metal plate. Season with salt and pepper and place them on a metal plate in the oven for 4–5 minutes.

Dump the rice into the sauce and season with salt and pepper. Ladle it onto plates, letting it run to the edges, lay the fish on the rice. Sprinkle the grated orange and lime rind over the fish.

Monkfish, bass and salmon are also good in this risotto.

*Trout is the princess of freshwater fish, as fishermen everywhere will be quick to agree. It is often served simply floured and sautéed (meunière), or sautéed with almonds (amandine), or in a boiling vinegar court bouillon. Here are three recipes for trout that I think you will find a little different.*

# TROUT POACHED IN VINEGAR
*Truite pochée au vinaigre*

2 whole trout
½ large onion
1 medium-sized carrot
¾ cup red wine vinegar
1 tablespoon green
    peppercorns
A fresh bouquet garni of basil,
    parsley and thyme (if
    available; p. 182)
Sea salt
2 slices white bread
4 tablespoons oil
2 eggs
Freshly ground black pepper
Garniture: parsley sprigs, 1
    lime

SERVES 2

Puncture a small hole in the tail of a trout, insert the tail into the mouth and secure with a toothpick. (You may find this difficult; if so, use a metal brochette.) Repeat with second fish.

Peel the onion and slice into thin slices. Peel the carrot, and slice it thinly crosswise. (See *Note* p. 62 to cut the carrot slices in the shape of a flower petal.) Bring 8 cups water to boil in a large saucepan along with the onion, carrot, vinegar, peppercorns, bouquet garni and 1 generous teaspoon sea salt.

Cut off the bread crusts and cut each slice into 2 triangles. Sauté triangles quickly in hot oil until brown on both sides. Reserve on a towel.

Place the trout into boiling water; when it returns to the boil, cook fish for about 6 minutes over medium-high heat. Then turn the trout over and break the eggs into the water.

After 2 more minutes, remove the trout to a platter on which you have placed a towel. Lift out the poached eggs, place one in the curl of each tail and grind some black pepper onto them. Spoon the carrots and onions over the fish, and serve with toast triangles, sprigs of parsley and lime halves.

# TROUT STUFFED WITH VEGETABLES
*Truite farcie aux légumes*

Preheat oven to 350°–400°. Cut the trout through the back to remove the backbone and the dorsal fin. The fish will still be attached at the head and the tail. (I like to serve trout with the head and tail on, but it is not necessary, so remove them if you wish.) Heat the oil; when it is hot, add 1 tablespoon of the shallots, the garlic, basil and scallion, then the julienne vegetables. Season with a pinch of salt and pepper and sweat them for 5–6 minutes over medium heat.

Generously butter a baking pan and place the trout in it. Season the insides of the trout with a pinch of salt and a few grindings of black pepper. Spoon the vegetables onto one side of each trout and fold the other side over on top. Pour 1 cup cream and ¾ cup wine around the fish, and sprinkle the remaining chopped shallots into the liquid. Salt and pepper the outside of the trout. Cover the pan with a buttered rectangle of aluminum foil or parchment paper. Bring the liquid to a boil on top of the stove, then cook fish in the oven for 15 minutes.

Carefully lift the trout onto plates with a long spatula. (You may want to scrape off the skin from the tops of the trout for a more attractive presentation.) Pour the cream and wine through a strainer into a clean pot. Rinse the pan in which the fish were cooked with the remaining 2 tablespoons each of cream and wine, and strain into the pot. Add the port, if desired, and the chopped parsley, and season with salt and pepper. Reduce. Finish sauce with butter, if desired, and pour it over and around the trout. Serve with steamed spinach or snow peas on the side.

Mackerel or salmon trout are other possibilities.

*2 whole trout*
*1 tablespoon oil*
*2 tablespoons chopped shallots*
*¼ teaspoon chopped garlic*
*1 teaspoon chopped fresh basil*
*1 tablespoon chopped scallion*
*1 generous cup julienne carrots, leeks and zucchini*
*Salt, white pepper*
*Butter*
*Freshly ground black pepper*
*1 cup heavy cream plus 2 tablespoons*
*¾ cup white wine plus 2 tablespoons*
*1 tablespoon port (optional)*
*1 tablespoon chopped parsley*
*1½ tablespoons butter, softened (optional)*

*SERVES 2*

# SMOKED TROUT SALAD
*Salade de truite fumée*

1 pair smoked trout filets
4 very small red potatoes
1 tablespoon red wine vinegar
1 tablespoon imported French
    mustard
Freshly ground black pepper
4 tablespoons olive oil
1 tablespoon chopped scallion
1 generous teaspoon chopped
    shallots
¼ teaspoon garlic (optional)
1 tablespoon chopped parsley
1 teaspoon chopped fresh
    thyme or chopped fresh
    basil
Lettuce for salad: Boston,
    radicchio

SERVES 2

Cut the trout filets in half lengthwise.

Cook the potatoes; do not peel them. Cut them into slices. Mix the vinegar with the mustard, and season with a few grinds of black pepper. Whisk in the olive oil. Add the scallion, shallots, garlic, parsley and thyme. Put the potato slices into the dressing to marinate for a minute or two.

Arrange the Boston lettuce and radicchio leaves on each plate so that there are 3 leaves of each, alternating. Spoon the potatoes and sauce into the middle. Lay 2 pieces of trout on top of the potatoes on each plate.

*Skate is less popular than other more well-known fish, but I hope you will try it. It is sold in wings, which may be already skinned. If you cannot find skate, look at the end of each recipe for other fish suggestions.*

1 pound skate
1 orange
½ lemon
5–6 fresh coriander leaves
Butter
Salt, white pepper
Garniture: orange zest

SERVES 2

# STEAMED SKATE WITH ORANGE
*Raie à la vapeur d'orange*

Remove the skin from both sides of the fish and separate the meat from the bone so that you have 2 filets.

Put hot water in the bottom half of a steamer. With a vegetable peeler, cut the skin off the orange in thin strips, and reserve. Cut the orange in half, squeeze the juice into the water in the steamer and add the squeezed orange halves, the lemon and 3–4 coriander leaves. Butter the perforated top section of the steamer and bring the water to a boil.

Cut 2–3 strips of orange peel into thin julienne strips. Season the filets with salt and pepper. Place a few orange strips and a coriander leaf on each filet, and place the filets in the top part of the steamer.

Cook the fish in the steamer for about 10 minutes. Lift the filets out of the steamer carefully, so as to keep them in one piece. Discard orange strips and coriander leaves. Serve with white rice or a puree of potatoes, steamed vegetables or spinach. Garnish with additional julienne strips of orange peel.

Many fish are nice simply steamed in this manner, for example, bass, red snapper, salmon, sole, flounder, etc.

# SKATE WITH RED CABBAGE
*Raie au chou rouge*

*1–1½ pounds skate (1 wing)*
*½ red cabbage*
*1 tablespoon chopped shallots*
*1 tablespoon butter*
*1 cup red wine vinegar*
*Salt, white pepper*
*2 tablespoons oil*
*Lemon wedges*
*Sauce suggestions: veal stock,*
*reduced (p. 219) or*
*Lemon Butter Sauce*
*(p. 228)*

*SERVES 2–3*

Preheat oven to 350°–400°. Trim the skate by removing the dark skin from the top and the white skin from the bottom of the fish. Cut the red cabbage into quarters across, instead of along the length, so that the center white core is evenly distributed among the slices.

Sweat the shallots in the butter in a medium-size saucepan and add the cabbage. Cook over medium-high heat for less than 1 minute, stirring with a wooden spoon. Add the vinegar and a pinch of salt and pepper; mix again and bring to a boil. Cover the pan and cook the cabbage over medium-high heat for about 6 minutes. Then drain and keep it warm.

Heat the oil in a frying pan until it is very hot. Season the skate with salt and pepper; then, using tongs, add it to the hot oil. Start with the thin side down (the side of the fish that had the white skin). Brown for about 2 minutes, then turn fish over and continue cooking over high heat until the skate is crispy, about 3 minutes. Remove the pan to oven for 8–10 minutes.

When the fish is done, pat off any fat with a towel. Spoon the cabbage onto the plates and place the fish pieces on top with a lemon wedge on the side. If you would like a sauce, reduced veal stock or Lemon Butter Sauce is a good choice.

Use halibut or monkfish if skate is not available.

1 pound skate
3 large onions
¾ cup oil plus 1 tablespoon
Paprika
Salt, white pepper
1 teaspoon sugar
½ teaspoon chopped garlic
2 tablespoons chopped parsley
1 tablespoon chopped basil
Juice of 1 lemon
1 tablespoon capers
A few drops Tabasco

SERVES 2

# SKATE WITH ONIONS
## Raie au confit d'oignons

Preheat oven to 350°–400°. Remove the skin from both sides of the skate, and separate each half of the fish from its center bone by gliding a sharp, flexible knife between the fish and the bone. Cut the filets into big pieces.

Peel the onions and slice very thinly. Heat the ¾ cup oil in a large frying pan over very high heat until the oil is very hot. Dump in the onions and shake the pan to agitate them (or mix with a wooden spoon if you prefer not to shake the pan). Season the onions with 2 pinches paprika, 2 pinches salt and a pinch of pepper, and cook over high heat for 20–30 minutes. Shake the pan occasionally. In the middle of the cooking, add the sugar, and near the end, add the garlic, parsley and basil.

In another pan, heat the 1 tablespoon oil until it is very hot. Season the fish with a pinch of salt and pepper, and then cook it very briefly over high heat, about 30 seconds on each side. Remove the pan to the oven for 6–10 minutes.

When the onions are cooked, pour them into a colander to drain off the extra fat. Squeeze the lemon juice into a small pot and add the capers and Tabasco to it. Reduce liquid a little. Pile the onions onto 2 plates, put the fish pieces on top and pour the lemon juice over them.

Halibut, monkfish, bass and red snapper are some other fish that would be good in this recipe.

¾ pound monkfish filets
2 shallots
1 small carrot
1 small zucchini
1 tablespoon butter
1 teaspoon flour
1 cup heavy cream
4 tablespoons white wine
6 tablespoons fish stock
    (p. 222) or any white stock
Salt, white pepper
1 tablespoon Pastis (anise
    liqueur)
Hot cooked white rice
Garniture: 1–2 dill sprigs

SERVES 2

# MONKFISH STEW WITH ANISE
## Blanquette de lotte à l'anis

Monkfish (lotte) is almost a universal fish that can be found in many different countries; it marries well with meat sauces or with highly seasoned sauces. Its flesh contains more water than that of most fish, so to make the fish crispy, start it cooking in a very hot pan with very hot oil so that it does not boil in its own juice.

Trim off any dark skin or bloody parts from the monkfish filets. Cut each filet into 6 pieces. Dice the shallots. Peel and blanch the carrot. Carve the carrot and zucchini into 6 oval pieces each.

Melt the butter in a medium-size saucepan. When it is very hot, add the fish pieces and the shallots. Cook for about 1 minute over medium-high heat, until fish begins to turn white, mixing it around in the butter with a wooden spoon.

Add the flour, cream, zucchini, carrot, white wine and stock. Season with 2 pinches salt, 1 pinch pepper. Cook for about 2 minutes longer, then turn the fish pieces over with tongs. Cook another 2 minutes, then add the Pastis. Cook for about 1 more minute; the total cooking time for the stew is 8–10 minutes.

Serve in wide soup bowls over hot cooked white rice. Place the fish pieces on the rice and pour the sauce and vegetables over them. Sprinkle with chopped dill.

# MONKFISH BROCHETTES
## Lotte en brochette

*Here is a simple recipe for monkfish that would do well on an outdoor barbecue in the summer.*

Preheat oven to 350°–400°, or preheat broiler. Trim the monkfish filets and cut them into chunks (about 6 for each brochette). Remove the core and seeds from the peppers and cut them into chunks; peel the onion and cut it and the tomato, lemon and lime into chunks.

Thread the fish, vegetables and citrus onto 2 brochettes, placing a piece of lemon or lime next to each fish piece. Season with 2 pinches salt and a pinch of pepper. Pat all over with oil.

Brown brochettes briefly, about 1 minute, either on a griddle or under the broiler. Remove them to a metal plate and sprinkle them with paprika and a few drops of olive oil. Finish brochettes in the oven for 6–8 minutes, turning them once, or under the broiler, about 3 minutes on each side. Serve with wedges of lemon or either Tartare Sauce (p. 237) or Hollandaise (p. 229). Garnish with fresh thyme.

*Note:* If you are doing the brochettes on an outdoor grill, season with the paprika and olive oil before putting them on the grill.

Other suitable fish for brochettes are bass, red snapper and salmon.

*¾ pound monkfish filets*
*1 green pepper*
*1 red pepper (sweet)*
*1 onion*
*1 tomato*
*⅓ lemon*
*½ lime*
*Salt, white pepper or herbed*
*    pepper*
*Oil*
*Paprika*
*A few drops olive oil*
*Garniture: 4 fresh thyme*
*    sprigs*

*SERVES 2*

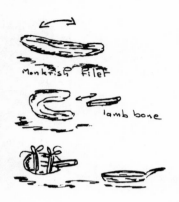

# *MONKFISH MASQUERADING AS A LITTLE LEG OF LAMB*
*Gigot de lotte au jus d'agneau*

*This combination of lamb juice and monkfish is unusual, as is its somewhat fanciful presentation. You need to ask your butcher for lamb bones and scraps.*

½ carrot
½ onion
2 tablespoons oil
About 1 pound lamb scraps
1 generous teaspoon tomato
    paste
1 tablespoon flour
¾ pound monkfish filets
Freshly ground black pepper
1 shallot
1 large basil leaf
A few drops olive oil
2 small bone ends of 2 rib
    lamb chops
½ cup white wine
1½ cups water
Salt, white pepper

**SERVES 2**

Preheat oven to 400°. Make the lamb juice first: peel the carrot and onion, and cut them into large pieces. Put 1 tablespoon oil in a medium-size frying pan over high heat and let it get very hot. Add the lamb scraps, onion and carrot, and cook quickly, still over very high heat, for about 2 minutes. Shake the pan back and forth a few times. Add the tomato paste and flour, mix them in quickly, and after another minute's cooking, transfer the pan to the oven for about 15 minutes.

Trim the monkfish filets and make an incision lengthwise so that each filet lies flat. You may want to make several shallow side incisions also. Season with several grinds of black pepper. Chop the shallot and basil, and sprinkle them over the fish along with a few drops of olive oil. Fold the filets over once (end to end) and tie them in 4 places. Insert a small rib lamb chop bone in the open end of each filet before you tie the final string.

Heat the remaining 1 tablespoon oil in another medium-size frying pan, and when it is very hot, add the monkfish filets. Cook them for about 3 minutes over high heat, turning once, then put them in the oven for about 15 minutes.

Remove the pan with the lamb and vegetables from the oven and pour off the fat. Return the pan to top of stove, over high heat, and pour in the wine and water. Cook, uncovered, over high heat until liquid is reduced by half. Strain the sauce through a sieve into a clean pot, reduce it again a little, and season with salt and pepper.

Remove the fish from the oven and cut away the strings. Decorate the chop bones with little paper hats and place the fish on plates. Ladle the sauce over the fish and serve with baked or sautéed potatoes, or spicy rice, or green vegetable.

*Red mullet (rouget) is the finest fish in the south of France. It has a
delicate, intense flavor and an attractive red skin. Mediterranean
mullet are small; 2 filets make a serving. The Atlantic red mullet
from Brittany that is imported into the United States is larger, so
only 1 filet is needed per serving. Country cooks in France call red
mullet the woodcock of the sea.*

# MOLDED RED MULLET
## Chartreuse de rouget

*You could use red snapper or bass filets for this recipe, with other
vegetables cut into julienne strips, but I like it best with cabbage
and rouget.*

Preheat oven to 350°. Slice the cabbage and blanch it briefly, about
half a minute, in boiling water. Peel the carrots and cook whole, in
boiling water, for 3–5 minutes. Refresh them under cold water and
slice them crosswise in thin slices.

Butter 4 individual soufflé molds that are about 3 inches in diameter.
Line the sides and bottoms of the molds with the mullet filets, trimming
them to fill the space completely. (See illustration.) Season the fish with
a pinch of salt and white pepper.

Cut the blanched cabbage slices into smaller pieces and place a small
amount in the center of each mold. Put about 1 tablespoon or more of
the sliced carrots on the top of the cabbage in each mold, then add more
cabbage, about 3 tablespoons in all. Season with a pinch of salt and
white pepper, and sprinkle ¼ teaspoon of gelatin in each mold, then 3
tablespoons fish stock. (The very best would be mullet stock.) Add a very
small pinch of crushed juniper berries.

Cover each mold with buttered aluminum foil. Press the foil down
over the sides. Place molds in a pan filled with very hot water (a bain-
marie). The water level should come over halfway to the top of the
molds. Cook in the oven for 20 minutes.

Remove the molds from the pan and let them rest at room temperature until they are cool. Refrigerate them for about 6 hours. To
serve, run a knife around the edges to loosen the chartreuses, and
unmold them onto plates. Serve with Fresh Tomato Sauce.

*Variation:* Serve the chartreuses hot. Omit the gelatin. After removing
the molds from the hot water, pour off the juice from each one into a
small pan. Reduce the juice by half over medium heat. Add 1–2
tablespoons softened butter and swirl it around in the pan until it is
incorporated. Unmold the fish and vegetables onto plates and pour the
juice over them.

½ head green cabbage
1–2 carrots
2 teaspoons butter plus a little
   extra
1½ pounds red mullet filets
Salt, white pepper
1 teaspoon unflavored gelatin
1 cup fish stock (p. 222)
⅓ teaspoon crushed juniper
   berries
Sauce suggestion: *Fresh
   Tomato Sauce (p. 239)*

***SERVES 4***

2 carrots
2 zucchini
2 leeks
2 tomatoes
10 basil leaves or 4–5 dill
    sprigs or leaves from 3
    branches tarragon
4 mushroom caps (optional)
1½ pounds red mullet filets
Salt, white pepper
4 tablespoons olive oil
4 tablespoons white wine

**SERVES 4**

# RED MULLET COOKED IN AN ENVELOPE
### Papillote de rouget

*I often serve fish cooked this way at the restaurant. The delicately steamed fish and vegetables, lightly perfumed with the herb and wine, make a colorful presentation. Parchment paper is traditional for this kind of cooking, but aluminum foil is far easier to use because you probably have it in your kitchen and the envelope can be hermetically sealed with no worries. When the fish is cooked, the envelope puffs up like a little balloon. The envelopes can be prepared some hours ahead of time, and you can use many different kinds of fish instead of mullet; see Note.*

*This is a very easy recipe to understand and to follow; it will take you almost less time to prepare the envelopes than it will to read the recipe!*

Preheat oven to 350°. Peel the carrots; cut off the carrot and zucchini ends. Cut off the green tops of the leeks; halve the leeks lengthwise and wash thoroughly. Cut all 3 vegetables into fine julienne strips about 2–3 inches long. Cut out small stem part of the tomatoes, blanch them briefly, then remove their skins. Squeeze out water and seeds, and chop the tomatoes coarsely. Chop the basil leaves. Slice the mushroom caps thinly. If the filets are large, cut them in half.

Place a piece of heavy-duty aluminum foil (about 15 × 18 inches) on your work surface and fold it half lengthwise. Open it up again.

Place a small handful of julienne carrots, zucchini and leeks on the bottom half of the foil, just below the fold. Place 2 pieces of mullet on the vegetables, then add another small handful of carrots, zucchini and leeks (and the mushrooms, if you are using them). Add ¼ of the chopped tomato, ¼ of the chopped basil, and season with a pinch of salt and white pepper. Pour 1 tablespoon olive oil and 1 tablespoon white wine over the fish and vegetables.

Bring the top half of the foil down to the bottom edge and fold inward so that the fold measures 1 inch. Fold again, this time making the fold about ½ inch. Repeat again with a final ½-inch fold. Turn the foil around and repeat the same folding process on both sides. (See illustration.)

Fill remaining 3 foil envelopes in the same manner. Place the envelopes on 2 baking sheets and cook in oven for about 10 minutes. If at the end of this time the envelopes are still flat, cook for a few minutes longer.

To serve, cut one end of the envelopes open with a pair of scissors. Use a rubber spatula to gently push the fish and vegetables out onto the plates.

The papillotes can be prepared as much as 5 hours ahead of time; if they need to wait over an hour before cooking, they should be refrigerated, in which case they will need a few extra minutes' cooking time.

*Note:* Salmon, red snapper, bass, halibut, monkfish, sole and trout filets are all good choices for this recipe; fish steaks are not. If a thick filet is used, for example, red snapper as it is usually found in the market, allow 5–10 minutes more cooking time. If using salmon or sea trout, be sure to remove the skin before cooking.

While dill and tarragon are good in this recipe, sage is not.

*Variation:* Add a few shellfish to the papillotes. For each package allow 4–6 scallops, or 3 clams or mussels that have been steamed very briefly and removed from their shells. (See p. 45 or p. 103.) If the scallops are large, cut them in quarters.

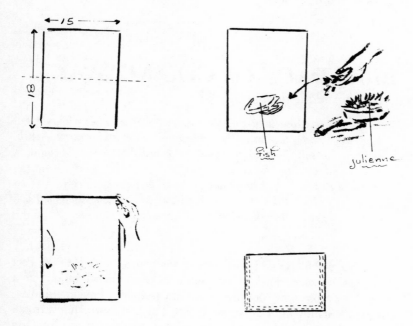

# RED MULLET MEUNIÈRE WITH BASIL
### Rouget meunière au basilic

¾ pound red mullet filets
Flour
2 tablespoons oil
Salt, white pepper
4 tablespoons butter
1 tablespoon finely chopped
  basil

**SERVES 2**

Roll the filets lightly in flour. Heat the oil in a heavy frying pan and sauté the filets briefly, about 2 minutes on each side, over medim heat. Turn them once during the cooking with a spatula. (If the filets are large, allow half a minute more on each side.) Remove the filets to warm plates or to a platter, and season them with a pinch of salt and white pepper.

Dump the oil out of the pan and return the pan to the fire. Add the butter to the pan, swirl it around, and, just at the moment when it bubbles, add the chopped basil. (This brief immersion in the hot butter keeps the basil strong and aromatic.) Pour over the fish filets and serve immediately with a pureed vegetable, or steamed snow peas, or steamed spinach, and fresh noodles.

# BRANDADE OF COD MY WAY
### Ma brandade de morue

*Cod is the fish I knew best as a child. The recipes I am giving you here are my adaptations of the traditional recipes of Provence, which use dried or salted cod to make well-known dishes such as brandade or cod with aïoli (garlic mayonnaise).*

2 pounds filet of cod
1 medium-size onion
1 tablespoon oil
2 tablespoons flour
½ teaspoon chopped garlic
2 cups heavy cream
Salt, white pepper
2 slices dense white (or
  brown) bread
4 tablespoons oil
2 potatoes

**SERVES 4–6**

*I like this version of brandade because the fresh cod makes a lighter dish than the traditional dried cod. You can serve this hot or cold; either way, it makes a very nice appetizer or canapé with drinks.*

Cut the cod filets into cubes; remove any bones you might find. Peel the onion and dice. Put 1 tablespoon oil and the chopped onion into a large, heavy pot and cook over medium heat for about 3 minutes, stirring constantly until the onion is soft, but not brown. Add the fish pieces and cook for a few minutes more, still stirring. Add the flour and mix it in vigorously with a wooden spoon. Do not be alarmed that it all becomes very dry; that is as it should be. Add the garlic, cream, 2 pinches salt and 1 pinch pepper. Let come to a boil, then lower the heat and let fish cook slowly, uncovered, for about 15 minutes. Stir once or twice during this time.

Trim the crusts off the bread and cut the slices into cubes. Heat the 4 tablespoons oil in a heavy frying pan until it is very hot; sauté the bread cubes in the oil, shaking the pan often to prevent the pieces from burning, or use a spatula to turn them evenly and often. When the croutons are uniformly browned, pour them into a strainer and pat them between paper towels to remove any excess fat.

Peel the potatoes, steam them and cut into slices. Spoon 3 large spoonfuls of the cod onto each plate. Place 2 slices of potato on each side of the cod, then a small pile of croutons on each of the other two sides. Serve hot.

To serve cold, let the brandade come to room temperature, then store in the refrigerator, where it will keep for 1–2 days. Mix it with a spoon before serving. The potato slices should be cold also.

# COD WITH VEGETABLES
## Morue à la basquaise

*Here is a little perfume of the south of France all on one plate. Prepare this recipe in the summer and soak yourself in an atmosphere of a Mediterranean vacation.*

Cut each filet in half, removing any bones you may find. Roll the filets in flour. Remove the seeds from the green pepper and slice it into thin strips. Peel and dice the shallots; crush the garlic; chop the scallions, including the green tops. Peel the tomato, squeeze out juice and seeds, and dice it.

In a large frying pan, heat 1 tablespoon of the oil until it is very hot. This is necessary to keep the fish from disintegrating while cooking. Add the cod filets and cook them very briefly, about 1 minute on each side. Turn them several times with a long spatula to be sure they are completely brown. Remove the fish from the pan and keep warm.

Dump out any oil remaining in the pan and add the remaining 1 tablespoon of oil. When it is hot, dump in the green pepper strips, shallots, garlic, tomato, scallions, thyme and green peppercorns, and sauté for about 2–3 minutes. Shake the pan back and forth several times to prevent sticking. Add the white wine and cook for 1 minute longer. If desired, swirl the butter into the pan and shake the pan vigorously to incorporate butter.

Season the fish filets with a small pinch of salt and a generous pinch of herbed pepper, pour the vegetables and sauce over them and serve immediately.

Bass, red snapper, monkfish and halibut filets would also be good for this recipe.

*¾ pound cod filets*
*Flour*
*½ green pepper*
*2 shallots*
*½ clove garlic*
*2 scallions*
*½ tomato*
*2 tablespoons oil*
*Leaves of 1 stalk fresh thyme*
*    or ⅛ teaspoon dried thyme*
*    (or herbed pepper)*
*½ teaspoon green*
*    peppercorns*
*2 tablespoons white wine*
*1 tablespoon butter, softened*
*    (optional)*
*Salt, herbed pepper*

***SERVES 2***

1 clove garlic
2 shallots
½ medium-size carrot
½ tomato
½ medium-size zucchini
4 green leek leaves (outside
    leaves)
4 thin slices onion
2 tablespoons chopped
    scallion
¾ pound cod filets
Herbed pepper
1 cup white wine
1 cup water
1 tablespoon olive oil
1 teaspoon green peppercorns
4 basil leaves
Salt
Garniture: 2 teaspoons olive
    oil

Garlic Mayonnaise
1 egg yolk
½ teaspoon mild mustard
2 cloves garlic
½ cup olive oil

SERVES 2

# COD IN COURT BOUILLON WITH GARLIC MAYONNAISE
*Morue au court bouillon et aïoli*

*Cod with Garlic Mayonnaise is the traditional national dish of Provence. It is always served on special occasions. I like this simplified version, which is easy to make but still keeps some of the feeling of Provence.*

Peel the garlic and shallots and cut into 3–4 pieces. Peel and slice the carrot thinly; slice the tomato. Cut the zucchini into thin slices and the leek leaves into pieces. Season the cod filets with a generous pinch of herbed pepper.

Put the wine, water, 1 tablespoon olive oil, the vegetables, peppercorns and basil in a medium-size saucepan, add a pinch of salt and bring to a boil. Cook at the boil for about 10 minutes. Meanwhile, follow either of the procedures for making mayonnaise on p. 236. Smash the garlic cloves before adding them to the mayonnaise.

Add the cod filets to the court bouillon and cook over medium heat for about 2 minutes. Turn them over with tongs, and cook another 2 minutes. Be careful not to let the heat get too high or the fish will fall apart.

Carefully lift the fish onto plates and run a thin line of olive oil along each filet, just to perfume the fish. Spoon the vegetables and juice over the filets and serve with Garlic Mayonnaise.

*Note:* You can use bass, monkfish, halibut or flounder if you do not have cod.

4 mackerel
1 onion
1 tomato
A few fresh thyme or basil
    leaves
1 tablespoon oil
2 teaspoons flour
¼ teaspoon chopped garlic
1 tablespoon chopped scallion
2 tablespoons chopped parsley
½ cup white wine
¾ cup olive oil
Salt, white pepper

SERVES 2–3 as a main course
4–6 as an appetizer

# MACKEREL RILLETTES
*Rillettes de maquereaux*

*Although mackerel is a fatty fish with a strong taste, it should not be ignored; Mackerel Rillettes can be an unforgettable dish, particularly served cold in the summertime.*

Filet the mackerel by separating the flesh from the bone on both sides. Cut out the bony spine down the center of each filet. Remove the skin and cut the filets into large pieces. Peel the onion and slice thinly; peel the tomato, cut out the center core, squeeze out any excess water and chop. Chop the fresh herb leaves.

In a medium-size saucepan, over medium-high heat, sweat the onion in the tablespoon of oil. After about 1 minute, before onion starts to color, dump in the mackerel pieces and mix around with a wooden spoon. Add the flour, mix well; fish will be quite dry. Now add the tomato, garlic, scallion, parsley and thyme or basil, then the white wine and olive oil. Season with 2 pinches salt and 1 pinch pepper. Mix vigorously with a wooden spoon, still over medium-high heat, then turn the heat down and cook very slowly for 8–10 minutes.

When cooking is finished, pour the fish and vegetables into a fine-meshed sieve and shake a few times to remove some of the liquid and fat. Turn into a small bowl and mash with a wooden spoon.

Let rillettes cool to room temperature, then chill in the refrigerator, where they will keep up to 1 week. Serve cold on toast. Use skate if good mackerel is not available.

# STEAMED MACKEREL ROLLS
*Rouleaux de maquereaux à la vapeur*

Fill the bottom of a steamer with hot water; add 2 sprigs thyme or a large basil leaf and a few drops of olive oil. Bring to a boil. Filet the mackerel, being sure to remove the bony spine from the center of each filet. Leave the skin on. Slap each filet a few times with the flat of a knife blade to make the filets easier to roll. Season the filets with salt and freshly ground black pepper.

Peel the fresh tomato, squeeze out water and seeds, and chop; chop the remaining thyme or basil leaves. Mix together in a small bowl along with the garlic and parsley. Slice the sun-dried tomato lengthwise so that you have 8 thin pieces. Lay 2 pieces of the sun-dried tomato on each filet, then add the chopped tomato mixture all along the center of the filet. Starting with the tail, the small part of the filet, roll up the mackerel and tie the roll with a string. Repeat with other filets.

Spread a little olive oil in the top of the steamer, stand rolls on end, then sprinkle a few drops of oil on top of the rolls. Steam the mackerel rolls for 10–15 minutes. Serve garnished with lemon wedges and freshly ground black pepper. Fresh noodles or steamed spinach would be good with the rolls.

*3–4 thyme sprigs or large basil leaves*
*Olive oil*
*2 mackerel*
*Salt, freshly ground black pepper*
*1 fresh tomato*
*¼ teaspoon chopped garlic*
*1 tablespoon chopped parsley*
*4 pieces sun-dried tomato*
*Garniture: lemon wedges, freshly ground black pepper*

**SERVES 2**

*¾ pound bluefish filets*
*Salt*
*Flour*
*2 round slices fresh (or*
*canned) pineapple*
*3 tablespoons oil*
*Herbed pepper or white*
*pepper*
*2 teaspoons sugar*
*Juice of a ½ a lemon*
*1 tablespoon water*
*1 tablespoon butter, softened*
*Garniture: chopped parsley*

*SERVES 2*

# BLUEFISH WITH PINEAPPLE
## Bluefish à l'ananas

*I never knew bluefish before I came to the United States. It is a fish with a strong taste and a moderate price tag. The skin is terrible, so be sure to remove it before cooking.*

*This combination of bluefish and pineapple works very well because the acid, yet sweet pineapple complements the flavor of the fish. Bluefish cooks very rapidly; to determine if it is done, press with your finger in the middle of the piece. When it is cooked, it will be soft to the touch.*

Remove the skin from the bluefish filets, cut them into 4 pieces, salt very lightly and roll them in flour. Remove the hard center core from the pineapple slices and cut each slice in half.

You will need 2 frying pans to cook the bluefish and pineapple separately. In one pan, heat 2 tablespoons oil. When it is hot, start sautéeing the fish over high heat. Season the fish with herbed pepper; after 1 minute, turn the pieces over and cook them for another 5–6 minutes, seasoning again with pepper.

Heat 1 tablespoon oil in the other pan and, when it is hot, add the pineapple slices. Turn the heat to low and sauté them for about 5–6 minutes, until they are nicely browned. Halfway through the cooking, sprinkle them with 1 teaspoon of the sugar, turn the pieces over and sprinkle with the remaining 1 teaspoon sugar. Remove the pineapple pieces to a plate and pour out any oil remaining in the pan. Squeeze the lemon juice into the pan, add the water and let cook for half a minute. Drop in pieces of the softened butter and agitate the pan to incorporate the butter into the sauce. Season with a pinch of salt and pepper.

Place the bluefish pieces on plates, put the pineapple slices on top of them and spoon the sauce over all. Garnish with a sprinkling of finely chopped parsley.

*Note:* If you wish to omit the butter in the sauce, add a little more lemon juice and water.

# BRAISED BLUEFISH
### Bluefish braisé

*Here is a country way of cooking bluefish that is very welcome on a cold day.*

Remove the skin from the bluefish filets, and cut each into 3 pieces. Peel and slice the shallots and garlic. Remove the outer leaves of the lettuce and reserve 4 of them; cut the remaining head into quarters. Cut the tomato into large dice and the carrot in half lengthwise, then into thin slices. Chop the basil leaves.

In a medium-size saucepan melt 1½ tablespoons butter. Add the shallots and garlic before it gets very hot. Cook for about 1 minute over medium heat, then add the bluefish, the quartered head of lettuce, the tomato, carrot and basil. Pour in white wine and season with a pinch of salt and pepper. Cook over a hot fire, turning the fish pieces once. Add the water and the remaining 1½ tablespoons butter, and lower the heat. Fold a piece of aluminum foil double and press it down over the fish. Let cook over low heat for about 6 minutes.

Lay out 2 of the reserved large lettuce leaves on each plate and place the fish on them. Cook the vegetables 2 minutes longer and spoon them over and around fish. Ladle several spoonfuls of juice over each plate.

¾ *pound bluefish filets*
*2 shallots*
*2 cloves garlic*
*1 head Boston lettuce*
*1 tomato*
*1 medium-size carrot, peeled*
*4 basil leaves*
*3 tablespoons butter*
*5 tablespoons white wine*
*Salt, herbed pepper*
*2 tablespoons water*

**SERVES 2**

# SHELLFISH

LOBSTER WITH
  TARRAGON
STEAMED LOBSTER
  WITH TOMATO
  SAUCE
WARM LOBSTER AND
  ASPARAGUS SALAD

SHRIMP IN SPICY
  BOUILLON
SHRIMP SOUFFLÉ
SHRIMP AND
  VEGETABLE STEW
SHRIMP AND MASHED
  POTATOES

SAUTÉED SOFT-SHELL
  CRABS
SOFT-SHELL CRABS
  WITH SCALLION
  BUTTER
MOUSSE OF SOFT-
  SHELL CRABS

MUSSELS GRATIN
MUSSELS AND RICE
MUSSEL SALAD

OYSTERS GRATIN
  WITH TRUFFLES
OYSTER AND
  VEGETABLE SALAD

SCALLOPS WITH
  FRESH TOMATOES
SCALLOPS WITH
  OYSTER
  MUSHROOMS

MUSSEL SOUP WITH
  SAFFRON (p. 44)
SHRIMP SOUP (p. 44)
CLAM SOUP (p. 45)
CLEAR VEGETABLE
  AND LOBSTER PÂTÉ
  (p. 27)
SHELLFISH OR
  VEGETABLE
  FRITTERS (p. 18)

Lobster is the very best of shellfish, especially American lobster, which is exceptionally fine. If you live near the ocean or are vacationing in Maine, cook your lobsters in a very little sea water with some seaweed thrown in and serve them warm with hollandaise sauce. The other delicious way to enjoy lobster is to grill it (see directions further on).

Shrimp are very popular in the United States, and they lend themselves well to any number of recipes. Two easy ways to cook them are to poach them in a court bouillon and serve warm with mayonnaise, or to sauté them with a little oil and parsley and finish them in the oven.

Soft-shell crabs are new to me; we do not have them in France. I like them immensely, and when they are in season, I love to work them into my menus.

Mussels are as old as the world; we have evidence that prehistoric man ate mussels. They arouse great suspicion: some people think they are dangerous, but others claim they are absolutely wonderful for eating. You may be surprised to know that in France many people eat mussels raw with a little lemon or vinegar during the proper season, that is, the months that contain an R—September, October, etc. Usually the French do not eat shellfish during the months without an R—May, June, etc.—and I think mussels taste better during the colder months. Mussels also have the great advantage of being very reasonably priced.

We know that oysters were also eaten by early man because piles of prehistoric oyster shells have been found on the coasts of Scandinavia. The ancient Romans valued oysters highly and, according to Apicius, brought them fresh to Rome all the way from the coasts of Brittany and Scandinavia. I suggest you enjoy oysters raw with a little shallot vinegar, but I have also given you two uncomplicated recipes for hot oysters.

Scallops are among the most refined and succulent of shellfish. During the time of the great pilgrimages in France, a belt of scallop shells identified its wearer as a pilgrim, and carved scallop shells are a recurring motif on fine furniture. For me, scallops recall my mother's wonderful gratin of scallops in a light béchamel sauce strengthened with grated Swiss cheese, eggs, nutmeg, butter and bread crumbs.

Raw clams are good served simply with lemon or vinegar, or cooked in puff pastry with saffron, or gratin with spinach. You will find a recipe for Clam Soup on p. 45.

### Lobster

Grilling lobsters on a barbecue or under the broiler preserves their taste perfectly. Be careful, though, not to overcook them—about 8–10 minutes is ample. If they burn, the meat will be too dry. (An old lobster needs more cooking than a young, juicy one.)

Split lobsters down the middle and place them shell side up on a barbecue, shell side down under a broiler, so that the direct heat reaches the exposed meat. If the lobsters came with coral, you might like to try this: Remove the coral before cooking the lobsters and mix it with 4 tablespoons hollandaise (for 2 lobsters), salt and pepper. One or two minutes before the lobsters are finished cooking, paint this mixture down the center of the lobster halves and return them to the fire.

Here are three lobster recipes that I think you will find interesting. Except for the Warm Lobster and Asparagus Salad, the lobsters must be alive and kicking.

# LOBSTER WITH TARRAGON
## Homard à l'estragon

*The subtle taste of tarragon in this very easy recipe will delight your palate.*

Cut the lobsters in half lengthwise. Cut off the claws and crack them slightly. Remove the intestine. You now have 8 pieces of lobster, 4 from each lobster.

Peel and dice the shallots; chop the tarragon leaves. Sweat the shallots in 2 tablespoons of the butter in a large sauteuse or frying pan. Add the lobster pieces to the pan open side down, and cook them over medium-high heat for a few minutes. Turn them over, add the wine, cream and a pinch of salt and pepper. Cover the pan and cook for 6–8 minutes.

Remove the 4 body halves from pan, and add the tarragon, garlic, parsley and peppercorns. Cook the claws a few minutes longer. Remove the claws from the pan and finish the sauce with the remaining 1½ tablespoons butter.

Separate the tail meat from the shells in large pieces and arrange it back in the shells. Take the claw meat entirely out of the shells and discard the claw shells. Place the lobster pieces in wide, shallow soup plates and pour the sauce over them.

Serve with white rice and a puree of vegetables or with carrots and zucchini that you have carved into small ovals and poached. Or throw a handful of julienne leeks, carrots and zucchini into the sauce with the lobster when you add the wine and cream. Spoon these vegetables onto the lobsters with the sauce.

*Note:* When I make lobster this way in the restaurant, I strain the sauce before serving it to remove the little bits of coagulated blood. I like my home cooking more natural, however, and so do not strain the sauce before serving.

*2 live lobsters (1 pound each)*
*3 shallots*
*1 stalk fresh tarragon (do not use dried tarragon)*
*3½ tablespoons butter, softened*
*1 cup white wine*
*1½ cups heavy cream*
*Salt, white pepper*
*⅛ teaspoon chopped garlic*
*1 tablespoon chopped parsley*
*¼ teaspoon green peppercorns (optional)*

**SERVES 2**

1 live lobster (1 pound)
3–4 thin slices of a large
  onion
1 thin, long slab each of
  carrot, zucchini and leek

Tomato Sauce
½ tomato
1 small clove garlic or ½ a
  large clove
½ scallion, green and white
  part
2 fresh basil leaves
½ teaspoon fresh lemon juice
1 teaspoon olive oil
A pinch of white pepper

SERVES 2

1 cooked carrot
4 basil leaves
1 small tomato
8 cooked asparagus spears
Tail and claw meat of 2
  cooked lobsters
1 teaspoon olive oil
Salt, white pepper
Lettuce for salad: endive,
  radicchio, Boston lettuce

Dressing
1 tablespoon lemon juice
6 tablespoons olive oil
1 tablespoon canned truffle
  juice
Chopped parsley
Salt, white pepper

SERVES 4 as an appetizer
2 as a main course

# STEAMED LOBSTER WITH TOMATO SAUCE

Homard cuit à la vapeur sauce provençale

*For those who like light food with very few calories, this recipe is perfect. It is also good without the tomato sauce.*

Make a small incision in the middle of the hard body shell of the lobster behind the eyes. (While this incision is not absolutely necessary, it has the beneficial result of cleaning out the white gelatinous substance often found inside a lobster after cooking.) Steam the lobster for about 10–15 minutes. Twist the tail from the body and remove the intestine from the tail. Trim off the end near the stomach, remove the shell and cut the tail in half lengthwise. Break open the top part of the claws and carefully remove the meat in one piece. Cut the thin slabs of carrot and zucchini into very thin julienne strips about 1 inch in length. Cut the slice of leek crosswise into very thin strips. Return the lobster meat to the steamer. Separate the onion slices into rings and lay them on the lobster pieces; sprinkle the vegetable strips over them. Cook for 5 minutes.

Make the tomato sauce: peel the tomato half and squeeze out the seeds and extra water. Chop the tomato finely. Flatten the garlic clove and chop it finely; chop the scallion; chop the basil leaves. Squeeze the lemon juice into a bowl and mix in all the other sauce ingredients.

Arrange the lobster meat on plates and pour any lobster juice over them. Place 1 tablespoon tomato sauce on each plate.

# WARM LOBSTER AND ASPARAGUS SALAD

Salade de homard aux asperges

*If you do not have a steamer, you can sauté the lobster and vegetables in a frying pan.*

From the carrot, cut 6 thin slices on an angle. Chop the basil leaves; peel the tomato, squeeze out water and seeds, and chop. Cut off the asparagus tops and cut them in half lengthwise.

Place the lobster, asparagus, carrot, tomato, basil, olive oil, 2 pinches salt and 1 pinch pepper in the top of a steamer and cook for 4 minutes (after the water in the bottom of steamer has come to a boil).

Arrange the lettuce leaves so that each plate has an arrangement of 4 endive, 2 radicchio and 3 Boston lettuce leaves. Mix all dressing ingredients together. Remove the lobster and vegetables from the steamer; drain them and arrange on the lettuce. Pour the dressing over top.

# SHRIMP IN SPICY BOUILLON

*Crevettes au bouillon épicé*

*These spicy shrimp are delicious served hot on a bed of rice, or cold with a piquant mayonnaise.*

Peel the shrimp and remove the intestines. Bring the wine and water to a boil and add the remaining bouillon ingredients; use 2 pinches salt. Boil for 5 minutes, uncovered. Add the shrimp and cook for another 5 minutes over medium-high heat, turning the shrimp once during the cooking.

Serve shrimp and vegetables hot on white rice; remove the parsley and basil leaves before serving. Or serve cold with lemon wedges, or with Spicy Mayonnaise.

*Note:* Mix the Spicy Mayonnaise a few hours ahead of serving time to let the flavor develop. It will keep 2–3 days in the refrigerator.

*12 large shrimp*
*1 cup white wine*
*2 cups water*
*½ carrot, sliced thinly*
*½ onion, sliced thinly*
*½ leek, cut into thin slices*
*½ tomato, cut into small pieces*
*1 clove garlic, peeled and smashed*
*1 tablespoon chopped scallion*
*6 large basil leaves*
*1 parsley sprig*
*1 teaspoon allspice (whole)*
*½ teaspoon ground cumin*
*½ teaspoon curry powder*
*½ teaspoon anise seeds*
*3 whole cloves*
*½ teaspoon green peppercorns*
*Salt*

*Spicy Mayonnaise (optional to serve with cold shrimp, see Note)*
*5 generous tablespoons Mayonnaise (p. 236)*
*¼ teaspoon curry powder*
*¼ teaspoon ground cumin*
*2 tablespoons ketchup*
*¼ teaspoon Worcestershire sauce*
*¼ teaspoon chopped garlic*
*2 tablespoons sesame seeds*
*2 large basil leaves, finely chopped*
*1 generous teaspoon chopped parsley*
*1 tablespoon chopped scallion*
*A few drops Tabasco*

**SERVES 2**

# SHRIMP SOUFFLÉ

## Soufflé de crevettes

18–20 raw, shelled shrimp
   (about 1 pound)
Filet of monkfish or bass,
   snapper or other whitefish
   (about 1 pound; sole is
   good, but expensive)
1 teaspoon chopped shallots
¼ teaspoon chopped basil (or
   tarragon or dill)
1 teaspoon butter
2 whole eggs
2 tablespoons heavy cream
Salt, white pepper
5 egg whites
Sauce suggestions: Lobster
   Sauce (p. 234) or Fresh
   Herb Sauce (p. 230)

**SERVES 4**

*This is a very delicate recipe that you must treat with care. You can prepare the soufflés some minutes in advance and keep them, uncooked, in the refrigerator. They only need 15–20 minutes in the oven and must then be served immediately.*

Preheat oven to 350°. Clean out any intestine you may find in the shrimp. Cut the fish filet into 8–9 large chunks. Sweat the shallots and basil in the butter. Put the shrimp and fish into the bowl of a food processor and process about half a minute. Add the whole eggs, cream, shallots and a generous pinch of salt and pepper to the processor bowl, and process about 1 minute, until the mixture is well blended. (It is important not to run the processor too long because the eggs and cream will break down into granules.)

Using a rubber spatula, scoop and scrape the mixture into a fine-meshed sieve or a tamis. Mash the mixture through the sieve with the spatula. This important step takes strength and perseverance but is necessary because both the shrimp and monkfish are fibrous. After about 5 minutes of hard work, you should have about 1½–2 cups of shrimp-fish mixture.

Beat the egg whites in the bowl of an electric mixer until firm but not dry. Mix the beaten egg whites into the shrimp-fish mixture carefully so as not to break the egg whites.

Butter 4 individual soufflé dishes, 4 inches in diameter. Spoon the mixture into the molds, slapping each mold lightly on the table after it is filled to let mixture settle. Trace a small circle in the center of soufflé with your finger, then run your thumb around the edge of the molds to clean off any extra mixture and make a small depression.

Cook the soufflés in the oven for about 15–20 minutes, until they rise 1–1½ inches above the molds. Make a slit in the top of each soufflé with a spoon and fill each one with 2 tablespoons Lobster Sauce. Serve immediately.

*Note:* This fragile soufflé works better in individual molds than in one large mold.

# SHRIMP AND VEGETABLE STEW
*Navarin de crevettes*

*The origin of the word* navarin *(a lamb stew) has been attributed both to* navet *(turnip) and to Navarin, the site of a battle in 1827. For me, navarin means spring, when the new, young vegetables arrive in the markets.*

Holding the shrimp flat on your work surface, cut through the back so that they are butterflied but held together at the base by the small piece of shell on the tail. Remove any intestine.

Blanch the carrot and cut it into 6 small pieces about the size of the top of your little finger. Peel the turnip and cut it and the zucchini in the same manner. Cut the scallions lengthwise into 6–8 pieces; peel the tomato and cut it into 4 pieces. The vegetables are cut in this manner so that their size is compatible with that of the shrimp.

In a small pan, sweat the shallots in the butter. Grill the shrimp briefly on each side, just to brown and firm the flesh. Mix the vegetables (including the mushrooms, if used), the white wine, basil and saffron into the shallots, and cook over medium-high heat for 1–2 minute. Add the shrimp and Lobster Sauce, and continue cooking for another 3–5 minutes. Season sparingly with salt and pepper. The Lobster Sauce is strong, so you do not need much more seasoning. Sprinkle with a few sprigs of dill and serve with rice.

8 raw shrimp, shelled except
    for tail piece
½ carrot
1 turnip
½ zucchini
2 scallions
½ tomato
1 teaspoon chopped shallots
1 teaspoon butter
6 small pieces shiitake
    mushrooms (optional)
3 tablespoons white wine
1 teaspoon chopped fresh
    basil (or tarragon or
    marjoram)
A pinch of saffron (optional)
½ cup Lobster Sauce (p. 234)
Salt, white pepper
**Garniture:** *a few dill sprigs*

**SERVES 2**

# SHRIMP AND MASHED POTATOES
*Crevettes aux pommes de terre*

Preheat oven to 350°–400°. Peel the shrimp and remove the intestines. Peel the potatoes and cook them in boiling water or a steamer until done. Mash them in a food processor with 1 tablespoon of the grated cheese, the sour cream and butter, pulsing the processor off and on quickly—just enough to puree the potatoes. Add the horseradish, cream, salt and pepper, and mix briefly.

Brown the shrimp in hot oil, 2 minutes on each side, then finish cooking them on a metal plate or baking dish in the oven for 2 minutes. Transfer the potatoes to an oven-proof dish and arrange the shrimp on top. Sprinkle the remaining ½ cup of grated cheese over the shrimp and potatoes and brown under the broiler for about 3 minutes.

12 large shrimp
3 large or 4 medium potatoes
½ cup plus 1 tablespoon
    grated Swiss cheese
1½ tablespoons sour cream
2 tablespoons butter
2 teaspoons horseradish
3 tablespoons heavy cream
Salt, freshly ground black
    pepper
1 tablespoon oil

**SERVES 3**

### Crab

Poach blue crabs in a court bouillon and eat them warm with a little mayonnaise. They only need to cook for the amount of time it takes to bring the bouillon to a boil after adding the crabs. Then turn off the heat and let the crabs sit in the liquid until they reach room temperature. (If you need them quickly, cook them for about 5 minutes in the bouillon.) Stone crabs are larger and need to cook for the same amount of time as lobster.

To prepare soft-shell crabs for cooking, lift up the back of the crab and pull out the 3 or 4 lungs that are on each side. Cut off the eyes in a crosswise cut. Remove the gelatinous triangular carapace on the underside. If there is coral in the crab, leave it in. (See illustration.)

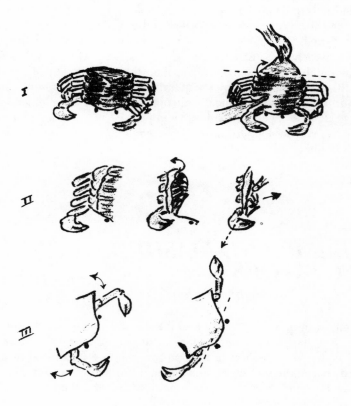

# SAUTÉED SOFT-SHELL CRABS
*Soft-shell crabes meunières*

*This simple recipe adapts well to soft-shell crabs, but you must be careful: the crabs will spit at you when they cook in the hot butter. Cover the pan with a grease screen to protect yourself.*

Lightly flour cleaned crabs on both sides. Melt 1 tablespoon of the butter in a pan until it is very hot and bubbling. Cook the crabs in the hot butter, back side down first, for about 2 minutes on each side over high heat. Season with salt and pepper. Turn the heat down toward the end of cooking time.

Remove the crabs to a plate, throw out the butter in the pan and melt the remaining 1 tablespoon of butter in the pan. When the butter just begins to brown, add the lemon juice; pour over the crabs. Sprinkle with chopped parsley and serve.

*Flour*
*2 soft-shell crabs, cleaned*
  *(p. 100)*
*2 tablespoons butter*
*Salt, white pepper*
*1 teaspoon lemon juice*
*Garniture: freshly chopped*
  *parsley*

**SERVES 1**

# SOFT-SHELL CRABS WITH SCALLION BUTTER
*Soft-shell crabes au beurre de scallion*

*The combination of vinegar, fresh thyme and scallions with the crabs creates an interesting taste.*

In a small pot, combine the lemon juice, water and scallion, and reduce the liquid by half, about 3 minutes.

Flour the crabs. Heat the oil in a frying pan; when it is extremely hot, cook the crabs over high heat for about 2 minutes on each side, back side down first. The high heat is necessary to get the crabs crisp.

Cut the butter into large chunks. Whisk it into the reduced lemon juice mixture, piece by piece. You do not want the butter to melt, you must beat it in. Season with 2 pinches salt, 1 pinch pepper, the thyme and vinegar.

Remove the crabs to a linen or paper towel and pat off any extra fat. Ladle 2 tablespoons of sauce on each plate and place the crabs on the sauce. Garnish with parsley.

*1 tablespoon lemon juice*
*2 tablespoons water*
*2 tablespoons chopped*
  *scallion*
*Flour (about 2 tablespoons)*
*8 soft-shell crabs, cleaned*
  *(p. 100)*
*3 tablespoons oil*
*½ pound butter*
*Salt, white pepper*
*1 generous teaspoon freshly*
  *chopped thyme or parsley*
*1 tablespoon wine vinegar*
*Garniture: finely chopped*
  *parsley*

**SERVES 4**

# MOUSSE OF SOFT-SHELL CRABS
*Mousse de soft-shell crabes*

3 cooked soft-shell crabs
1 cup raw bay scallops
1 tablespoon sour cream
2 eggs
4–5 basil leaves, chopped
Salt, white pepper
1 teaspoon chopped shallots
¼ teaspoon chopped garlic
¼ cup heavy cream
Butter
4 cooked crab legs

Sauce
2 tablespoons sour cream
1 teaspoon wine vinegar
1½ teaspoons chopped
    tarragon
2 teaspoons chopped parsley
1½–2 tablespoons finely
    chopped cucumber
    (peeled)
¼ teaspoon ground cumin

**SERVES 4**

Preheat oven to 350°. Place the 3 crabs, scallops, sour cream, eggs, chopped basil leaves and 2 pinches of salt and pepper in the bowl of a food processor, and process until well blended. It is nicer if the mixture is not too smooth, if there are still some distinguishable pieces of crab. Add the shallots, garlic and heavy cream and process for about half a minute.

Butter the bottoms and sides of 4 1-cup mousse molds. Place a crab leg in the bottom of each mold and pour in the crab-scallop mixture. The molds should be just ¾ full.

Place the molds in a bain-marie of hot (not boiling) water that comes up just 1 inch on their sides. Cook for about 15–20 minutes in the oven, until firm but still moist.

Whisk the sauce ingredients together in a bowl; you will have about ¾ cup. Ladle a generous tablespoon of sauce on each plate. Unmold the mousse by running a knife around the sides of the molds and inverting them onto plates.

### Mussels

For the following recipes you must first open the mussels. Scrub them under cold water; place mussels (about 16–20) in a saucepan with 3–4 tablespoons white wine, 4 tablespoons water, 1 finely chopped shallot and 1 teaspoon chopped parsley. Cover the pan and cook for 1–2 minutes over medium heat, until the mussels just open. They are now ready for further cooking. Strain the juice and reserve for a mussel recipe or for a fish dish. It will keep in the refrigerator for 3–4 days, or in the freezer.

# MUSSELS GRATIN
## Moules gratinées

16 mussels
16 mussel shells (halves)
1 shallot
1 clove garlic
2 walnuts
8 tablespoons butter, softened
1 tablespoon chopped parsley
1 tablespoon finely diced scallion
Salt, white pepper
½ teaspoon Pastis (anise liqueur)
2 tablespoons fine dry bread crumbs

SERVES 2 as an appetizer
1 as a main course

Preheat broiler. Open the mussels (see above), free them from their shells and replace each mussel in half its shell on a metal platter. Peel and finely dice the shallot and garlic; finely chop the walnuts. In a small bowl, mash the softened butter together with the shallot, garlic, parsley and scallion. Add a pinch of salt, pepper, the Pastis, walnuts and bread crumbs, and mix it all together.

Spread a small amount of the butter mixture on each mussel, just to cover it. Place the platter under the broiler for about 2 minutes.

# MUSSELS AND RICE
## Moules au riz

16–20 mussels
2 shallots
1 leek
1½ cups heavy cream
Pinch of saffron threads or ½ teaspoon curry powder
Salt, white pepper
2 cups cooked white rice

SERVES 2

*My mother often made risotto when I was young, and this recipe reminds me of it.*

Open the mussels (see above), and remove all but 4–5 plump, juicy ones from their shells. Strain the juice from this first brief cooking through a fine-meshed sieve into a heavy saucepan.

Peel the shallots and dice finely; wash the leek and cut it into large julienne strips. Add the shallots and cream to the mussel juice; bring to a boil and reduce over medium-high heat for about 10–15 minutes. Halfway through this cooking add the julienne leek. Season with the saffron or curry and a small pinch of salt and a pinch of pepper.

Add the rice and mussels, including the ones with shells. Cook for about 2 minutes. Serve in wide soup plates; this is meant to be liquid.

# MUSSEL SALAD
## Salade de moules

*This succulent salad is truly a diet recipe and is very simple to prepare.*

16 mussels
Herbed pepper
2 teaspoons chopped basil
½ teaspoon chopped parsley
2 teaspoons finely chopped
   scallion
¼–½ teaspoon chopped
   garlic
Grated rind of 1 lemon
1 small carrot
1 leek
1 small zucchini
1 teaspoon lemon juice
¼ teaspoon olive oil
Lettuce for salad: radicchio,
   Bibb lettuce

**SERVES 2**

Cook the mussels for 3–5 minutes and remove them from their shells (p. 103). Discard the shells and marinate the mussels in a small bowl in which you have mixed the pepper, 1 teaspoon chopped basil, the parsley, 1 teaspoon chopped scallion, the garlic and the lemon rind, for at least 15 minutes. (You can do this a few hours ahead of time, in which case, keep in the refrigerator.)

Peel the carrot and cut it into julienne strips; wash the leek and cut it and the zucchini in the same manner. Place vegetables in top of a steamer. Sprinkle with the remaining 1 teaspoon basil and 1 teaspoon scallion, 2–3 generous pinches herbed pepper, the lemon juice and olive oil. Cook in the steamer for 6–8 minutes.

Just before the vegetables are cooked, start to build the salads, placing 6–7 small leaves of Bibb lettuce and 3 leaves of radicchio on each plate. Using tongs, remove the steamed vegetables to the plates, then add the mussels, at room temperature.

*Note:* I like this highly seasoned, but if you prefer it somewhat less so, use less herbed pepper.

### Oysters

To open oysters, cook them, covered, in a small pan with ½ cup water and 2 whole peeled shallots for about 5 minutes. Fried oysters, like other fried shellfish, or thin slices of fried fish are popular canapés or appetizers; see Shellfish or Vegetable Fritters (p. 18).

## OYSTERS GRATIN WITH TRUFFLES

*Huîtres gratinées aux truffes*

Preheat broiler. Open the oysters and place them in their shells on a metal plate or broiling pan. Mix the truffles, truffle juice and Hollandaise, and spoon it over the oysters. Season with freshly ground black pepper.

Place the oysters under the broiler for about 1½ minutes, just to heat the sauce. Sprinkle with finely chopped parsley.

*12 medium-size oysters or 16 small ones*
*3 teaspoons slivered truffles*
*2 teaspoons truffle juice*
*4 tablespoons Hollandaise (p. 229)*
*Freshly ground black pepper*
*Garniture: finely chopped parsley*

*SERVES 4 as an appetizer*
*2 as a main course*

## OYSTER AND VEGETABLE SALAD

*Salade d'huîtres et légumes*

*A well-known food critic asked me for an elaborate consommé for a benefit dinner. I garnished the consommé with fresh coriander leaves, steamed vegetables of different colors and quenelles of oysters. The consommé was very well received, but I am just as happy with a simple oyster salad like this one.*

Open the oysters and remove them from their shells (see above). Quarter the zucchini and carrot lengthwise, and cut them into pieces about 2½ inches long. Trim the snow peas. Cook the vegetables very briefly in boiling water, then refresh in cold water after cooking. The carrots need 1–2 minutes to cook, the zucchini 1 minute, the snow peas only half a minute. Cut them all into thin julienne strips. Arrange the lettuce on plates and strew the vegetables on top. Place the oysters on the vegetables.

Mix the vinaigrette ingredients together in a small bowl and spoon over the salad. Garnish with a few sprigs of dill and very thin slices of lime or avocado.

*8 oysters*
*½ zucchini*
*½ carrot*
*12 snow peas*
*Lettuce for salad: Bibb heart, 8 endive leaves, 8 radicchio leaves*

*Vinaigrette*
*2 tablespoons olive oil*
*1 teaspoon French mustard*
*Juice of ½ lime*
*1 tablespoon chopped tomato*
*1 teaspoon finely chopped dill*
*Salt, white pepper*

*Garniture: dill sprigs, very thin lime slices or very small, thin slices of avocado*

*SERVES 2 as an appetizer*
*1 as a main course*

### Scallops

Scallops in France come to the market with the coral attached, but that is not true in this country, where the coral is thrown away before the customer ever sees it. If you can find scallops with coral, do not throw it out; the taste is good and the appearance interesting. I prefer bay scallops because I think their taste sweeter than the larger Maine scallops. If you use the large scallops, cut them in half horizontally before cooking.

There are many easy ways to cook scallops. They are good steamed with fresh herbs, poached in a court bouillon, sautéed with scallions or au gratin with cream and cheese.

*4 tomatoes*
*3 shallots*
*1 large clove garlic*
*1 tablespoon butter*
*2 generous tablespoons*
  *chopped scallion*
*1 generous tablespoon*
  *chopped fresh basil*
*1 cup cream*
*4 tablespoons white wine*
*Salt, white pepper*
*1 tablespoon oil*
*Flour*
*1 generous cup scallops*
*2 tablespoons chopped parsley*
*¼ teaspoon finely chopped*
  *garlic*

*SERVES 2*

# SCALLOPS WITH FRESH TOMATOES
*Coquilles Saint-Jacques au coulis de tomates fraîches*

Peel the tomatoes, squeeze out the water and seeds, and chop finely. Peel the shallots and slice them thinly; smash and chop the garlic clove. Sweat the shallots in a saucepan with the butter and cook them for 1 minute. Add the tomatoes, garlic, scallion and basil, and let sweat for another minute. Add the cream and the wine, season with 2 pinches of salt and 1 pinch pepper, and reduce over medium-high heat.

Heat the oil in a medium-size frying pan. Flour the scallops lightly. When the oil is very hot, drop in the scallops and cook them very fast until they are crispy. Just before they are done, drop in the parsley and chopped garlic. Spread the tomato mixture onto plates and spoon the scallops onto the tomato.

# SCALLOPS WITH OYSTER MUSHROOMS

*Coquilles Saint-Jacques aux pleurottes*

Clean the mushrooms by rubbing them with a dry towel; do not wash them as they will retain too much water. Heat 2 tablespoons of the oil until very hot. Add the mushrooms and sauté them until they are brown, about 4–5 minutes, over high heat. Season them halfway through the cooking with a pinch of salt and pepper. Remove the mushrooms to a dry towel and keep them warm.

Dump out any oil in the pan, add the remaining 2 tablespoons of oil and heat until very hot. Lightly flour the scallops and add them to the hot oil. Sauté them very quickly on both sides over high heat, seasoning them with a pinch of salt and pepper after you turn them over. Turn them once again; cook about 2 minutes in all.

Remove the scallops to a dry towel and throw out the fat in the pan. Add the butter, parsley, scallion, shallots and garlic to the pan. Mix them all around off the heat, and add the water. Heat briefly. Divide the mushrooms between the 2 plates, place the scallops on top of them and pour the sauce over all.

*3 cups oyster mushrooms*
*4 tablespoons oil*
*Salt, white pepper*
*Flour*
*8 French scallops with coral*
*    or 16 sea scallops*
*1 tablespoon butter*
*1 tablespoon chopped parsley*
*1 tablespoon chopped scallion*
*1 tablespoon chopped shallots*
*¼ teaspoon chopped garlic*
*1 tablespoon water*

**SERVES 2**

# CHICKEN AND OTHER DOMESTIC FOWL

OLD-FASHIONED
ROAST CHICKEN
POACHED CHICKEN
POACHED CHICKEN
WITH CREAM
POACHED CHICKEN
WITH CABBAGE
CHICKEN LEGS LIKE A
LITTLE LEG OF LAMB
CHICKEN PROVENÇAL
CHICKEN FRICASSEE
WITH LEMON AND
LIME
CHICKEN BREAST
WITH CALVADOS
AND APPLES
CHICKEN BREAST
WITH BEER

CHICKEN BREAST
WITH PINEAPPLE
AND STRAWBERRIES
CHICKEN BREAST
WITH WHISKEY
CHICKEN BREAST AND
LIVER
CHICKEN WINGS
MINUTE
CHICKEN SALAD

CORNISH GAME HENS
STUFFED WITH
SHRIMP
CORNISH GAME HEN
WITH CARROTS
STEAMED CORNISH
GAME HEN
CORNISH GAME HEN
FRITTERS

ROAST DUCK WITH
FIGS
QUICK DUCK BREAST
STEW WITH
VEGETABLES
DUCK CONSERVE
CRISPY DUCK FAT
SALAD

DUCK CONSERVE
SALAD WITH SLICES
OF PEAR (p. 24)
CHICKEN SAUSAGE
(p. 25)
CHICKEN LIVER
CUSTARD (p. 25)
CHICKEN
FRICANDEAU WITH
VIOLETS (p. 181)

Chicken and other members of the poultry family, Cornish game hens and capons, are prized for their versatility. You can prepare chicken a thousand different ways and the next day find yet another tasty recipe. With so many possibilities, you need never tire of chicken.

Like most farm children, I helped feed the chickens after school and collected the newly laid eggs in a little basket. My mother raised baby chickens in the wintertime, and sometimes we would have a hundred little chirping babies to feed. It may seem strange, but we fed them chopped hard-boiled eggs; of course, I threw out grain to our regular chickens, but sometimes they found new ways to expand their diet. One memorable day the chickens were pecking around the yard when they found the residue of crushed grapes from my grandfather's wine making. The chickens threw themselves on the fermented stuff and became quite tipsy, staggering back to the hen house in zigzag motions. Happily their intoxication lasted only two days.

The illustration below shows you how to cut a chicken into pieces for cooking. (After you roast or poach a whole chicken, you may want to carve it into four parts for serving, the two breasts with wings and the two thighs and legs.) There are two different ways to prepare a whole chicken for roasting, with string or with a needle.

# OLD-FASHIONED ROAST CHICKEN

*Poulet cuit à l'ancienne*

*A perfectly roasted chicken is one of the best meals in the world. It requires your attention, however. To attain a crispy skin, you must brown the chicken on top of the stove before putting it in the oven, and you also must turn it several times during the cooking.*

Mix the sour cream, basil, parsley and garlic. Preheat oven to 350°–400°. Salt and pepper the body cavity of the chicken and rub the cavity with sour cream mixture. Chop off the outer wing tips and truss the bird (p. 112).

Heat the oil in a pan just large enough to hold the chicken. Season the chicken with salt and pepper, and brown it on all sides in the hot oil, starting with the breast down. Use tongs or 2 wooden spoons to turn the chicken, not a fork, because you do not want to pierce the skin. Spread butter on top of the chicken when it is completely browned, and continue cooking it in the oven for 45–60 minutes, or until the juice of the chicken runs clear.

After you put the bird in the oven, peel the potatoes and cut them to a uniform size. Dry them and salt them lightly. Add them to the roasting pan about 30 minutes before the chicken will be done. These risolé potatoes are a fine complement to the roast chicken.

*2 generous tablespoons sour cream*
*1 teaspoon fresh, chopped basil or ¼ teaspoon dried*
*1 teaspoon chopped parsley*
*¼ teaspoon chopped garlic (optional)*

*Salt, herbed pepper*
*1 3½-pound chicken*
*4 tablespoons oil*
*1 tablespoon butter*
*10 small new red potatoes*

**SERVES 4**

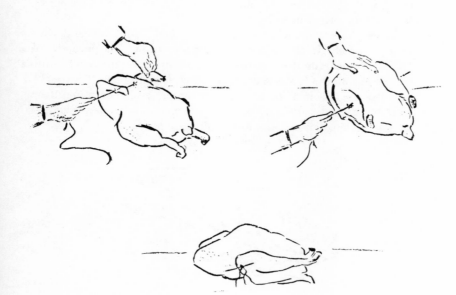

1 whole chicken
Salt, white pepper
2–3 stalks fresh thyme or ¼
    teaspoon dried thyme
3–4 basil leaves
1 large onion
8 whole cloves
Oil
1 whole head of garlic,
    unpeeled
A bouquet garni of parsley,
    thyme and basil or
    rosemary (p. 182)
1 tablespoon sea salt
Cold water
2 large carrots
4 leeks
3 zucchini
12–14 small new potatoes,
    unpeeled

**SERVES 4**

# POACHED CHICKEN
## Poulet poché

*Henry IV was the French king well remembered for his wish that all the families in his kingdom have a chicken in the pot every Sunday. That is why you will find "La poule au pot Henri IV" on French country restaurant menus. You can easily modify the basic recipe: see the two following variations. Poached chicken is delicious hot or cold.*

Cut off the end wing tips of the chicken and the large glob of fat in the body cavity. Sprinkle a pinch of salt and pepper in the cavity along with the thyme and basil leaves. Tie the chicken legs together, then tie the wings to the body. Peel the onion, cut it in half, stick 4 cloves in each half and brown quickly, cut sides down, in a very small amount of oil. Cut the whole head of garlic partially across, so that the cloves are still attached. Make a large bouquet garni by tying together 4–5 parsley sprigs, 3 thyme sprigs, and either a branch of basil or 2 stalks of rosemary.

Place the chicken in a large, heavy pot with the onion, garlic, bouquet garni, sea salt and water to completely cover (about 30 cups). Bring the water to a boil over medium-high heat. This will probably take about 20 minutes. While the chicken is cooking, peel the carrots and cut them into large pieces. Wash the leeks well, discard most of the green tops and cut the leeks lengthwise down to, but not through, their bases. Cut ends off the zucchini and cut each zucchini into 3 pieces, then cut the pieces in half.

When the water reaches a good, rolling boil, turn the heat down a bit and cook chicken for 20 minutes. Add the carrots to the pot and cook for 15 minutes; add the potatoes and leeks and cook another 15 minutes. Ten minutes before serving, add the zucchini.

Carve the poached chicken into serving pieces and surround them with the vegetables and juice from the cooking. Serve with mustard, or with a combination of sour cream and horseradish.

# POACHED CHICKEN WITH CREAM
### Poulet poché à la crème

Prepare the chicken and poach as directed in the preceding recipe. Then, 20 minutes before the end of the cooking, ladle out 1 cup of the chicken broth into a small pan, add the heavy cream and reduce for about 10 minutes. Mix the arrowroot with the cold water, add it to the cream and reduce further, until sauce is glossy, about 6 minutes. Whisk occasionally. Pass sauce through a fine-meshed sieve and return it to a clean, medium-size saucepan. Add a pinch of freshly grated nutmeg, taste and correct seasoning if necessary; add salt and pepper if desired.

Carve the chicken into pieces and heat the pieces in the sauce briefly, about half a minute. Serve hot with white rice and cooked vegetables. Garnish with chopped parsley.

*1 whole chicken*
*Salt, white pepper*
*2–3 fresh thyme sprigs or ¼ teaspoon dried thyme*
*3–4 basil leaves*
*1 large onion*
*8 whole cloves*
*Oil*
*1 whole head garlic, unpeeled*
*A bouquet garni of parsley, thyme, and basil or rosemary (p. 182)*
*1 tablespoon sea salt*
*Cold water*
*1 large carrot*
*1 leek*
*1 zucchini*
*1 cup heavy cream*
*½ teaspoon arrowroot*
*2 teaspoons cold water*
*Freshly grated nutmeg*
Garniture: *chopped parsley*

**SERVES 4**

# POACHED CHICKEN WITH CABBAGE
### Potée de poulet

Cut off the end wing tips of the chicken and the large glob of fat from the body cavity. Sprinkle a pinch of salt and pepper into the cavity. Tie the chicken legs together, then tie the wings to the body. Peel the carrots and the onion and cut them in half. Cut the head of garlic partially across, so that the cloves are still attached.

Place the chicken in a large pot with 30–35 cups of water, the carrots, onion, garlic, bouquet garni and sea salt. Bring to a boil and cook over high heat for about 45 minutes.

Cut the head of green cabbage into 6 sections (do not remove the core) and add to the pot 15 minutes after it reaches the boil. Turn the heat up slightly when you add the cabbage and push it down with a wooden spoon several times during the cooking process. If you wish, flavor with crushed juniper berries.

Carve the chicken into pieces and serve hot with the carrots, onion and cabbage. Ladle juice over the chicken and vegetables, and serve with bread on the side.

*1 whole chicken*
*Salt, white pepper*
*3 large carrots*
*1 medium-size onion*
*1 whole head of garlic, unpeeled*
*Cold water*
*A bouquet garni of parsley and thyme (p. 182)*
*1 tablespoon sea salt*
*1 head green cabbage*
*¼ teaspoon crushed juniper berries (optional)*

**SERVES 4**

2 drumsticks and thighs, not
    separated
Salt, white pepper (or herbed
    pepper)
1 scallion or 1 shallot
4–5 fresh basil leaves or fresh
    thyme or tarragon or sage
Oil (optional)
Chicken stock or white wine
    (optional)
2 tablespoons butter, softened
    (optional)

**SERVES 2**

# CHICKEN LEGS LIKE A LITTLE LEG OF LAMB
## Gigot de poulet

*Here is an amusing way to prepare chicken legs when you need to make stock from a whole chicken.*

First, remove the bone from the thigh so that the meat is still attached to the drumstick. This is not hard to do, but allow about 5 minutes for each leg the first time you do it. (See illustration below.) Lay a leg on your work surface, and with a small, sharp knife, cut down to the bone of the thigh, then cut along it. By a combination of cutting and scraping, separate the bone from the meat. Be careful not to cut through the meat that is connected to the drumstick. When the bone is free of the meat, remove it by cutting through the socket connecting it to the drumstick. Repeat with the other leg.

Spread the boneless thighs out flat and season them with salt and pepper. Chop the scallion and fresh herb leaves, and place them on the flattened meat. Tie the meat together in several places as you would a boneless leg of lamb.

There are 2 ways you can cook these little legs. Either steam them for 30–40 minutes, or sauté them briefly in a little oil, then cover the pan and cook in a medium oven (350°) for about 25 minutes. If desired, just before serving, deglaze the pan with chicken stock or white wine, and finish sauce with butter.

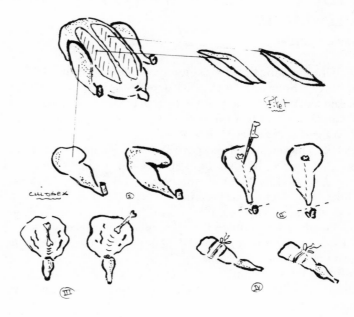

# CHICKEN PROVENÇAL
## Poulet à la provençale

Preheat oven to 300°. Remove the skin and bones from the breast but not from the legs. Bone out each thigh to produce a flat piece of meat attached to the drumstick. (See illustration and directions, p. 114.) If you do not want to take the time to bone out the thighs, season the skin of the drumsticks and thighs with salt, pepper and basil, and cook as directed in the next paragraph.) Season the flattened thigh meat with salt and herbed pepper, and sprinkle with 2 chopped basil leaves. Tie the meat together in several places. If you are using bacon, put a strip of bacon around the center of each thigh and tie with a piece of string so that the bacon encircles the folded meat.

Heat 1 tablespoon of the oil in a medium-size saucepan. Over high heat, brown the chicken legs on one side in the hot oil for about 1 minute, then turn them over, cover the pan and continue cooking over low heat for about 15 minutes.

Chop the remaining basil leaves, the tomato, green pepper, garlic and scallion. Sprinkle the eggplant slices with salt. Heat 2 tablespoons of oil in a sauté pan and brown the eggplant slices in the hot oil over medium-high heat. Remove the pan to the oven and continue cooking the eggplant in the oven until the chicken is done.

Add the chopped vegetables, basil and white wine to the chicken, agitate the pan several times to mix things around, re-cover the pan and cook for another 15–20 minutes. Halfway through this process, check the chicken; if the vegetables have released a lot of liquid, finish cooking with the lid off.

Just before the chicken legs are done, cook the breasts. Salt and pepper them, and sauté quickly in a small pan with a very little oil. Cut them in long diagonal slices so that the uncooked part is exposed. Run them under the broiler on a lightly oiled pan for about 2 minutes, turning them once.

Remove the eggplant slices from the oven and pat them with a towel to pick up any extra fat. Put an eggplant slice on each plate and lay a chicken leg on top of it. Fan the breast slices out beside them.

Return the saucepan in which the chicken legs cooked to the heat and reduce liquid slightly. Finish the sauce with the butter and pour it over the chicken. Garnish the plates with basil leaves.

*Breast, drumsticks and
  thighs of 1 chicken (do
  not separate the
  drumsticks from the
  thighs)*
*Salt, herbed pepper*
*6–7 basil leaves or fresh
  thyme leaves or ¼
  teaspoon of either herb,
  dried*
*2 pieces bacon (optional)*
*3 tablespoons oil plus a
  little extra*
*1 tomato*
*½ green pepper*
*1 clove garlic*
*1 scallion*
*2 slices eggplant (about ¾
  inch thick), unpeeled*
*1 tablespoon white wine*
*2 tablespoons butter,
  softened*
*Garniture: 4 basil leaves*

*SERVES 2*

# CHICKEN FRICASSEE WITH LEMON AND LIME
### *Fricassée de coq aux deux citrons*

*1 3½-pound chicken, cut into
   12 pieces*
*Flour*
*Salt, white pepper*
*4 tablespoons oil*
*3 tablespoons butter*
*2–3 large shallots, peeled and
   finely diced*
*3 cups chicken stock (p. 221)*
*1 cup white wine*
*1 lemon*
*2 limes*
*A pinch of nutmeg*
*Garniture: lemon and lime
   slices*

*SERVES 4*

Cut each chicken breast half into 2 pieces, separate the drumsticks from the thighs, cut the wings into 2 pieces at the joint. Reserve the back, neck, etc., for stock, or freeze them until you have time to make stock.

Flour the chicken pieces lightly and season them with salt and pepper. Heat the oil in a large pan and sauté the chicken pieces in the hot oil until they are brown on all sides. Remove them to a platter lined with a paper or linen towel.

Pour off the fat from the pan, add the butter and the shallots. Sweat them, stirring with a wooden spoon. Return the chicken to the pan and shake the pan vigorously. Add 2 tablespoons flour and cook for 2–3 minutes, stirring several times to mix well. Add the chicken stock and white wine, and season with salt and pepper. The liquid should cover the chicken. If you need more liquid, add some white wine, and, if you do not have more chicken stock, water and ½ a bouillon cube.

Turn the heat to medium low and partially cover the pan. Cook for 5 minutes. Turn the chicken pieces over and continue cooking, uncovered, for about 45 minutes, turning the chicken several times. Grate the lemon and lime peels, and 15 minutes before the chicken is done, add the grated peel and a sprinkling of nutmeg.

Serve the chicken with hot rice. Garnish with slices of lemon and lime that you have sectioned out from between the white membranes of the grated lemon and limes. Arrange these slices in a fan beside the chicken and rice.

*Salt, white pepper*
*1 whole chicken breast
   (2 halves), boned and
   skinned*
*2 tablespoons calvados*
*2 Granny Smith apples*
*2½ tablespoons butter,
   softened*
*1 teaspoon sugar*
*1 tablespoon oil*
*2 tablespoons heavy cream*
*Garniture: chopped parsley*

*SERVES 2*

# CHICKEN BREAST WITH CALVADOS AND APPLES
### *Blanc de poulet au calvados*

Preheat broiler. Salt and pepper the chicken breasts and marinate them for about 5–10 minutes in 1 tablespoon of the calvados. Peel and core 1 apple. Cut ⅓ of the apple into small dice. Make a lengthwise cut in each chicken breast to form a pocket, and fill the pockets with the chopped apple. Halve the remaining ⅔ of the apple, cut the halves into slices (you will have about 10 slices) and place them on a buttered metal plate. Sprinkle them with the sugar and dot with 1 teaspoon butter. Run the plate under the broiler for 3–4 minutes to caramelize the sugar and color the apple pieces.

Heat 1 teaspoon of the oil in a small pan. Sauté the chicken breasts over high heat for 2–3 minutes, turning them once. Put the pan in a 400° oven and continue cooking the chicken breasts for about 6 minutes.

Heat the remaining 2 teaspoons of oil in another small pan. Cut 2 thick (1-inch) slices from the middle of the remaining apple; remove the core but do not peel. Sauté apple slices in the hot oil just to color each side; they should be *al dente*, not soft.

Throw out the fat in the pan in which the chicken breasts have cooked and add the remaining 1 tablespoon of calvados. Heat it slightly, but do not let it boil. Flame it by carefully lighting the warmed liquid with a match. When the flame subsides, remove the chicken breasts to a warm plate or platter and add the cream to the pan. Reduce liquid for about 2 minutes, stirring occasionally. Finish the sauce with butter, if you wish.

Place each chicken breast on top of one of the thick apple slices; arrange the caramelized apple slices in a fan around the chicken. Pour the sauce over the chicken and garnish with chopped parsley.

# CHICKEN BREAST WITH BEER
## Blanc de poulet à la bière

Cut the chicken breasts in half lengthwise, then crosswise into large pieces. Cut the shallots into thin slices and sweat them briefly in the butter. Add the chicken pieces and sauté them on all sides for about 1 minute.

Add the flour to the pan and let it cook for about 1 minute until it is very dry, then pour in the beer and season with a pinch of salt and pepper. Cook very slowly, uncovered, for 10–15 minutes.

Cut the snow peas in half. Blanch the carrot and cut it into thin slices. Steam the snow peas and carrot, lightly sprinkled with olive oil, salt and pepper, for 3 minutes.

Dump the vegetables into the pan with the chicken and season with salt and pepper, if necessary. Finish sauce with the butter, if desired. Serve with rice.

*1 whole chicken breast (2 halves), boned and skinned*
*3 shallots*
*1 tablespoon butter*
*1 teaspoon flour*
*1 cup beer*
*Salt, freshly ground black pepper*
*12–16 snow peas*
*1 carrot*
*Olive oil*
*1 tablespoon butter, softened (optional)*

**SERVES 2**

# CHICKEN BREAST WITH PINEAPPLE AND STRAWBERRIES
*Suprême de poulet à l'ananas et aux fraises*

1 whole chicken breast
(2 halves), boned and
skinned
2 slices fresh or canned
pineapple
6 strawberries
1 teaspoon oil
Flour
Salt, white pepper
4 teaspoons butter, softened
3 tablespoons white wine
1 teaspoon fresh lime juice
Garniture: 2 strawberries
(from above), fresh parsley
and dill sprigs

SERVES 2

Slice the chicken breasts in half lengthwise to get 4 thin slices. (Boned and skinned chicken breasts sold separately at the supermarket are larger than those found on most whole chickens; these breasts should be cut into 6 slices.) Cut the pineapple slices into 8 wedge-shaped pieces. If using fresh pineapple, discard the core. Cut 4 of the strawberries in half, reserve the other 2 for the garniture.

Heat the oil in a frying pan. Flour the chicken pieces lightly and brown them on both sides in the hot oil. Season with salt and pepper. When you turn the chicken pieces over, add the pineapple slices and season with salt and pepper again.

When the chicken is just browned, remove it to a warm plate. Add 1 teaspoon of the butter to the pineapple and, after a few minutes, the white wine and strawberries. Finish the sauce with the remaining 1 tablespoon of butter and the lime juice.

Serve the chicken surrounded by the pineapple and strawberries. Cut the 2 remaining strawberries into fan shapes by slicing them up to the top hull section, but not all the way through. Flatten the partial slices with your thumb and place beside the chicken along with sprigs of parsley and dill.

1 whole chicken breast
(2 halves), boned and
skinned
½ green pepper
½ red pepper
4 scallions
2–3 shallots
1 tablespoon oil
Flour
Salt, white pepper
1 tablespoon butter
½ cup whiskey (Scotch, rye or
bourbon)

SERVES 2

# CHICKEN BREAST WITH WHISKEY
*Escalopes de poulet au whisky*

Slice the chicken breasts in half lengthwise to get 4 thin slices, then cut in half crosswise to attain 8 thin pieces. Remove the white membrane and seeds from the peppers and cut each one into about 12 pieces. Trim the scallions, keeping just the center sections; peel and slice the shallots.

Heat the oil in a pan. Flour the chicken pieces lightly and sauté them in the hot oil to brown them. Add the shallots and peppers, cook for 1 minute, then add the scallions. Season with salt and pepper.

When the chicken pieces are lightly browned, remove them to a warm place and continue cooking the vegetables for a few minutes. Add the butter and cook for another 3 minutes. Add the whiskey and swirl it around in the pan, being careful not to let it flame. Spoon the vegetables and sauce over the chicken and serve with rice or fresh spinach.

# CHICKEN BREAST AND LIVER

*Suprême de poulet aux foies de volailles*

*If you like the taste of liver, here is an unusual recipe that will appeal to you. Lemon Butter Sauce (p. 228) goes nicely with this.*

Preheat oven to 350°–400°. Butterfly each breast half, splitting it almost entirely and spreading the meat open so that it lies flat. Remove the connecting tissue and fat from the chicken livers and chop them finely.

Peel and chop finely the garlic and shallot. Sweat the shallot in the butter for 1–2 minutes. Cut the crusts off the bread and crumble it in a bowl with the cream. Beat the egg with a fork. Add the garlic, sweated shallot, chicken livers, egg and parsley to the bowl with the bread and cream, and season with salt and pepper.

Heat the oil in a sauté pan and quickly brown the chicken breasts, about 1–2 minutes a side. Place the breasts on a lightly buttered metal plate and spoon the chicken liver mixture over them. Cook for 10 minutes in the oven, then serve on top of a Potato Pancake (p. 166) or with a green salad.

*1 whole chicken breast (2 halves), boned and skinned*
*2 chicken livers*
*1 clove garlic*
*1 shallot*
*½ teaspoon butter*
*1 slice soft bread*
*2 teaspoons heavy cream*
*1 egg*
*1 teaspoon chopped parsley*
*Salt, herbed pepper*
*1 tablespoon oil*

**SERVES 2**

# CHICKEN WINGS MINUTE

*Ailerons de poulet*

*I like to serve radicchio with these crispy little wings because the dark red leaves set them off so nicely.*

Salt and pepper the chicken wings; heat the oil, and when it is very hot, add the wings. Cook them over high heat until they are brown, about 5 minutes, turning them once or twice.

Peel the carrot, steam it briefly and cut it into pieces. Chop the scallion and cut the snow peas into pieces. Add the vegetables and the sugar to the chicken, shake the pan vigorously and continue cooking another 5–10 minutes.

Form the radicchio leaves into cups and transfer the chicken wings and vegetables onto the lettuce. Squeeze lemon juice over the wings just before eating.

*Salt, white pepper*
*12 chicken wing halves (the 2 end joints, not the meatier first section)*
*2 teaspoons oil*
*1 small carrot*
*1 scallion*
*12 snow peas*
*1 teaspoon sugar*
*Radicchio or other lettuce*
*Juice of ½ a lemon*

**SERVES 2**

1 whole chicken breast
   (2 halves), boned and
   skinned
Olive oil
Salt, white pepper
3 small cooked new potatoes
1 teaspoon lemon juice
1 teaspoon chopped basil
½ teaspoon chopped shallot
⅛ teaspoon chopped garlic
Freshly ground black pepper
Chopped tomatoes (optional)
Chopped green and/or red
   peppers (optional)
Chopped celery (optional)
Chopped parsley (optional)

SERVES 2

# CHICKEN SALAD
## Salade de poulet

*Here is an easy chicken salad that travels well for a picnic.*

Rub chicken breast with a little olive oil and season with salt and pepper. Cook in a steamer for about 10 minutes. Let the chicken cool, then cut it into cubes. Peel the potatoes and cut them into slices.

Mix the lemon juice with 2 tablespoons olive oil, the basil, shallots, garlic, salt and black pepper. Pour over the chicken and potatoes and mix well. Add chopped tomatoes, bell peppers, celery, parsley, if desired.

Stuffing
1 shallot
¼ teaspoon chopped garlic
1 teaspoon butter
5 medium-size cooked shrimp
   and their shells
2 slices soft white bread
1 egg
1 scallion (green part only)
4 tablespoons heavy cream
Salt, white pepper

Salt, white pepper
2 Cornish game hens
2 tablespoons oil
2 teaspoons butter
¼ onion
¼ carrot
1 clove garlic
1 teaspoon flour
4 tablespoons white wine
4 tablespoons chicken stock
   (p. 221)
1½–2 tablespoons butter,
   softened (optional)

SERVES 4

# CORNISH GAME HENS STUFFED WITH SHRIMP
## Coquelets farcis aux crevettes

*I think you will like this recipe for the useful little Cornish game hens; you can, of course, also use the shrimp stuffing for chicken. (See Note.)*

Preheat oven to 350°–400°. Make the stuffing: peel and chop the shallot. Briefly sweat the shallot and the ¼ teaspoon chopped garlic in the 1 teaspoon butter. Remove the shrimp from their shells, discard the intestines, and chop the shrimp finely. Reserve the shells. Cut the crusts off the bread and cut the bread into cubes. Beat the egg with a fork. Chop the scallion. Mix the shallot, garlic, shrimp, bread, egg, scallion and cream together in a small bowl, and season with a pinch of salt and pepper to taste.

Sprinkle a pinch of salt and pepper in the body cavities of the birds, then spoon in the stuffing. Truss the birds so that the string does not cross the breasts and make a mark.

Heat 1 tablespoon of the oil in a sauté pan until it is very hot. Brown the birds on all sides in the hot oil, turning them with tongs. When they are entirely brown, dot each bird with 1 teaspoon butter and put the pan into the oven. Cook for about 30 minutes, turning the game hens every 10 minutes.

While the birds are cooking, peel the onion and carrot and cut them into large pieces; peel and smash the garlic. After 30 minutes of cooking, remove the game hens from the oven onto a plate. Pour off the fat in the pan, and any stuffing that has leaked out; clean the pan and return it to the top of the stove. Heat the remaining 1 tablespoon of oil in the pan and quickly brown the birds, the onion, carrot, garlic and the shrimp shells. Return the pan to the oven for another 10–15 minutes.

Remove the birds to a warm plate. Pour off any fat in the pan and add 1 teaspoon flour. Stir it in vigorously over medium-high heat until just dry, then immediately add the white wine, chicken stock and a pinch of salt and pepper. Cook for 2–3 minutes. Strain the sauce into a small pan and reduce it for 2 minutes. Finish with butter, if desired, and serve the birds on a Little Doormat of Leek and Zucchini (p. 161) with the sauce poured over them.

*Note:* This amount of stuffing is enough for a 3½–4-pound chicken; cook the chicken about 1 hour and 15 minutes.

1 Cornish game hen
3 large carrots
Salt
1 large onion
2 large cloves garlic
Flour
3 tablespoons oil
1 tablespoon butter
2 tablespoons chopped parsley
2 tablespoons chopped fresh
    basil
2 tablespoons chopped
    scallion
White pepper
2 tablespoons red wine
    vinegar
2 pieces orange peel
1 cup chicken stock (p. 221)
Garniture: grated orange peel

*SERVES 2*

# CORNISH GAME HEN WITH CARROTS
### Coquelet aux carottes

Cut the game hen into 8 pieces, discard the backbone. Peel the carrots and slice them, not thinly. Poach them in boiling, salted water, about 3 minutes after the water returns to a boil; drain, refresh in cold water and dry. Peel the onion and slice thinly. Peel and smash the garlic, then chop coarsely.

Roll the game hen pieces in flour. Heat the oil in a sauté pan until it is very hot. Cook the game hen in the hot oil over high heat for about 3 minutes, turning pieces with tongs to attain even browning.

Melt the butter in a medium-size saucepan. Cook the onion slices in the butter until just brown, then add the garlic, carrots, parsley, basil and scallion. Season with salt and pepper. Cook over high heat for 6 minutes. Add the game hen pieces, vinegar, orange peel and chicken stock. Let come to a boil, then cover the pan and cook very slowly over low heat for 30 minutes. Turn the pieces once during this process.

Serve the game hen with the vegetables. Garnish with grated orange peel.

*Note:* You can, of course, substitute cut-up chicken for the game hen pieces; cook the chicken 15 minutes longer.

1 Cornish game hen
Salt, herbed pepper
1 onion
1 carrot
1 stalk celery
3 Belgian endives
Juice of ½ lemon
1 tablespoon olive oil
Butter

*SERVES 2*

# STEAMED CORNISH GAME HEN
### Coquelet à la vapeur

*This simple recipe is very light and will be a welcome addition to a diet menu.*

Cut the game hen in half along the backbone. Remove the breast bone so that you have 2 boneless breast halves. Separate the thighs from the body, but keep the drumsticks attached to the thighs. Remove the thigh bones by scraping and cutting the meat away from them; sever the thigh bones from the drumsticks. (See p. 114.) Sprinkle the pieces with salt and herbed pepper.

Peel the onion and carrot, andcut them and the celery into large pieces. Cut out the bitter end of the endives and halve lengthwise. Sprinkle them with the lemon juice.

Fill the bottom of a steamer with hot water; add the onion, carrot, celery and olive oil, and bring to a boil. Butter the perforated top section of the steamer to prevent the game hen from sticking. Place the game hen pieces and the endives in the steamer top; dot a few small pieces of butter on the endive. Cook, covered, for 20–25 minutes.

# *CORNISH GAME HEN FRITTERS*
## Coquelet en beignet

*Here is a new version of fried chicken. Serve the fritters with lemon wedges or Fresh Tomato Sauce (p. 239).*

Remove the skin and bones from the breast of a Cornish game hen and cut each breast half into thin diagonal slices, about 4–5 slices per half. Remove the skin from the legs and thighs and cut the meat off the bones in thin slices.

Beat the flour and beer together in a bowl until smooth. In a separate bowl, beat the egg whites until light and fluffy; incorporate them into the beer batter.

Heat the oil in a sauté pan. Season the game hen pieces with salt and herbed pepper. When the oil is very hot, dip each piece into the batter, then slide it into the hot oil. (It is better to fry the fritters in 2 batches.) After about 1 minute, when the fritters color on one side, turn them over, and cook for another 2 minutes. Remove the pieces to a platter covered with a paper or linen towel and cook the second batch. Serve immediately with lemon wedges and a salad.

*Breast, thighs and drumsticks*
*of 1 Cornish game hen*
*1 cup flour*
*1 cup beer*
*2 egg whites*
*½ cup oil*
*Salt, herbed pepper*
*Lemon wedges*

***SERVES 2***

## Duck

You can make any number of interesting recipes with duck. Roast duck is good with fresh or dried fruits, and a number of sauces go well with duck. When you are feeling ambitious sometime in the cold winter months, please make the confit. It is a grand old recipe from southwestern France.

I use Long Island ducklings, a domestic duck readily available in supermarkets in the Northeast. They are fatty but very tasty.

Wild duck has a different flavor from domesticated duck, but it is also good roasted with fresh fruit, with a *sauce poivrade*, or in a salmi (a ragoût of game cooked in a rich sauce). Sometimes wild duck has a strong odor a little like that of fish.

And do not forget goose. It too is splendid for confit, but is also delicious simply roasted with its own juice, served with glazed turnips lightly perfumed with a zest of orange. If you are the happy recipient of a wild goose, cook it with red cabbage; it is wonderful.

I bought a little white goose at the market when I was twelve years old and named her Zézé. Of course she grew bigger, and when she did so, she became very tame and full of love for my mother, whom she followed around everywhere. Sometimes she would even go into the village, because she had the naughty habit of hiding herself in the car whenever the windows were open. As she got older, Zézé became more aggressive and bit the heels of anyone who came to the farm. She was so bad, my father finally had to get rid of her.

1 tablespoon oil
1 Long Island–type duckling
    (about 5–6 pounds)
Salt, white pepper
16 dried figs
2 cups red wine
6 tablespoons sugar
1 cup duck stock (p. 220)
Salt, white pepper
1½ tablespoons butter,
    softened (optional)

SERVES 4

# ROAST DUCK WITH FIGS
*Canard rôti aux figues*

*Roast duck marries well with many fruits, but I urge you to try this recipe with figs. I think you will like it.*

Preheat oven to 400°. In a pan on top of the stove, heat the oil until it is very hot. Season the duck with salt and pepper, and brown it on all sides in the hot oil. Place duck on a rack in a roasting pan and cook it in the oven for about 1½ hours. Turn it 3 times during the cooking so that it cooks on its side as well as on its back. The rack is very important for cooking this type of duck because it is so fatty. You should also be careful at the end of the cooking to let the fat cool somewhat before you throw it out or you may give yourself a bad burn.

Poach the figs in the red wine and sugar for about 20 minutes. Remove the figs and continue reducing the liquid until it is very syrupy. Return the figs to the wine just before servng so that they become shiny and coated with the wine.

Carve the duck so that the breast meat, the legs and thighs retain their skin. Reduce the duck stock. Finish sauce with butter, if desired. Place the figs around the duck pieces on a platter and spoon sauce over them.

Breast of 1 duck (2 halves),
    boned and skinned
10 baby carrots
4 scallions
1 leek
½ zucchini
3 basil leaves
1 tablespoon oil
Salt, white pepper
Herbed pepper (optional)
1 tablespoon butter
5 tablespoons duck stock
    (p. 220)

SERVES 2

# QUICK DUCK BREAST STEW WITH VEGETABLES
*Canard aux légumes*

*You only need the breast of the duck for this recipe, so it makes great sense to make duck stock with the rest of the bird. You can also reserve the legs for confit. (You can, of course, save the legs and the bones in the freezer until you are ready to use them.)*

Remove all the white fat and tear off the thin membrane from around the breast. Cut each breast half crosswise into 5 diagonal slices.

Peel the carrots and cook them for about 3 minutes in salted water. Cut the scallions in half lengthwise and then into 1–1½-inch pieces. Wash the leek and quarter lengthwise, then cut it crosswise; cut the zucchini into wide, flat julienne strips, then into pieces so that the pieces of scallion, leek and zucchini are approximately the same size. Use only the outside pieces of the zucchini; the skin gives a good color. Chop the basil coarsely.

Heat the oil in a sauté pan until it is very hot, then add the strips of duck breast. Season them with salt and pepper, and sauté them briefly. Agitate the pan back and forth while they cook. After the breast slices begin to color a little, add the vegetables and basil, and season with salt and herbed pepper. Add the butter and continue cooking on very high heat, agitating the pan occasionally, for about 7 minutes. Add the duck stock and cook for an additional 2 minutes.

# DUCK CONSERVE
## Confit de canard

*Originally created as a means of keeping meat safely before refrigeration, confit has come to be considered one of the most refined of food preparations.*

Cut the breast pieces off the duck, leaving the wings attached to the breasts. Cut off the thighs, leaving the drumsticks attached to them. Cut off all the obvious pieces of fat on the remaining duck and reserve. You will have about 2 cups of fat. Reserve the duck carcass for duck stock.

You now have 4 pieces of duck that have a layer of fat between the skin and the meat. Place skin side down on a cutting board and trim any extra fat around the edges of the meat so that the fat does not overlap the meat edges. Salt the pieces on both sides with the sea salt, place on a plate, cover with plastic wrap and refrigerate for 24 hours.

Put the reserved duck fat in a saucepan with the water and bring it just to a boil. Reduce the heat and cook very slowly for 1½ hours. If any scum rises to the top, skim it off. Strain the fat into a bowl, let it cool to room temperature, then refrigerate.

Rinse the salt off the duck pieces and pat them dry. The salt will have firmed up the meat, and it will not be bloody. Again trim off any fat overlapping the edges of the meat pieces. In a medium-size pot, melt the refrigerated fat, which now looks light and fluffy. Add the duck pieces, skin side down, and cook over medium heat, uncovered, until the meat rises to the top of the fat, about 1¼ hours. If the pieces do not rise after this time, cook for another 15 minutes.

Place the duck pieces in a stainless-steel or enamel container. Ladle in enough fat to completely cover the duck pieces. Let the duck and fat cool to room temperature, then refrigerate. The duck will keep in the refrigerator for up to 6 months.

When you are ready to prepare the duck (it should have been refrigerated at least 24 hours first), cut the pieces in half with a cleaver. If you do not like the skin, cut it off. Preheat the oven to 350°–400°. Heat the oil in a sauté pan. When it is very hot, add the cold duck pieces and cook them over high heat for about 3 minutes on each side. Remove the pan to the oven for 15–20 minutes. Serve the duck on Crispy Potato (p. 167).

1 Long Island duckling (about 5–6 pounds)
1 generous tablespoon sea salt
5 tablespoons water
1 tablespoon oil

**SERVES 4**

Fat from a fresh duck
¾ cup water
1 tablespoon oil
Freshly ground black pepper
3 tablespoons wine vinegar
Lettuce for salad: Boston
    lettuce, radicchio, endive
Fresh basil leaves
1 slice or crust of French
    bread (optional)
1 clove garlic (optional)
Salt (optional)

SERVES 2

# CRISPY DUCK FAT SALAD
## Salade de gratillons

*Next time you cook a duck, instead of throwing out the fat, make this original salad. It is an economical use of the duck fat and far from banal.*

Cook the fat with the water in a small saucepan over medium heat for 20–30 minutes. Strain off the liquid yellow fat. You can use this to make confit or to preserve meat or poultry without refrigeration, as was the custom in the old days.

Cut the pieces of solid fat into strips and pat them dry. Sauté them with the oil in a small frying pan over a high heat. Turn the pieces so that they become crispy on all sides. Pour off any extra fat halfway through the cooking. Season strips with a few grinds of black pepper, and remove them from the pan to a paper towel. Throw out any fat and pour the vinegar into the pan to deglaze it.

Pile the lettuce leaves and basil into a bowl. If you wish, add a piece of French bread rubbed with a cut garlic clove and cut into pieces. Add the crispy fat strips and the pan juices; season with a pinch of salt, if desired, and toss well. This salad needs no other dressing.

# *MEAT*

QUICK LAMB CHOPS
 WITH SHALLOTS
LAMB CHOPS IN THE
 STEAMER
SOFT LEG OF LAMB

VEAL IN AN
 ENVELOPE WITH
 CORIANDER
BRAISED VEAL CHOPS
STUFFED BREAST OF
 VEAL

CALF'S LIVER WITH
 ENDIVE
CALF'S LIVER WITH
 SCALLIONS
CALF'S LIVER
 PACKAGES

VEAL KIDNEY WITH
 WATERCRESS
VEAL KIDNEY IN RED
 WINE

SWEETBREAD WITH
 FRESH NOODLES
SWEETBREAD IN A
 SALAD

LEAN PHEASANT AND
 VEAL PÂTÉ IN
 LETTUCE *(p. 26)*
LIGHT LAMB PÂTÉ
 *(p. 26)*

This is a short chapter because the emphasis in my cooking is more on fish than meat. But I do want to give you these few easy recipes for lamb and veal, to me the best of meats.

Lamb is a delicate meat that does not have the strong odor of mutton. The neck, breast and top of the ribs are best suited for a stew, for sautéing or even for a pot-au-feu with lamb. The little steaks (*noisettes*) taken from the saddle or the ribs are superb when served with lamb juice and morels or fresh thyme. I call your attention to the illustration below, which shows you how to cut the noisettes.

If you cut the steaks into thin slices, they will cook very quickly, no more than 1 minute or less on each side, in hot oil. When asparagus is in the market, sauté cooked asparagus tips with the lamb and serve them with lamb stock that you have reduced along with the asparagus stalks.

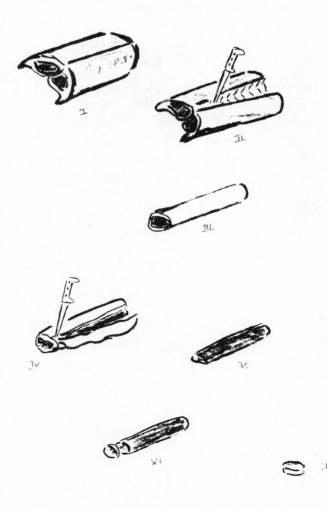

### Baby Lamb

If you can find baby lamb in the spring, cook it simply because the meat is so good unadorned. The lamb must be no older than 3 weeks and still milk-fed; the taste of the meat changes after the lambs start eating grass. Season baby lamb chops with salt and white pepper. Brown them quickly in oil, then put the pan in a preheated 400° oven until the meat is done to your taste, about 8 minutes. A baby lamb leg will take about 30 minutes in the oven (400°) after browning. You can paint mustard on the lamb 5 minutes before it is finished.

## QUICK LAMB CHOPS WITH SHALLOTS

*Côtes d'agneau aux échalotes cuisson minute*

*Here is a quick, easy recipe, well balanced in taste, and suited for family meals.*

Trim off the extra fat around the lamb chops and season them with salt and pepper. Cut the shallots into quarters and poach them in a steamer or in a little boiling water. Peel the garlic clove, smash it and cut it into small dice.

Sauté the chops and shallots in the hot oil until the chops are done to your taste. (I like mine rare, so I do not cook them very long.) Remove the chops and continue cooking the shallots until they are very brown.

Put the chops back in the pan, sprinkle with the flour, mix it in a bit, add the white wine and agitate the pan. Remove the chops to a warm place, add the lamb stock or water, parsley, garlic, thyme, and a little salt and pepper. Reduce this sauce over high heat and serve over the chops.

*4 thin lamb chops*
*Salt, white pepper*
*6 large shallots*
*1 clove garlic*
*1 tablespoon oil*
*1 teaspoon flour*
*2 tablespoons white wine*
*2 tablespoons lamb stock*
*(p. 220) or light lamb*
*stock (Note p. 219)*
*1 tablespoon chopped parsley*
*Fresh thyme leaves or ¼*
*teaspoon dried thyme*

**SERVES 2**

## LAMB CHOPS IN THE STEAMER

*Côtes d'agneau à la vapeur*

*This dish is very light and contains very few calories; it is perfect for those on a diet.*

Season the water in the bottom of a steamer with a few drops of olive oil, the garlic cloves (whole, unpeeled and lightly crushed) and 1 of the thyme branches. Salt and pepper the lamb chops, and sprinkle them with the leaves from the remaining thyme branches. Cook for about 25 minutes in the buttered top perforated section of the steamer. Serve with lemon juice or Fresh Tomato Sauce.

*Olive oil*
*A few cloves garlic*
*3 large fresh branches of*
*thyme or ¼ teaspoon dried*
*thyme*
*Salt, white pepper*
*4 very thin lamb chops*
*Lemon juice*
*Sauce suggestion: Fresh*
*Tomato Sauce (p. 239)*

**SERVES 2**

# SOFT LEG OF LAMB

## Compote de gigot

*This is a lovely way to surprise your family and guests. The lamb cooks for a long, long time, and it becomes so soft and juicy that you serve and eat it with a spoon.*

Lamb stock (p. 220) or light
   lamb stock (Note p. 219)
1½ cups dried beans (white
   beans are the best choice)
2 carrots
2 onions
1 whole head garlic
2 tablespoons oil
1 leg of lamb
Salt, freshly ground black
   pepper
White wine
Water
¼ cup port
A fresh bouquet garni with
   thyme (p. 182)
A handful of dried
   mushrooms
A few peppercorns

**SERVES 6**

If you do not have lamb stock, get a few bones when you buy the leg and make a light stock. Soak the dried beans for a few hours.

Peel and slice the carrots and onions. Do not peel or separate the garlic head. In a large heavy pot, heat the oil until very hot and brown the leg of lamb on all sides. Season with salt and pepper. Add the carrots and onions just to brown them a little.

Pour out the oil. Cover the lamb and vegetables with the lamb stock, white wine, water and port. The stock should make up a little more than half the liquid, the other half should be ⅓ white wine and ⅔ water. Add the bouquet garni, garlic, dried beans, dried mushrooms, peppercorns and salt to taste. (You do not have to soak the mushrooms.) Bring to a boil and cover the pot closely with heavy aluminum foil and then with a tight-fitting pot cover. Cook the lamb in a very slow oven (250°) for 7–8 hours.

To serve, place the lamb, vegetables and sauce in a large earthenware bowl (something rustic-looking). Spoon onto individual plates at the table.

*Veal*

Veal is the meat of a calf during its first year of life. It is at its best at about 3 months of age, when the meat should be white or very lightly pink. Too much color indicates that the "veal" is from an animal no longer a calf, but an adult.

# VEAL IN AN ENVELOPE WITH CORIANDER
*Papillote de veau au coriandre*

*This is the same method as for Red Mullet Cooked in an Envelope, the recipe for which you will find on p. 84. It works nicely for veal.*

*2 thin slices filet of veal*
*1 leek*
*A few coriander leaves*
*A few drops of olive oil*
*1 tablespoon white wine*
*A soupçon freshly grated nutmeg*
*Salt, freshly ground black pepper*

*SERVES 1*

Preheat oven to 350°–400°. Cut the veal slices in half. Wash the leek well and cut it crosswise into slices. Lay a piece of aluminum foil (about 15 × 18 inches) on your work surface and fold it in half lengthwise; open it up again. Spread half of the leek pieces on the bottom half of the foil, in the center just below the fold. Lay the veal slices on them, then add the rest of the leek, the coriander, olive oil, white wine and nutmeg. Season with salt and pepper.

Bring the top half of the foil down to the bottom edge and fold it in so that the first fold measures 1 inch. Repeat with 2 more folds of about ½ inch each. Turn the package around and fold the 2 sides in the same way. Place the envelope on a baking pan in the oven and cook for 15 minutes, or until the envelope puffs up.

*Note:* You can prepare the envelopes a few hours ahead of time; keep them in the refrigerator and remember to cook them a few minutes longer.

6 button mushrooms
2 shallots
½ carrot
1 teaspoon oil
1 tablespoon butter
Flour
2 veal chops (½-inch thick)
Salt, white pepper
⅛ teaspoon chopped garlic
1 tablespoon chopped parsley
2 tablespoons chopped
  scallion
1 tablespoon chopped basil
2 tablespoons cognac

SERVES 2

# BRAISED VEAL CHOPS
## Côtes de veau étuvées

Slice the mushrooms. Peel and slice the shallots. Peel the carrot and cut into small dice. Heat the oil and butter in a pan. Flour the chops lightly and brown them on one side over medium-high heat. Turn the chops over, add the mushrooms, shallots and carrot, season with salt and pepper, and cook, covered, for about 6 minutes.

Turn the chops again, add the garlic, parsley, scallion and basil, and cook for another 6 minutes. Then, 2 minutes before the chops are done, add the cognac.

Season with salt and pepper, if desired, and serve with the vegetables spooned over the chops.

1 boned breast of veal (about
  2½ pounds)
Salt, freshly ground black
  pepper
1 stalk celery
½ leek, washed
½ carrot
⅓ zucchini
7 cloves garlic
4 basil leaves, chopped, or
  ¼ teaspoon dried basil
2 tablespoons chopped
  scallion
3 tablespoons oil
White pepper
6 large shallots
1 cup white wine

SERVES 6

# STUFFED BREAST OF VEAL
## Poitrine de veau farcie

*This easy recipe using an inexpensive cut of veal is perfect for entertaining because it can be prepared ahead of time. Cook the stuffing and roll it up in the veal. Keep the rolled meat in the refrigerator until an hour before serving. Cook as directed. Or cook ahead of time and reheat meat just before serving (see Note), or serve it cold with mayonnaise.*

Preheat oven to 350°–400°. Trim excess fat off the veal, lay it flat on your work surface and season it with salt and black pepper. Cut the celery, leek, carrot and zucchini into thin julienne slices. Smash 1 garlic clove and dice it into small pieces.

Heat 1 tablespoon oil in a pan, and when it is hot, add the celery, leek, carrot, zucchini, diced garlic, scallion and basil; season with a pinch of salt and white pepper. Cook the vegetables for about 3 minutes over medium-high heat, agitating the pan occasionally.

Pour the vegetables onto the veal and spread them out. Leave a margin around the edge of the vegetable stuffing. Roll up the meat lengthwise and secure it in 7–8 places with string.

Heat the remaining 2 tablespoons oil in a baking pan. When the oil is hot, add the veal, the 6 remaining garlic cloves and the shallots (both shallots and garlic are whole and unpeeled). Sauté the meat on all sides until it is brown, about 3–5 minutes; sprinkle with a generous pinch of salt. Remove the pan to the oven and cook veal for about 45 minutes.

Halfway through the cooking, pour off all the fat in the pan and add the white wine. Return the pan to the oven.

Just before serving, remove the meat to a platter and reduce the juices over medium-high heat. Spoon the juice, shallots and garlic over the meat. Carve into slices.

*Note:* To reheat, place the veal in a pan with a little water and white wine or chicken stock and cook for 15 minutes in a 250°–300° oven.

# CALF'S LIVER WITH ENDIVE
*Sauté de foie de veau aux endives*

**4 thin slices calf's liver (about 10 ounces)**
**½ carrot**
**2 endives**
**1 tablespoon oil**
**Salt, white pepper**
**1 tablespoon chopped parsley**
**1 teaspoon chopped shallots**
**1 tablespoon sugar**
**3 tablespoons port**

**SERVES 2**

Cut the calves liver into short strips. Blanch the carrot and cut it crosswise into thin slices. Cut off the stem end of the endives and cut them in half across, then cut each leaf in half lengthwise.

Heat the oil in a frying pan until it is very hot. Season the liver with salt and pepper, then sauté quickly over high heat. After a few minutes, add the parsley and shallots, then the carrot and endives. Add the sugar; shake and agitate the pan continuously. After 1 minute, add the port, cook for only a bare half minute longer, just to reduce the port, and serve.

# CALF'S LIVER WITH SCALLIONS
*Foie de veau aux scallions*

**Flour**
**4 thin pieces calf's liver (about 10 ounces)**
**1 tablespoon oil**
**4 tablespoons chopped scallion**
**1 tablespoon red wine vinegar**
**2 tablespoons brown stock (pp. 219–220)**
**1 tablespoon butter, softened (optional)**
**Salt, white pepper**

**SERVES 2**

Flour the calves liver pieces lightly. Heat the oil in a sauté pan until it is very hot. Add the liver and sauté over very high heat for about half a minute. Add the scallion, turn the liver pieces over and cook another half minute.

Add the vinegar and the stock. Remove the liver to warmed plates and finish the sauce with butter, if desired. Season with salt and pepper. Ladle the sauce over the liver and serve immediately.

**4 thin pieces calf's liver
(about 10 ounces)
Salt, herbed pepper
2 teaspoons chopped shallots
plus 2 whole shallots
2 teaspoons chopped scallion
1 teaspoon chopped parsley
1 teaspoon chopped basil or
¼ teaspoon dried basil
½ carrot
½ leek
1½ teaspoons oil**

**SERVES 2**

# CALF'S LIVER PACKAGES
*Foie de veau alouette sans tête*

Preheat oven to 350°–400°. The calves liver pieces should be narrow. Lay them on your work surface and season them with salt and herbed pepper. Lay 1 piece of liver vertically and place another piece on top of it horizontally; repeat with the other 2 pieces so that you have 2 separate servings. (See illustration.)

Mix the chopped shallot with the scallion, parsley and basil, and spoon this mixture into the center of the liver pieces. Fold up the liver into little packages and tie them with string.

Peel the 2 whole shallots and cut them into quarters. Peel the carrot, cut it in half, then crosswise into thin slices. Wash the leek and cut it crosswise into thin slices. Heat the oil in a medium-size saucepan until it is very hot. Add the liver packages (top side down), the quartered shallots, the carrot and leek. Brown the liver quickly over high heat, turn the heat down and cook over low heat for a total of 5 minutes from the time you started. Turn the packages over, cook another 5 minutes over low heat; finish cooking the liver in the oven for about 5 minutes.

*Note:* You can prepare the liver packages and cut the vegetables several hours in advance and keep them in the refrigerator until you are ready to cook them.

**1 large veal kidney
2 bunches watercress
1 tablespoon sea salt
1–1½ tablespoons oil
Salt, white pepper
1 tablespoon butter
2 tablespoons cream**

**SERVES 2**

# VEAL KIDNEY WITH WATERCRESS
*Rognon de veau au cresson*

Preheat oven to 350°–400°. Cut the kidney into large pieces and cut these pieces into slices. Do not remove the fat from the kidney. As you make your slices, you will find that the fat in the center of each slice is necessary to hold the slices in one piece.

Wash the watercress and chop off the stem ends. Put the sea salt in a large pot of water, bring to a boil and add the watercress. Cook for about 3 minutes; drain.

Brown the kidney slices quickly on both sides in the hot oil. Season them with a pinch of salt and pepper, and put them in the oven for 3–5 minutes.

Put the drained watercress in a food processor and whirr briefly. Add the butter and cream and whirr again. Add a generous pinch of pepper. Spoon the watercress onto 2 plates and spread it out so that it covers the plate. Place the kidney slices on the cress and serve.

# VEAL KIDNEY IN RED WINE
*Rognon de veau au vin rouge*

Cut the kidney into medium-size pieces; cut off and discard the fat. Flour the kidney pieces lightly. Cut the shallots into small dice; mince the garlic.

Heat the oil in a medium-size frying pan; when it is very hot, add the floured kidney pieces. Sauté them for about 1 minute, then add the shallots and garlic; season with a generous pinch of salt and pepper. Agitate the pan during the cooking process.

After the shallots and garlic have cooked for 1 minute, add the 1 teaspoon of flour and the red wine. Stir with a wooden spoon and continue to agitate the pan. Cook for only 2 minutes. With tongs, remove the kidney pieces to a plate; keep them warm while you finish the sauce.

Season the sauce with a further pinch of salt and pepper. Add the port and let the sauce reduce for about 1 minute. Drop in pieces of the softened butter and agitate the pan to incorporate the butter into the sauce.

Place the kidney pieces on plates, spoon the sauce over them and sprinkle chopped parsley on top. Serve with rice, potatoes or noodles, and spinach.

*Note:* The kidney will be rare, that is, a little red on the inside, which is the way I like it. If you prefer them better done, cook a few minutes longer when you first add the pieces to the pan.

*1 veal kidney*
*Flour*
*2 shallots*
*1 clove garlic*
*1 tablespoon oil*
*Salt, white pepper*
*1 teaspoon flour*
*½ cup red wine*
*2 tablespoons port*
*1 tablespoon butter, softened*
**Garniture:** *chopped parsley*

**SERVES 2**

*Sweetbread*

A sweetbread is the thymus gland of a calf. You need to precook it slightly before it is ready for use. Blanch it in salted water to which you have added 1 tablespoon vinegar, a carrot, an onion and a bouquet garni (p. 182). Let it come to room temperature after the blanching; then refrigerate the sweetbread in the liquid; it will keep up to 2 days.

# SWEETBREAD WITH FRESH NOODLES
## Ris de veau aux pâtes fraîches

*1 sweetbread, prepared for cooking (see above)*
*Freshly cooked or reheated noodles*
*1 shallot*
*4 basil leaves*
*1 tablespoon oil*
*Salt, white pepper*
*1 cup veal stock (p. 219)*
*Garniture: a few basil leaves*

**SERVES 2**

Remove the skin from a blanched sweetbread and cut into slices. Cook the noodles in boiling, salted water, or reheat already cooked noodles in the top of a steamer that you have buttered slightly; season the water in the bottom of the steamer with a tablespoon of butter.

Chop the shallot and basil leaves. Heat the oil in a small frying pan. Over high heat, sauté the sweetbread slices, basil and shallot quickly, for about 2 minutes, turning them once with tongs and seasoning them with salt and pepper. Holding the sweetbread pieces in the pan with a spatula, pour out the oil. Add the veal stock to the pan, just to heat it through. Serve the sweetbread on top of the pasta, topped with 2–3 leaves of basil.

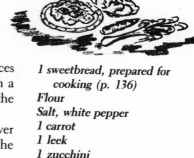

# SWEETBREAD IN A SALAD
## Salade de ris de veau

Remove the skin surrounding the sweetbread and slice it into pieces (not ultra-thin slices). Flour the slices lightly and season them with a small pinch of salt and pepper. Peel and blanch the carrot, wash the leek. Slice the carrot, zucchini and leek crosswise.

Heat the oil in a small frying pan. Sauté the sweetbread slices over high heat for about 2½ minutes on each side. Remove them from the pan and keep warm on a towel.

Add the carrot, zucchini and leek slices to the same pan, season them with salt and pepper, and sauté them quickly over high heat along with the parsley, shallot, garlic and basil.

Arrange the lettuce leaves on plates, perhaps 4 radicchio and 4 endive leaves on each, and spoon the vegetables over the lettuce. Place the sweetbread slices on top, spoon the vinaigrette over them and sprinkle with freshly ground black pepper.

*1 sweetbread, prepared for cooking (p. 136)*
*Flour*
*Salt, white pepper*
*1 carrot*
*1 leek*
*1 zucchini*
*2 tablespoons oil*
*1 tablespoon chopped parsley*
*1 teaspoon chopped shallots*
*¼ teaspoon chopped garlic*
*1 teaspoon fresh chopped basil*
*Salt, white pepper*
*Lettuce for salad: radicchio, endive (or any other lettuce)*
*2 tablespoons vinaigrette of your choice (pp. 174–176)*
*Freshly ground black pepper*

**SERVES 2**

# GAME

STUFFED PIGEON
PIGEON SALAD

QUAIL WITH BEANS
QUAIL IN THE
 STEAMER

PHEASANT AND
 CABBAGE
FILET OF PHEASANT
ROAST PHEASANT

LEAN PHEASANT AND
 VEAL PÂTÉ (p. 26)

GRILLED RABBIT
 BREAST
GIGOT OF RABBIT
QUICK RABBIT PIE
WILD RABBIT

RIBS OF VENISON
 WITH RED CABBAGE
WILD BIRD STUFFED
 WITH VENISON, THE
 CROWN OF THE
 CHASE

Fresh game in season offers the cook a nice variety of possibilities, but remember that different kinds of game require different cooking techniques. Wild birds such as pheasant, woodcock, quail, pigeon, thrush, etc., are usually eaten fresh and are easily digestible. Rabbit and other small animals and larger animals like deer (venison) often need a marinade (p. 150) before cooking to remove their gaminess and strong odor. (My own feeling is that if your wild rabbit is not too strong, you can eliminate the marinade. And of course it is not necessary for domesticated rabbit that you buy at the store.)

The best parts of venison are the saddle, roasted whole or cut into steaks; the loin, roasted whole or cut into chops; the shoulder, roasted or braised whole or cut into pieces for a stew or terrine; and the haunch, roasted or braised whole. The inferior parts of venison can be made into an excellent stew with rabbit.

*1 whole pigeon*
*Salt, white pepper*
*2 teaspoons chopped shallots*
    *plus 4 whole shallots*
*1 teaspoon butter*
*1½ slices white bread*
*⅓ cup heavy cream*
*1½ teaspoons chopped fresh*
    *basil, thyme or tarragon*
    *(or dried herbs, see Note)*
*¼ teaspoon chopped garlic*
*2 tablespoons chopped*
    *scallion*
*1 tablespoon beaten egg (1*
    *egg will do 4 pigeons)*
*1 generous teaspoon sour*
    *cream*
*2 slices bacon (optional)*
*½ carrot*
*½ tablespoon oil*
*1 teaspoon flour*
*½ cup white wine*
*½ cup water*

**SERVES 1–2**

# STUFFED PIGEON
## Pigeon farci

With a heavy knife, cut straight through the back of the pigeon. With a small, very sharp knife, remove the backbone and the liver by cutting and scraping away the meat clinging to the bones. Using this method, remove all the bones except those of the drumsticks and the wings; the thigh bones must come out also. Chop off the wing tips and first section of the wings. Reserve the wing pieces and all removed bones. (See illustration p. 141.)

With the pigeon still lying on its breast, season it with 2 pinches salt and a pinch of pepper. Where the breast is thick in the middle, slice it toward the outside edge so that you have an extra breast flap.

Make the stuffing: sweat the chopped shallots in the butter in a small pan for 1 minute. Cut the crusts off the bread and tear it into pieces. Mash the bread and cream together in a bowl with a fork. Add the sweated shallots, chopped fresh herbs, garlic, scallion, egg and sour cream. Mix this all together; it will be runny, not stiff.

If desired, lay 2 slices of bacon crosswise under the pigeon. Lay 4 pieces of string crosswise under the pigeon (2 of them under the bacon strips, if used). Spoon the stuffing onto the pigeon, fold the edges over the stuffing, and tie bird up. Do not worry if some of the stuffing runs out when you tie the strings.

Peel the carrot and the 4 whole shallots; cut the carrot into large pieces, leave the shallots whole. Heat the oil in a small sauté pan, and when it is hot, add the pigeon, breast side up, the reserved bones and wings, the carrots and shallots. Sauté the pigeon for 2–3 minutes over high heat, then turn it over and sauté it on the other side. Season it with salt and pepper.

After the bird is thoroughly browned on both sides, lower the heat, cover the pan and cook it for 30–35 minutes. If you like your birds well done, cook it a little longer.

Remove the pigeon to a platter and keep it warm. Pour out any fat remaining in the pan, but not the bones and vegetables. Mix in the flour, then add the white wine and water. Reduce over high heat for 10–15 minutes. Place the whole shallots and carrot pieces around the pigeon and strain the sauce over the bird. Crispy Potato (p. 167) goes nicely under the pigeon.

*Note:* If you do not have any of these fresh herbs, mix chopped parsley with ¼ teaspoon of a dried herb. You can also stuff a pigeon with wild rice, fresh herbs, garlic and scallions.

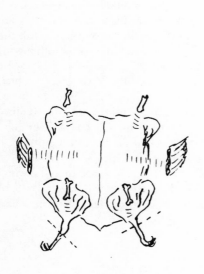

1 pigeon
1 cooked artichoke heart
2 cooked asparagus spears
¼ carrot
¼ medium-size zucchini
¼ tomato
½ scallion
Leaves from several stalks of
  fresh thyme or 3 basil
  leaves
2 tablespoons oil plus a little
  extra
Salt, freshly ground black
  pepper
Lettuce for salad: mache,
  radicchio
Sauce suggestions: Veal stock
  (p. 219) or lamb stock
  (p. 220) reduced and
  finished with butter, or
  Vinaigrette of your choice
  (pp. 174–176)
Garniture: chopped parsley, a
  tomato-peel rose (p. 11)

**SERVES 1**

# PIGEON SALAD
## Salade de pigeon

*This is particularly nice with squab (young pigeon). If you are doing it for more than one person, it would be worth your time to make stock from the remaining parts of the pigeons; be sure to remove the livers and kidneys before making the stock.*

Preheat broiler. Remove the breast meat from the pigeon by cutting down along the breastbone on each side of the bird with a sharp knife. Cut off the legs and wings and discard the small wing tips. Remove the skin from the breast pieces and any extra flapping skin from the legs. (See illustration.)

Slice the artichoke heart crosswise and cut the slices into halves. Cut the asparagus spears in half lengthwise. Peel the carrot and steam it briefly. Cut the carrot and the zucchini into vertical slices (but not thin julienne). Peel the tomato and slice it thinly, chop the scallion.

You will need 2 sauté pans. Place 1 tablespoon oil in each one. Cook the pigeon legs and wings in one pan on very high heat until they are browned all over, about 5–6 minutes. Sprinkle the vegetables with the thyme or basil leaves and cook in the same manner in the other pan, but only for 1 minute. Season with salt.

Push the pigeon pieces to one side and add the breast pieces, which you have salted lightly and rubbed with a little oil. Sauté the breast pieces very quickly on each side (about half a minute in all). Remove them from the pan and slice them very thinly on a diagonal. Run them under the broiler on a lightly oiled metal plate for just 1 minute to brown them. Season with a few grinds of black pepper.

Arrange the lettuce on the plate, then the vegetables, then the wings and legs, with the breast slices on top. Dress lightly with a vinaigrette or a hot brown sauce and sprinkle with chopped parsley. Garnish with a tomato-peel rose, if desired.

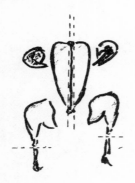

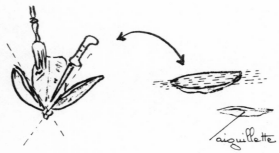

l'aiguillette

# QUAIL WITH BEANS
## Cailles aux flageolets

Preheat oven to 350°–400°. Season the quail body cavities with salt and pepper. Smash and chop the garlic, chop the shallots. Sweat the shallots in the butter in a medium-size saucepan. Drain the beans and rinse them with cold water. Add the beans, garlic and 2 tablespoons of the white wine to the shallots. Remove the beans from the heat until 5 minutes before serving.

Heat the oil in a baking pan, and when it is very hot, brown the quail on both sides. Put the pan in the oven for about 10 minutes. Turn the quail once in the middle of the cooking time.

Lower oven temperature to 300°–350°. Put the quail in the saucepan with the beans and pour off the fat from the baking pan. Deglaze the pan with the 3 remaining tablespoons white wine and the water. Pour the juice over the quail and beans, cover the saucepan and cook slowly in oven for 5 minutes.

4 quail
Salt, white pepper
1 clove garlic
3 shallots
1 tablespoon butter
1 15-ounce can flageolet
    beans
5 tablespoons white wine
2 tablespoons oil
3 tablespoons water

*SERVES 2*

# QUAIL IN THE STEAMER
## Cailles à la vapeur

4 quail
Salt, freshly ground black
    pepper
2 large basil leaves
2 tablespoons chopped
    scallion
2 leeks
Juice of 1 lemon
2–3 teaspoons olive oil

*SERVES 2*

Remove most of the bones from the quail: make a cut down the back of the quail and flatten the birds out. Remove the backbones and breastbones and as many of the other bones as you can while leaving the meat in one piece. (Do not worry about the wings and drumsticks, you can leave those bones in.) Season quail with salt and pepper.

Chop the basil leaves. Sprinkle the scallion and basil over the 4 quail. Clean the leeks well and cut them crosswise, both the white and green parts.

Perfume the water in the bottom of a steamer with the lemon juice and olive oil. Steam the quail for 10 minutes in the buttered top perforated section of the steamer. Add the leeks, sprinkle them with a few drops of olive oil, salt and pepper, and cook for another 5 minutes.

# PHEASANT AND CABBAGE
*Faisan au chou*

*The pheasant is an ancient, noble bird although many think its flesh is dry and sometimes hard. On the contrary, I think pheasant belongs in the top realm of gastronomy. I like to cook the breast meat very quickly on top of the stove and serve it with vegetables.*

*My friend Pierre, our barman, is a great hunter, and in the restaurant we hear many good hunting stories. Last year, he told of shooting a pheasant so plump and so beautiful that it broke the branch of a tree as it fell to the ground. I hope you too will have many plump, juicy pheasants for your kitchen.*

*I particularly like this combination of crunchy cabbage and tender pheasant meat, perfumed with the aroma of juniper berries.*

1 medium-size cabbage
1 teaspoon olive oil
1 small carrot
Juniper berries
2 pheasant
Salt, white pepper
6 shallots, peeled
1 tablespoon oil
1 teaspoon flour
1 cup white wine
1 cup water or chicken stock
(p. 221)
1½ tablespoons butter,
softened

**SERVES 4**

Preheat broiler. Remove the outer leaves from a head of cabbage and keep 4 nice ones. Slice the remaining cabbage and sprinkle with olive oil. Peel the carrot and slice into small, thin pieces. Steam the cabbage and half of the sliced carrot, sprinkled with a few juniper berries, for about 8 minutes; add the outer cabbage leaves for the last minute.

Carve off the breast meat from the pheasant; carve off the legs and reserve them for another use. (See illustration p. 145.) Cut the remaining pheasant bodies and the wings into pieces; remove the liver and kidneys. Salt the pheasant breasts lightly and pat them with olive oil. In a sauté pan, brown them quickly on each side. (At this point you can stop the cooking process and let the pheasant breasts rest in a warm place.)

Brown the pheasant body pieces, the shallots and the remaining carrot slices in the tablespoon of oil in a pan over high heat. Add a pinch of crushed juniper berries and a very little salt and pepper. Reduce the heat to medium and cook for about 15 minutes until the pheasant is entirely browned, turning the pieces several times during the cooking. Pour off any extra oil, add the flour to the pan and vigorously stir in over high heat until dry. Add the wine and water or chicken stock and reduce until it is strong, about 5 minutes. Strain the juice into a clean pan.

Slice the pheasant breasts in half lengthwise, then cut each half into 3–4 thin slices. Run slices under broiler until they are cooked through.

Place a large cabbage leaf on each plate, then a mound of the sliced cabbage with a few of the sliced carrots on the leaf. Arrange the pheasant slices on the cabbage. Finish the sauce with butter and pour it over the pheasant.

*Note:* If you can find baby pheasant, it is very tender; allow 1 pheasant breast per person. It is better not to use pheasant legs for this recipe because they need longer cooking. Reserve them for Lean Veal and Pheasant Pâté (p. 26).

# FILET OF PHEASANT

## Paupiettes de faisan

Preheat oven to 400°. Carve off the breast meat from the pheasant; carve off the legs and reserve them for another use. Cut the rest of the pheasant and the wings into pieces; remove the liver and kidneys. Split the breasts lengthwise to create a pocket in each breast half.

Slice the mushroom caps. Peel the carrot and slice it into thin pieces; peel the shallots. Distribute the mushroom slices in the breast pockets and season them with salt, pepper and a sprinkling of the chopped fresh herbs.

Heat the oil in a sauté pan and add the pheasant breasts, carrot slices, shallots and pheasant body pieces. Brown everything over high heat for about 5 minutes. Remove the breast pieces to an oiled platter and continue cooking them in the oven for about 10 minutes.

Continue cooking the body pieces and vegetables in the sauté pan for another 5 minutes. Pour off any extra oil, add the flour to the pan and vigorously stir it in over a high heat until dry. Add the wine and water, and reduce until juice is strong, about 5 minutes. Remove the body pieces, and strain the juice into a clean pan. Place the pheasant breasts on a bed of steamed spinach, finish the sauce with butter and spoon it over the meat.

*1 pheasant*
*4 mushroom caps*
*¼ carrot*
*6 shallots*
*Salt, white pepper*
*Leaves of 1 stalk of fresh basil,*
    *thyme or parsley*
*1 teaspoon oil*
*½ teaspoon flour*
*1 cup white wine*
*1 cup water*
*1 tablespoon butter, softened*
*Steamed spinach*

**SERVES 2**

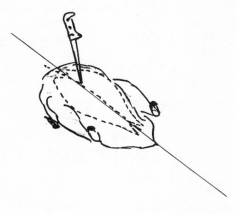

Aiguillette

Paupiette

# ROAST PHEASANT
*Faisan rôti*

*This simple recipe needs no sauce. The vegetables are brown and tender and add flavor to the pheasant, especially the roasted, unpeeled shallots.*

*1 stalk celery*
*1 large carrot*
*2 potatoes*
*1 medium-size tomato*
*3 scallions*
*8–12 shallots*
*2 cloves garlic*
*1 pheasant*
*Salt, herbed pepper*
*2 generous teaspoons sour cream*
*2 tablespoons oil*
*4 tablespoons white wine*

*SERVES 4*

Cut the vegetables so that they are all approximately the same size: cut the celery and carrot into 6 pieces each, peel the potatoes and cut them into 8 pieces each, cut off the top and bottom off the the tomato and cut it into 4 pieces, trim the scallions. Do not peel the shallots or the garlic; crush the garlic cloves.

Sprinkle the body cavity of the pheasant with salt and herbed pepper, then spread with the sour cream. Truss the pheasant by tying the neck to the leg ends with one piece of string, then the wings tightly to the body of the bird with another string. Sprinkle herbed pepper on the outside of the pheasant.

Heat the oil in a large, heavy pot. When it is hot, add the pheasant and brown it on both sides, turning it once with tongs. Add the celery, carrot, potatoes, tomato, scallions, garlic and shallots, and agitate the pan. Cover the pan, lower the heat and cook the pheasant for about 45 minutes. About 10 minutes into the cooking time, turn the pheasant over, shake the vegetables about again and add the white wine.

When the pheasant is cooked, carve off the breasts, wings and legs. Serve immediately, surrounded with the vegetables.

*Note:* You can also use a medium-size roasting chicken for this recipe, or 2 Cornish game hens or baby pheasants. (The smaller birds need about 5 minutes less cooking time.)

*1 rabbit breast*
*½ head green cabbage*
*Olive oil*
*Salt, freshly ground black pepper*
*Peanut oil or other cooking oil*

*SERVES 2*

# GRILLED RABBIT BREAST
*Filet de lapin rôti*

*It is a shame that many Americans never consider eating rabbit. It has a delicate taste, is reasonably priced and is becoming available in many supermarkets. It is best when young—at 3–4 months. There are so many ways to cook rabbit, I hope you will not hesitate to add it to your menus regularly. (See illustration for directions on cutting up a rabbit.)*

With a very sharp knife remove the bone from the breast of the rabbit; also remove the shiny skin from around the breast meat. Slice the cabbage, flavor it with a touch of olive oil, salt and a few grinds of pepper, and steam it.

Slice the breast into thin pieces diagonally (you will have about 6 slices from each breast half); rub the slices with cooking oil and brown them quickly, either on the griddle or under the hot broiler. Or sauté the breast halves (unsliced) in 1 teaspoon cooking oil in a frying pan for about 3–4 minutes, turning once; remove them from the pan, slice them lengthwise into 3 pieces each and finish the pieces under the broiler.

Serve the breast slices on a bed of cabbage.

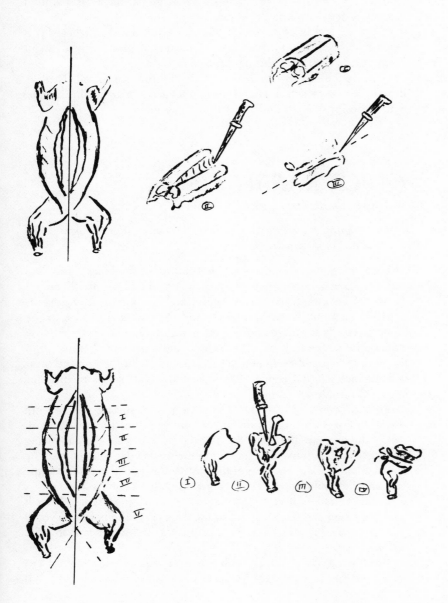

## GIGOT OF RABBIT
### Gigot de lapin

2 hind legs of a rabbit
1 shallot
Fresh basil leaves (or tarragon
    or thyme)
2 slices bacon (optional)
1 tablespoon oil
½ cup rabbit stock (p. 222) or
    ¼ cup white wine
1 tablespoon butter, softened
    (optional)

*SERVES 2*

Remove the thigh bones so that you have a boneless piece of meat that is still attached to the lower leg (see illustration p. 147). Peel the shallot and chop finely. Chop the fresh basil and sprinkle chopped shallot and herb on the flattened thigh meat. Fold the meat up and tie it with string in several places. If you wish to use bacon, wrap it around the thighs before you tie the strings.

Sauté the legs briefly on each side in the oil in a small, heavy pan over high heat. Lower the heat, cover the pan and cook slowly for about 25 minutes. Turn once during the cooking.

Remove the legs to a plate or platter and throw out the fat. Deglaze the pan with the stock or white wine and reduce it by half. Finish sauce with butter, if desired, and strain it over the rabbit.

## QUICK RABBIT PIE
### Tourte de lapin minute

*This fragrant pie would also be delicious made with other game, like pheasant, or even with chicken.*

1 rabbit (a scant 2 cups meat)
1 tablespoon port
1 teaspoon cognac
1 clove garlic
2 shallots
1 leek
1 tablespoon butter
½ teaspoon chopped fresh
    thyme or fresh basil
Salt, freshly ground black
    pepper
Flour
Puff pastry sufficient for top
    and bottom of the pie (see
    Note p. 185)
1–2 tablespoons olive oil
Egg wash (p. 13)

*SERVES 6–8 as an appetizer
3–4 as a main course*

Bone the rabbit. Remove the shiny skin from the breast, back legs and any other tender pieces of meat. I also like to use the liver and kidneys of the rabbit, but it is not necessary. Cut the meat into small, edible chunks and place in a bowl. Add the port and cognac to the rabbit pieces. Peel, smash and dice the garlic; peel and dice the shallots; wash and dice the leek. Sweat the garlic and shallots in 1 teaspoon of the butter, then add them and the leek to the rabbit. Season the meat with thyme, salt and pepper. Marinate the rabbit in this mixture for about 30 minutes at room temperature.

Preheat oven to 350°–400°. Flour your work surface and roll out pastry until it is thin. Cut it to comfortably fit a 9- or 10-inch tart pan. Butter the tart pan and place the pastry in it, crimping the pastry into the fluted sides with your fingers. Trim the pastry a little larger than the tart pan and prick the bottom of the pastry all over with a fork. Fill the tart with the rabbit mixture and sprinkle lightly with olive oil.

Roll out another piece of pastry so that it just fits the tart pan. Place it over the rabbit and stretch it out to the edge. Fold the bottom layer of pastry over the top and pinch the 2 pieces of pastry together so that the tart is closed.

Brush the top of the pastry with egg wash. You can decorate the tart by cutting thin strips of pastry to make a number of squares; inside each square place a little ball of pastry. Brush the pastry decorations with egg wash also.

With a knife, cut a hole in the middle of the tart, about ¼ inch in diameter. Roll a piece of aluminum foil about 2 inches high around a pencil to make a tube and place the tube in the hole as a chimney. Bake the tart about 30 minutes in the oven.

*Note:* You can make this tart up to 1 hour before serving, cook it, keep it warm near the stove and reheat it for 5 minutes when you need it.

# WILD RABBIT
## Civet minute

*Here is a flavorful, aromatic dish that is very welcome in the cold months of the rabbit season, October through February.*

Preheat oven to 350°–400°. With a sharp knife, separate the legs from the rabbit; use all four legs. Cut the breast into 2 pieces; you will have 6 pieces of meat. (Discard the rest of the body; it is too gamy for stock.) Peel the onion and cut into large dice; peel the carrot and cut it into large pieces.

In a medium-size sauté pan, heat 2 tablespoons of the oil until it is very, very hot. Brown the rabbit pieces in the hot oil for 2–3 minutes, turning them with tongs to ensure uniform browning. Remove the pan from the heat and pour off the fat. Warm the cognac, add it to the pan and flame it with a match. Return the pan to the heat.

In a medium-size, heavy saucepan, sweat the onion and carrot in the remaining tablespoon of oil over medium heat for about 1 minute, stirring continuously.

Add the rabbit pieces to the vegetables, then add the flour and stir well over medium heat until mixture is dry, about 1 minute. Add the red wine, bouquet garni, salt and pepper. Bring to a boil, then cover the pan and put in the oven for 35–40 minutes. If the rabbit does not seem tender at the end of this time, cook for another 10 minutes.

Just before serving, add the chopped garlic and parsley to the pan and season again with salt and pepper if needed. Serve with fresh noodles or boiled potatoes.

*1 wild rabbit (about 2 pounds)*
*1 medium-size onion*
*1 carrot*
*3 tablespoons oil*
*2 tablespoons cognac*
*1 tablespoon flour*
*2 cups red wine*
*A fresh bouquet garni of parsley, rosemary, thyme (p. 182)*
*½ teaspoon chopped garlic*
*1 tablespoon chopped parsley*
*Salt, white pepper*

**SERVES 3**

# RIBS OF VENISON WITH RED CABBAGE

*Côtes de chevreuil au chou rouge*

1 small head red cabbage
4 shallots
3 cloves garlic
2 tablespoons oil
10 chestnuts, peeled
Salt, white pepper
4 tablespoons red wine
   vinegar
4 small venison chops or 2 big
   ones
Freshly ground black pepper
2 tablespoons butter, softened
2 tablespoons chopped parsley
⅛ teaspoon crushed juniper
   berries
2 tablespoons gin
3 tablespoons port

**SERVES 2**

*Marinate venison for 1–2 days in the refrigerator before using. Here is a light game marinade suitable for venison and other game: ¾ red wine to ¼ vinegar, oil (the proportion of oil should be about ⅛ of the marinade), a carrot cut into large pieces, sliced onions, unpeeled garlic cloves, peppercorns and a lot of fresh herbs. Mix the ingredients together and completely cover the meat with the marinade. (See illustration for directions on cutting venison chops.)*

   *Traditionally venison is served with a game sauce or a sauce poivrade, but here is an easy recipe that does not require a sauce.*

Slice the red cabbage, discard the core. Peel and slice the shallots; peel and mash, then slice 2 of the garlic cloves. Do not mix the shallots and garlic together. Put the shallots and 1 tablespoon of oil in a medium-size frying pan and cook over high heat for about 1 minute. Add the cabbage, garlic and chestnuts. Shake the pan vigorously (or stir the ingredients). Season with a generous pinch of salt and white pepper, and cook for another 3–5 minutes. Pour the vinegar into the pan and reduce it slightly. Turn down the heat to keep the cabbage warm while you cook the venison.

Season the venison with salt and black pepper. Heat the remaining 1 tablespoon of oil in a pan and cook the chops in the hot oil until they are the way you want them. I like them medium rare, which takes about 3 minutes on each side.

Remove the chops to a warm plate and pour out the fat. Add 1 tablepoon butter to the pan, then add the parsley, juniper berries and the last garlic clove, peeled and chopped finely. Cook these together for about half a minute, then pour in the gin and port. They may flame a bit. Finish the sauce with the remaining 1 tablespoon butter and serve over the chops, which you have placed on the cabbage.

*Note:* Canned, peeled, unsweetened chestnuts from France are now available in many supermarkets.

*selle*

*Filet*

*noisette*

# WILD BIRD STUFFED WITH VENISON, THE CROWN OF THE CHASE

*Joyau de chasse*

*Wild birds, such as woodcock, pheasant, quail and pigeon, are good cooked very simply. Brown the bird in hot oil, then roast it in the oven and serve it with its own juices deglazed with a mixture of ⅔ white wine and ⅓ cognac. Or roast it with this unusual stuffing, which is not beautiful to look at, but has a wonderful taste.*

1 clove garlic
⅛ teaspoon juniper berries
1 slice white bread
2 tablespoons heavy cream
½ cup diced raw venison
Salt, freshly ground black
    pepper
2 tablespoons oil
1 tablespoon brandy
1 tablespoon port
1 woodcock or other wild bird
    of the same size
½ carrot
½ tomato
3 shallots
A few fresh thyme sprigs or 2
    basil leaves or ¼ teaspoon
    dried thyme

**SERVES 2**

Preheat oven to 350°–400°. Peel, mash and slice the garlic clove. Chop the juniper berries. Remove the crusts from the bread slice and cut it into cubes. Put in a bowl with the cream and mash together with a fork. Add the diced venison, garlic, juniper berries, salt and pepper to the bread, and mix it all together.

Heat 1 tablespoon oil in a small frying pan. Dump the stuffing mixture into the hot oil and cook it for about 1 minute, moving the pieces around with tongs to get them browned. Add the brandy and port, and remove pan from the heat. Spoon the stuffing into the body cavity of your wild bird and tie it up.

Heat the remaining 1 tablespoon of oil in a medium-size saucepan. Cut the carrot and tomato into large pieces. Put the bird into the hot oil and brown it on all sides over medium-high heat. Add the shallots, whole and unpeeled, the carrot and tomato, and place the saucepan, uncovered, in the oven for 30–40 minutes, turning the bird over every 10 minutes. Halfway through the cooking, add a few sprigs of fresh thyme. Serve with wild rice or Crispy Potato (p. 167).

*Note:* This stuffing is sufficient for 1 woodcock or baby pheasant. If you have smaller birds, it will do for 2. If the bird is larger, increase the stuffing and cook a little longer.

# *VEGETABLES*

ARTICHOKES
ASPARAGUS
BEANS
BEETS
GREEN CABBAGE
CARROTS
CAULIFLOWER
CELERY
CELERY ROOT
CUCUMBERS
EGGPLANT
ENDIVE
LEEKS
MORELS

ONIONS
SNOW PEAS
PEPPERS
POLENTA
POTATOES
PUMPKIN
SALSIFY
SPINACH
TOMATOES
TURNIPS
ZUCCHINI

RIBS OF VENISON
  WITH RED CABBAGE
  (p. 150)

EGGPLANT CAVIAR IN
  THE STEAMER (p. 28)
EGGPLANT CAVIAR MY
  WAY (p. 27)
A LIGHT RAGOÛT OF
  POTATOES AND
  TRUFFLES (p. 33)
TOMATO TARTS (p. 239,
  Note)
VEGETABLE TART
  (p. 22)
COLD STUFFED
  VEGETABLES (p. 29)

Thanks to rapid modern transportation, we can now enjoy many fresh vegetables all year. But these good gifts of nature still taste the best when they first appear in their proper season.

There is such a wide variety of vegetables that you have a wealth of choice and can change the emphasis of a recipe by your vegetable selection. There are the roots, bulbs and tubers—potatoes, carrots, turnips, radishes, celeriac, beets, salsify, etc.; there are stems and leaves—leeks, celery, spinach, sorrel, lettuce, etc.; there are fruits of plants—tomatoes, zucchini, cucumbers, etc.; and there are the family of seeds—corn, and the other cereals, dried beans, peas, etc. Vegetables contain nearly all the necessary minerals for our diet and to aid the operation of our digestive system.

I love to eat fresh vegetables, and the very best way to get them is to grow them yourself, even if your garden is just a window box with a few herbs. Even though I now live in New York City and see very few gardens except the potato fields of Long Island, I like to think of my friend Zona's small garden in Ohio, where she grows basil, sorrel, carrots, parsley, etc.

Steaming is a good way to conserve the sugar and rich taste of some vegetables, such as spinach and cabbage. Not all vegetables take well to steaming, however; see the directions for cooking green beans.

My family ate a lot of dried beans when I was young because that was one of our farm crops. We dried them during the hot summer months, then during the winter we cleaned them, saving the best for seed and eating the rest as warm bean salads or simply sautéed with garlic and parsley.

4 artichokes
1 onion
2 tablespoons olive oil
1 tomato
1 clove garlic
3 tablespoons chopped
    scallion
3 tablespoons chopped fresh
    basil, thyme or tarragon or
    1 tablespoon of dried herbs
Salt, white pepper
½ cup chicken stock (p. 221)
3 tablespoons white wine

*SERVES 4*

# ARTICHOKE RAGOÛT
### Ragoût d'artichauts

Cut the stems, outside leaves and spiny tips from the artichokes. Cook them in a large pot of boiling, salted water for 30–40 minutes. Drain them and squeeze out the water. Cut them into quarters and remove the choke.

Slice the onion and sweat it in 1 tablespoon of the olive oil until it begins to color. Peel the tomato, squeeze out the water and seeds, and chop into large pieces. Peel and chop the garlic. Add the tomato, garlic, scallion, fresh herbs, salt and pepper to the onion. Add the artichoke quarters, the chicken stock, white wine and the remaining tablespoon of olive oil, and cook the ragoût slowly for 10–15 minutes.

If you can find baby artichokes, the very tiny ones, they are perfect for this recipe; 8 will serve 4 people.

### Asparagus; asperges

When asparagus first appears in the markets in early spring, serve it very simply with a dressing of lemon juice, a little olive oil or a light vinaigrette.

Unless the asparagus is very thin, peel the stalks with a vegetable peeler. Place them in a large pot with 3 quarts of water and 2 tablespoons sea salt. Bring the water to a boil and cook for 8–10 minutes. Cover the asparagus with a napkin or towel to keep it immersed in water during the cooking time. If you prefer to cook the stalks upright, be sure the water covers the tops.

Cooked asparagus will keep 2–3 days in the refrigerator, covered with a linen napkin or plastic wrap.

# ASPARAGUS TART

## Tarte aux asperges

Preheat oven to 350°–400°. Cut off the very top green tips of the asparagus and slice each tip in half vertically. Cut the remaining asparagus stalks into 1-inch pieces. Discard the tough bottom ends.

Lightly butter an 8-inch tart pan with scalloped edges. Roll out pastry to a shape slightly larger than the pan. With your hand, fit the pastry into the pan, filling in all the scalloped indentations, and cut the pastry edges by rolling the rolling pin over the top of the pan. Prick the pastry with a fork.

Beat the eggs in a bowl with the nutmeg, 2 pinches salt and 1 pinch pepper. Beat in the cream and parsley. Cover the bottom of the pastry with the pieces of the asparagus stalks. Pour the egg and cream mixture over them and arrange the asparagus tips like the spokes of a wheel on top. Place the tart on a cookie sheet and bake for 20 minutes in the oven.

*6 cooked asparagus stalks*
*Short Pastry (p. 185) or puff*
*pastry*
*Butter*
*2 eggs*
*Freshly grated nutmeg*
*Salt, white pepper*
*1 cup heavy cream*
*1 tablespoon chopped parsley*

**SERVES 6**

2 slices bacon
6 cooked asparagus tops
1 scallion
2 teaspoons butter plus a little
    extra
2 large crêpes (7–9 inches;
    p. 184)
4 teaspoons sour cream
Salt, white pepper
2 basil leaves, chopped

**SERVES 2**

# ASPARAGUS CRÊPES
## Crêpes aux asperges

Preheat oven to 350°. Cook the bacon slices, pat dry with a paper towel and cut bacon into small dice. Cut the asparagus tops in half lengthwise; chop the scallion. Lightly butter a small broiling pan.

Lay the crêpes on your work surface and divide the asparagus between them, placing it just below the middle of the crêpes. Dot the asparagus with 2 teaspoons of the sour cream, then sprinkle with the bacon, scallion, a pinch of salt and pepper, and the chopped basil. Roll the crêpes, starting from the filled half. Place them on the broiling pan, seam side down, and spread 1 teaspoon butter along the top of each crêpe. Cook the crêpes in the oven for 5–6 minutes.

To serve, slide the crêpes off onto a plate and place a teaspoon of sour cream beside each one.

### Green beans; haricots verts

Green beans, like all green vegetables, should cook on high heat in a large quantity of salted, boiling water. (I like to use sea salt.) They do not take well to steaming. White vegetables, on the other hand, should start cooking in cold water.

The best way to cook green beans so they retain their vitality is to first soak them in an ice-water bath. Then plunge them into the boiling water and cook until they are *al dente*. Refresh them with icy water or ice cubes.

### Dried Beans

Dried beans, red, black, or white, should be rinsed and soaked for at least 8 hours before cooking in boiling salted water with a little seasoning (onion, carrot, garlic, bouquet garni). Serve as a warm salad. Lentils do not need soaking before cooking, but you should wash them carefully and pick out any small stones. Lentil salad with shallots goes beautifully with wild birds or chicken.

### Broad Beans

Remove the thin layer of skin that envelops new broad beans and cook them in boiling salted water with a little seasoning and a fresh bouquet garni. Sauté them in butter and serve with fish or meat.

# BEETS IN RED WINE
*Betteraves au vin rouge*

1 bunch beets
1 onion
1 tablespoon oil
2 cloves garlic
1½ tablespoons chopped
    parsley
2 tablespoons chopped fresh
    basil or thyme or ½
    teaspoon dried herb
1 tablespoon flour
½ cup red wine
¼ cup brown stock
    (pp. 174–176) or water
    and a small piece of a
    bouillon cube

Boil the beets, peel and slice them. Slice the onion and sweat it in the oil until it is just blond. Add 1½ garlic cloves, smashed, 1 tablespoon of the chopped parsley, the basil or thyme and the flour.

Stir the flour in until dry, then add the red wine and brown stock. Reduce the sauce for a few minutes and add the beets. When they are hot, add the remaining ½ garlic clove, chopped, and the rest of the chopped parsley.

**SERVES 4**

# GREEN CABBAGE ENVELOPES
*Chou vert en enveloppe*

1 head green cabbage
Salt, white pepper
2 tablespoons butter
6 tablespoons cottage cheese
3 shallots
2 cloves garlic
2 tablespoons chopped fresh
    basil or thyme or 1
    tablespoon chopped fresh
    coriander or 1 teaspoon
    dried herb
½ cup water or chicken stock
    (p. 221)
¾ cup bread crumbs
6 tablespoons grated Swiss
    cheese

Preheat oven to 300°. Remove 6 large outer leaves from the head of cabbage and poach or steam them until they are soft, about 3–5 minutes. Cut the remaining head into quarters and cook in boiling, salted water for about 20 minutes. Squeeze out the water and pat dry. Puree the cabbage quarters in a food processor along with a pinch of salt, pepper and 1 tablespoon of the butter.

Lay the outer cabbage leaves on your work surface and put a tablespoon of the puree on each leaf, then a spoonful of cottage cheese on the puree. Fold the leaves around the filling.

Chop the shallots and garlic. Sweat them in the remaining 1 tablespoon of butter in a gratin dish along with the chopped herbs. Place the cabbage envelopes in the dish and add the water or stock. Top the cabbage with bread crumbs and grated Swiss cheese, and cook in the oven for 20 minutes.

You can do this a few hours ahead of time and reheat the envelopes briefly in the oven.

**SERVES 6**

*Carrots; carottes*

Carrots are good cooked very simply. Peel and slice the carrots and cook them in boiling, salted water. Drain, refresh and dry. Finish cooking them in butter over medium-high heat; when they are crispy add chopped parsley and garlic.

## CARROT CAKE
*Gâteau de carottes*

3 large carrots
3 eggs
2 tablespoons heavy cream
½ teaspoon sugar
Salt, white pepper
Butter
Sauce suggestion: **Lemon Butter Sauce (p. 228)**
Garniture: *chopped parsley*

*SERVES 4*

Preheat oven to 350°–400°. Peel and slice the carrots and cook them in boiling, salted water. Drain them and pat dry. Put the carrots, eggs, cream, sugar and a pinch of salt and white pepper in a food processor. Process just enough to chop carrots thoroughly but still keep their texture. (If you puree them, they will be too watery.) Turn the carrots into buttered individual soufflé molds and cook in a bain-marie in the oven for about 15 minutes. Cool for 10 minutes, then invert molds onto plates. Serve with Lemon Butter Sauce and chopped parsley.

## PUREE OF CARROTS, CELERY ROOT AND PEAS
*Purée de carottes, céleri-rave et petits pois*

3 large carrots
1 small celery root
1 cup fresh or frozen peas
2 tablespoons butter
2 tablespoons heavy cream
Salt, white pepper
⅛ teaspoon nutmeg

*SERVES 6*

Peel the carrots and the celery root and cook them in separate pots of boiling, salted water. Cook fresh peas very briefly. Drain the vegetables and put them through a meat grinder or food mill along with the butter, cream, a pinch of salt, pepper and the nutmeg.

*Note:* A grinder or food mill works better for this recipe than a food processor because the resulting texture is rougher and more interesting.

# SAUTÉED CAULIFLOWER
### Chou-fleur en boulette

1 cauliflower
2 eggs
A pinch of freshly grated nutmeg
Salt, white pepper
1 tablespoon flour
2 tablespoons fine bread crumbs
1 tablespoon butter
1 tablespoon oil

SERVES 4

Cook the cauliflower head in boiling, salted water for about 10 minutes until it is tender. Very fresh cauliflower cooks quickly. Discard the stem and mash the flowerets with a fork.

Beat the eggs along with the nutmeg, a pinch of salt and pepper. Using a dessert spoon, make a ball of the cauliflower mixture and roll the ball in flour, then in the egg mixture, then in the bread crumbs. Sauté the ball on all sides in the butter and oil until hot, but not colored.

# CAULIFLOWER PANCAKE
### Galette de chou-fleur

1 cauliflower
2 whole eggs
2 tablespoons heavy cream
1 tablespoon chopped parsley
Salt, white pepper
1 egg white
2 tablespoons oil

SERVES 2

Cook the cauliflower head in boiling, salted water for about 10 minutes until it is tender. Discard the stem. Drain and dry the flowerets and puree them in a food processor along with the whole eggs, cream and parsley. Season with a pinch of salt and pepper. Beat the egg white and fold it into the puree. In a small pan, cook the cauliflower puree as a crêpe in the hot oil.

### Celery; céleris

Chop off the bottom and leafy tops of celery. Poach the midsections in salted water for 20 minutes. Drain, dry and sauté them in butter along with chopped garlic, salt and white pepper.

# CELERY ROOT PUREE
### Purée de céleri-rave

2 small celery roots
2 tablespoons butter
3 tablespoons heavy cream
1 tablespoon lemon juice
Salt, white pepper

SERVES 4

Peel celery roots and cook in boiling, salted water for 30 minutes, until al dente. Drain and dry. Grind in a meat grinder or food mill (not a food processor). Heat the ground celery roots with the butter and heavy cream. Mix it around with a wooden spoon, season with the lemon juice, salt and pepper, and serve hot. You can also mix peeled, cooked carrots and/or turnips in the grinder with the celery roots.

Variation: Boil, drain and dry celery roots as above. Slice and place on a buttered plate in a preheated 350°–400° oven, dot with butter, sprinkle with salt and pepper, cook until brown.

*Cucumbers; concombres*

Peel cucumbers and cut them into small finger-length sticks. Blanch them briefly and dry them well. Cook them in 2 tablespoons hot butter for a few minutes, season them with salt and white pepper.

# EGGPLANT WITH TOMATOES
### Aubergines à la tomate

*The two eggplant recipes in the Appetizers chapter are nice served cold for summer picnics.*

2 medium-size eggplants
½ cup oil plus 1 tablespoon
3 tomatoes
½ onion
3 cloves garlic
2 tablespoons chopped fresh
    basil
1 heaping tablespoon tomato
    paste
3 tablespoons chopped fresh
    parsley
2 tablespoons bread crumbs
Butter

SERVES 4

Peel the eggplants and cut into very thin slices lengthwise. Fry the slices quickly in the ½ cup of oil; pat off the oil when the eggplant is browned.

Peel the tomatoes, squeeze them to get rid of the seeds and water, and chop them coarsely. Chop the onion and garlic, and reserve ⅓ of the garlic. Sweat the onion and ⅔ of the garlic in the remaining 1 tablespoon of oil. Add the tomatoes, basil and tomato paste, and cook for 15 minutes.

Butter a gratin dish. Make several alternating layers of eggplant slices and the tomato sauce, starting with a layer of eggplant and ending with sauce. Sprinkle chopped parsley, the reserved chopped garlic and the bread crumbs on top, dot with butter and heat in the oven just before serving.

1 eggplant
Salt, freshly ground black
    pepper
Sour cream or butter or olive
    oil
Garlic
Fresh herbs

SERVES 1–2

# EGGPLANT IN THE OVEN
### Aubergine au four

Preheat oven to 400°. Place a whole, unpeeled eggplant on a broiling pan in the oven for about 45–60 minutes. Slash it lengthwise down the center and season it with salt and black pepper. Fill it with sour cream or butter or olive oil seasoned with chopped garlic and fresh herbs. Eat it with a spoon.

### Endive

Separate endive leaves and place them on a buttered baking sheet. Sprinkle them with sugar and butter, and put them under the broiler for about 5–6 minutes until they caramelize.

Or cut whole endives in half lengthwise and cook them very simply in the top perforated section of a steamer along with butter and lemon juice.

Or cook whole endives in boiling, salted water to which you have added lemon juice and a little sugar. Dry them and sauté in butter until they are golden.

# LITTLE DOORMAT OF LEEK AND ZUCCHINI

*Paillasson de poireaux et courgettes*

½ *large leek*
½ *large zucchini*
1 *egg*
*Salt, white pepper*
2 *tablespoons oil*

**SERVES 2**

Wash the leek well (see illustration below) and cut it into thin julienne strips. Cut the zucchini into julienne also. If the vegetables are of medium size, use an entire leek and zucchini instead of half of each. Beat the egg and add the vegetables to it; season with a pinch of salt and pepper.

Heat the oil in a small frying pan. When it is hot, turn the vegetables into the pan and brown them briefly on both sides, about 1 minute to a side. Cut in half and serve with chicken, game hen, roast fish, etc.

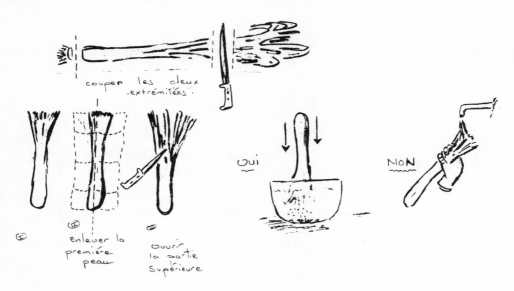

# RAGOÛT OF LEEKS AND TRUFFLES

*Ragoût de poireaux et truffes*

2–3 leeks
2 shallots
1 tablespoon butter
½ teaspoon oil
Salt, white pepper
1 truffle, chopped
2 tablespoons truffle juice

SERVES 4

Clean the leeks and cut them crosswise into small pieces. Chop the shallots and sweat them in the butter and oil in a pan. Add the leeks, season with a pinch of salt and pepper, and cook for a few minutes. Add the truffle and the truffle juice, heat and serve.

# LEEK MOUSSELINE

*Mousseline de poireaux*

3 leeks
1 generous teaspoon
    unflavored gelatin
1 tablespoon butter plus a
    little extra
1 whole egg
2 egg whites
⅓ cup heavy cream
A pinch of nutmeg
A pinch of ground cumin
Salt, white pepper

SERVES 2–4

Wash the leeks, cut them in half lengthwise and cook in boiling, salted water until soft. Drain and squeeze out the water. Puree the leeks in a food processor along with the gelatin, 1 tablespoon butter and the whole egg.

Beat the egg whites until they hold their shape; whip the cream. You should have equal proportions of these two ingredients. Turn the leeks into a bowl and mix in the egg whites and whipped cream. Season with nutmeg, cumin, salt and white pepper. Turn the mousseline into buttered individual soufflé molds and put them in the refrigerator. Serve them very cold in the summer.

# SAUTÉED MORELS

*Morilles sautées*

*If you are able to get fresh morels from Oregon in late spring or early summer, I suggest you try these easy recipes.*

4–5 large fresh morels
1 teaspoon oil
½ teaspoon chopped parsley
½ teaspoon chopped garlic

SERVES 1

Cut the morels into large pieces. Sauté them in hot oil for about 3 minutes. Add the parsley and garlic, and serve immediately.

*Variation:* Cook morels as directed above. Remove the morels from the pan; add ¼ cup cream to pan and reduce by half. Pour the cream over the morels, sprinkle with chopped parsley and serve.

# MORELS STUFFED WITH SCALLOP MOUSSE

*Morilles farcies à la mousse de coquilles Saint-Jacques*

*This very delicate recipe will not work with dried morels, you must have fresh morels in season.*

8 large fresh morels
1½ cups scallops
4 tablespoons heavy cream
Salt, white pepper
2 tablespoons chopped
  scallion
¼ teaspoon chopped garlic
1 tablespoon chopped parsley
1½ tablespoons oil
Sauce suggestion: *Veal stock
  (p. 219) or lamb stock
  (p. 220) reduced and
  finished with butter*

***SERVES 4***

Preheat oven to 350°–400°. Wash the morels in cold water and pat them dry. Cut of their stems and slice each morel in half lengthwise.

Put the scallops in a food processor along with the cream and a pinch of salt and pepper, and start processing. Add the scallion, garlic and parsley. Process the ingredients very briefly, just enough to mix them and chop the scallops. You do not want a puree.

Fill the morel halves with the scallop mixture. Heat the oil in a heavy frying pan, and when it is very hot, add the morel halves (filled side up), and sauté them for about half a minute over high heat. Transfer the pan to the oven and cook for 6–8 minutes. Put 2 spoonfuls of brown sauce on each plate and arrange the morel halves like the petals of a flower on top of sauce.

### Onions; oignons

To brown onions, heat the oil in the pan first, then add the onions. If you wish to cook onions without them coloring, start the oil and the onions in the pan at the same time and heat them together, stirring constantly.

To make baked onion slices, cut 1 large onion crosswise into slices. Steam or blanch to make them soft, then pat them dry. Heat 2 tablespoons oil in a frying pan, and when it is very hot, add the onion slices; brown each side thoroughly. Season with cumin, salt and white pepper, cover the pan with aluminum foil and cook onions in a preheated 350°–400° oven for 30–40 minutes.

### Snow Peas

Cook snow peas in the same way as you do green beans, but very briefly.

A good way to serve snow peas is to blanch them quickly to keep them green. Drain and dry. Sweat chopped shallots in butter with a few sliced lettuce leaves. Add the snow peas and cook for a few minutes. Season with salt and pepper.

# SMALL PÂTÉ OF PEPPERS
### Le petit pâté de légumes aux poivrons

*This recipe and the one following are designed for summertime, when red, yellow, green and light green (sweet Italian) peppers are readily available.*

⅓ to ½ of each of the 4
    different peppers described
    above
*1 large leek or 2 small ones*
*1 medium-size zucchini*
*1 carrot, peeled*
*Butter*
*4 eggs*
*Salt, white pepper*
Garniture: *blanched, julienne
    strips of the 4 peppers*
Sauce suggestions: *Lemon
    Butter Sauce (with hot
    pâté; p. 228) Fresh
    Tomato Sauce (with cold
    pâté; p. 239)*

**SERVES 4**

Preheat oven to 350°–400°. Discard the seeds from the peppers and cut them into thin julienne strips. Blanch the pepper strips in boiling water very briefly. Cook the leek, zucchini and carrot in boiling water for about 10 minutes (or steam them for 15 minutes) until just tender; drain and refresh.

Butter individual soufflé molds. Place 1 strip of pepper of each color in the bottom of each mold. Reserve a few strips of each pepper for the garniture; chop the remaining pepper strips into fine dice.

Put the drained leek, zucchini and carrot in the bowl of a food processor and season with several pinches of salt and pepper. Process until they are chopped finely but not pureed. Turn them into a bowl and add the chopped peppers. Beat the eggs together with a fork, and beat them into the vegetables.

Fill the molds to the top with the egg-pepper mixture. Place them in a pan of hot or boiling water (a bain-marie) so that the water level comes halfway up the molds. Cook for 15–20 minutes in the oven. The mixture will be slightly brown on top.

To serve hot, ladle 2 tablespoons Lemon Butter Sauce onto each plate. Cut around the edge of the molds with a knife and invert them onto the plates. Garnish with a few strips of the reserved peppers.

To serve cold, let the molds cool, then chill them in the refrigerator for at least 6 hours or, even better, overnight. (They will keep 3–4 days in the refrigerator.) Serve them with Fresh Tomato Sauce as a summer luncheon dish.

# POACHED EGG WHITES WITH PEPPERS
### Oeufs à la neige au poivron

Discard the seeds and chop the peppers in a food processor; you should get about 4 tablespoons finely chopped peppers. Reserve 1 tablespoon for garniture. Beat the egg whites along with 2 pinches salt and 1 pinch pepper until they are stiff, but still moist. Just at the end, mix in the chopped peppers.

Half fill a large skillet or sauté pan with hot, but not quite boiling water. Using a dessert spoon, scoop the egg white mixture into ovals, making 3–4 scooping motions to mold each spoonful, and place them carefully in the water. Dip the spoon in a pan of hot water to clean it before taking each new spoonful. You should have 8–9 ovals. Keep the pan over low heat so the water does not boil. Cook ovals for 1 minute, then using 2 rubber spatulas, turn each one carefully in the water and cook for 3 more minutes.

Remove ovals from the water onto a baking sheet that you have lined with a dish towel and chill them in the refrigerator.

Make the sauce: peel and squeeze seeds and water from the tomato. Mix the tomato with the other sauce ingredients in a food processor; season with 2 pinches salt and 1 pinch pepper. Ladle 2–3 tablespoons of the sauce onto each plate, top with the chilled ovals, each garnished with the reserved finely chopped pepper.

*⅓ to ½ of each of 4 different
    peppers—red, yellow,
    green and light green*
*6 egg whites*
*Salt, white pepper*
*Garniture: Finely chopped
    pieces of each of the 4
    peppers*

*Sauce*
*1 tomato*
*½ teaspoon chopped basil leaf*
*½ teaspoon chopped garlic*
*1 egg*
*½ cup olive oil*

*SERVES 4*

# FRIED POLENTA
## Polenta frite

Heat the milk in a saucepan. After it comes to a boil, reduce it a little over high heat, then spoon in the cornmeal. Stir with a whisk, then with a wooden spoon. The mixture will immediately thicken; keep stirring and cook it until it is a little dry. Remove from the heat and beat 1 tablespoon of the butter and 2 of the eggs into the cornmeal mixture for about 1–2 minutes. Season with a pinch of salt and pepper.

Generously butter a small square baking pan (about 6½ inches) and spoon the polenta into it. Refrigerate for at least 15 minutes.

Unmold the polenta by inverting it onto a plate. Cut it into 6 pieces and return it to the refrigerator. Heat the oil in a frying pan. Break the remaining egg into a shallow bowl and beat it quickly with a fork. Dip the polenta squares in the beaten egg, then cook them in the hot oil until brown, about 2 minutes on each side. Season with salt and pepper while they cook. Remove the squares, throw out the oil and dump in the parsley, basil, garlic, tomato and the remaining 1 tablespoon of butter. Cook for 1 minute only, and spread over the polenta squares. You can also serve the polenta squares with Fresh Tomato Sauce (p. 239).

*2 cups milk*
*¾ cup cornmeal*
*2 tablespoons butter plus a
    little extra*
*3 eggs*
*Salt, white pepper*
*1 tablespoon oil*
*2 tablespoons chopped parsley*
*1 teaspoon chopped fresh
    basil*
*¼ teaspoon chopped garlic*
*3 heaping tablespoons
    chopped tomato*

*SERVES 4–6*

2 cups milk
¾ cup cornmeal
1 tablespoon butter plus a
    little extra
2 whole eggs
Salt, white pepper
½ red pepper
6 egg whites
Flour

SERVES 4

# POLENTA SOUFFLÉ WITH RED PEPPER
### Soufflé de polenta au poivron rouge

Preheat oven to 350°–400°. Heat the milk in a saucepan. After it comes to a boil, reduce it a little over high heat, then spoon in the cornmeal. Stir with a whisk, then with a wooden spoon. The mixture will immediately thicken; keep stirring and cook it until it is a little dry. Remove from the heat and beat 1 tablespoon butter and the whole eggs into the cornmeal for about 1–2 minutes. Season with a pinch of salt and pepper.

Slice the red pepper into thin strips; chop the end pieces into small dice (about 1 teaspoon). Add all the pepper pieces to the cornmeal mixture and put the pan in the refrigerator for no longer than 10–15 minutes.

Whip the egg whites until firm, but not dry; fold them into the cornmeal mixture. Butter and flour 4 individual soufflé molds. Fill them with the mixture and bake them in the oven for about 15 minutes.

1 baking potato (Long Island)
1 egg
¼ teaspoon chopped garlic
¼ teaspoon chopped basil
    leaves
¼ teaspoon chopped parsley
Salt, white pepper
1 teaspoon oil

SERVES 2

# POTATO PANCAKE
### Beignet de pomme de terre

Peel the potato and grate into a small bowl. Add the egg, garlic, basil, parsley and a pinch of salt and pepper to the grated potato. Heat the oil in a small frying pan. When it is hot, add the potato mixture and mash it down with a fork. Cook over medium-high to high heat, shaking the pan back and forth frequently. Loosen the edges of the pancake with a spatula. After one side is brown, about 2–3 minutes, flip it over and cook it on the other side until it is uniformly browned.

3 baking potatoes (Long
    Island)
2 tablespoons butter
A pinch of nutmeg
Salt, white pepper
½ cup heavy cream

SERVES 2

# CREAMY PUREE OF POTATOES
### Purée crèmeuse

Peel and cook the potatoes and mash them in the bowl of an electric mixer or with a potato masher. Season them with butter, nutmeg, salt and pepper. Turn them into a metal bowl and place the bowl in a warm place on your stove. Whisk the cream into the potatoes and serve immediately.

# CRISPY POTATO
## Galette de pommes de terre

1 baking potato (Long Island)
¼ leek (optional)
2 teaspoons oil
Salt, white pepper

**SERVES 2**

Peel the potato and slice it very thinly. The best way to do this is with a mandoline. If you wish to use a leek, wash well and cut it into thin julienne strips.

Heat the oil in a small frying pan. When it is hot, lay the potato slices in the pan so that they overlap each other and cover the bottom of the pan. If using the leek, sprinkle over the potato near the center. Add another layer of potato slices, covering the leek entirely.

Cook the potatoes over medium heat for about 5 minutes, until they are brown on one side, then turn over. You might have fun flipping the galette like I do: pull the pan in toward you and toss the galette in the air so it turns over, catching it with the pan when it comes down. (See illustration.) Or turn it onto a plate, then slide it back into the pan, or turn it with a spatula. Cook until galette is completely brown on the second side, about another 5 minutes. Serve under stuffed pigeon or chicken.

*Note:* You can also add a thinly sliced truffle over the first layer of potatoes.

# POTATOES FORESTIÈRE
## Pommes de terre forestières

2 baking potatoes (Long Island)
6 button mushrooms
1½ tablespoons oil
2 tablespoons chopped parsley
1 clove garlic, chopped (optional)
Salt, white pepper

**SERVES 2**

Peel the potatoes and cut them into very small cubes. Cut button mushrooms into the same size cubes. Wash the potatoes and mushrooms and dry them very thoroughly.

Heat the oil in a pan, and when it is very hot, dump in the potatoes and mushrooms and cook them quickly. When they just begin to brown, add the chopped parsley and garlic; season with a pinch of salt and pepper. Cook until thoroughly brown. Drain off the oil and pat the vegetables with a paper towel to remove the last bits of fat. Serve with pigeon, wild game birds.

### Sweet Pumpkin; potiron confit

Peel and remove the seeds from a small pumpkin. Cut it into cubes; you should have about 2 cups. Make a sugar syrup by boiling 1 cup sugar and ½ cup water for a few minutes. Cook the pumpkin cubes in the sugar syrup until soft.

Mix the pumpkin cubes with vanilla ice cream or incorporate them into a cheesecake or a génoise.

### Salsify; salsifis

Peel the salsify and plunge it into water to which lemon juice has been added. Bring salted water to a boil and add ½ cup flour; cook the salsify until it is tender, about 30–40 minutes. The flour will keep the salsify white. Drain, dry and sauté in butter with fresh herbs.

### Spinach; épinard

To give steamed spinach a delicate flavor and glossy appearance, sprinkle the leaves with olive oil, salt and pepper. Steam for 2–3 minutes until the spinach is just *al dente*.

4 tomatoes
Salt, white pepper
2 tablespoons oil
3 tablespoons bread crumbs
3 tablespoons chopped parsley
1 tablespoon chopped garlic
½ shallot, chopped
1 tablespoon butter

*SERVES 4*

# TOMATOES PROVENÇAL
Tomates provençales gratinées

Preheat oven to 350°–400°. Cut the tomatoes in half and season them with salt and pepper. Sauté on both sides in the oil until they color slightly. Mix the bread crumbs with the chopped parsley, garlic and shallot. Spoon the mixture onto the tomatoes and dot with butter. Cook in the oven until crispy.

# SLICED TURNIPS
## Navets en lamelles

Preheat oven to 350°–400°. Peel the turnips and cut them into thin slices (a mandoline is good for this). Chop the shallots and garlic, and sweat them in the butter in a gratin dish. Pour the chicken stock into the dish and add the turnip slices. Season them with salt and white pepper. Cover with aluminum foil and cook 10 minutes in the oven; remove the foil and cook another 5 minutes.

*4 small or 2 large white*
  *turnips*
*2 shallots*
*1 clove garlic*
*1 tablespoon butter*
*1 cup chicken stock (p. 221)*
*Salt, white pepper*

*SERVES 2*

# GLAZED TURNIPS
## Navets glacés

Peel the turnips and cut them into little finger lengths. Cook them until *al dente* in boiling, salted water.

Mix the vinegar and honey in a gratin dish, or similar flameproof shallow casserole, and cook over medium-high heat; season with black pepper. Just as liquid begins to reduce, add the turnips and raisins. Cook for 5–10 minutes. Add the coriander leaves just at the end.

*4 small or 2 large white*
  *turnips*
*2 tablespoons vinegar*
*2 tablespoons honey*
*Freshly ground black pepper*
*2 tablespoons raisins*
*2–3 coriander leaves*

*SERVES 2*

# ZUCCHINI WITH CHEESE
## Courgettes au gratin

*Sliced zucchini cook very quickly in a steamer. Or roast them whole in the oven: sauté unpeeled, unsliced zucchini in hot oil with sliced onions, then finish in the oven for 1 hour. The onions cook with the zucchini.*

Preheat oven to 350°–400°. Slice the zucchini thinly (a mandoline is good for this). Cook the slices very quickly, either in a steamer or in boiling water, just to soften them. Drain.

Butter a gratin dish. Beat the eggs with a fork and mix them with the zucchini slices; season with nutmeg, salt and white pepper. Dump the zucchini and eggs into the gratin dish and cover them with a layer of grated Swiss cheese. Cook 15–20 minutes in the oven.

*3 medium-size zucchini*
*Butter*
*3 eggs*
*A pinch of nutmeg*
*Salt, white pepper*
*4 tablespoons grated Swiss*
  *cheese*

*SERVES 2*

# STUFFED ZUCCHINI
*Courgette farcie*

1 large zucchini
1 carrot
1 leek
1 egg
1 tablespoon heavy cream
2 tablespoons chopped fresh
 basil or thyme or ½
 teaspoon dried thyme
1 clove garlic, chopped
A pinch of ground cumin
Salt, white pepper
½ cup chicken stock (p. 221)
4 tablespoons grated Swiss
 cheese

SERVES 4

Preheat oven to 250°–300°. Cut the zucchini crosswise into 8 pieces. Scoop out (and reserve) the center of each piece to make a hollow for the stuffing. Very briefly blanch the scooped-out zucchini. Peel the carrot and wash the leek and blanch them. Drain and dry the blanched vegetables and mix them in a food processor along with the egg, cream, fresh herb, garlic, cumin, salt and pepper to taste.

Fill the hollowed-out zucchini pieces with the vegetable mixture. Pour the stock into an oven-proof dish, place the zucchini pieces in the dish and top with grated cheese. Cook in the oven for about 45 minutes.

# VINAIGRETTES, OILS AND BUTTERS

VINEGAR WITH
  MARIGOLDS
CORN CONDIMENT
  WITH VINEGAR

VINAIGRETTE
WALNUT SAUCE
TRUFFLE
  VINAIGRETTE
FRUIT VINAIGRETTE
LIGHT VINAIGRETTE
VINAIGRETTE
  WITHOUT OIL

GARLIC BUTTER
ONION BUTTER
ANCHOVY BUTTER
GREEN BUTTER
COLD BÉARNAISE
  BUTTER
SALTED BUTTER
SPICY BUTTER
HONEY BUTTER

### Vinegar

Vinegar is the product of the acetic fermentation of wine, alcohol or cider. Wine-based vinegar should have a lovely pink color and a good acid flavor. Vinegar made from alcohol is colorless, with less aroma and flavor, but its strength makes it the best for preserving cornichons, capers, condiments, etc. Cider vinegar is yellowish in color and sweet.

Before the Renaissance in France, vinegar makers were cooks who prepared sauces, stuffings and spices. Meat or fish was cooked at home, but the sauce was bought from a vinegar maker like Robert, Saupiquet, etc. If the order was an important one, it was delivered to the house in a wheelbarrow. This system lasted a long time in France, until housewives and cooks started to create their own sauces and vinegars.

There are an infinite variety of perfumed vinegars based on wine and alcohol. You can buy vinegars flavored with tarragon, shallots or raspberries, to name just a few, or why not create your own? Try the recipe for Vinegar with Marigolds or use other flowers from your garden.

Use white wine vinegar to preserve fresh tarragon, basil, dill or sage. Simply put sprigs of the herb in a jar and fill it with the vinegar. Cover with a screw-top lid. It is only necessary to refrigerate this vinegar after it has been opened. (You can combine different herbs together in the same jar.)

*10 marigolds (orange)*
*3 cups red wine vinegar*
*4 drops Tabasco*
*10 drops Angostura bitters*
*1 teaspoon Rose's lime juice*
*2 tablespoons port*

# VINEGAR WITH MARIGOLDS
### Vinaigre aux fleurs de soucis

*You can also use violets, gladiola or pansies; or use fresh herbs (and/ or the herb flowers), such as mint, basil or thyme.*

Dry the flowers on a windowsill in the sun for about a week. Pull the petals off the flower heads and boil them briefly with the vinegar, seasonings and port, for about 2 minutes. Cool to room temperature. Keep in the refrigerator, covered, for 1 week. Strain the vinegar into a clean jar and return to the refrigerator until needed.

# CORN CONDIMENT WITH VINEGAR

*Grains de maïs au vinaigre*

*Serve corn or other vegetables marinated in vinegar as a condiment instead of capers with meats, chicken, etc.*

Blanch the ear of corn briefly in boiling, salted water and refresh under cold water. Pat dry and cut the kernels off the cob into a bowl. Bring the vinegar to a boil and pour it over the corn, the tarragon leaves, some whole peppercorns, clove and a pinch of salt. Marinate the corn in the vinegar for a few hours.

Bring the corn, vinegar and seasonings to a boil, and pour them into a clean jar. Let liquid cool to room temperature, cover the jar and refrigerate it. The condiment should sit for 3–4 weeks in the refrigerator before using; it is good for 3–4 months.

For other vegetables, such as carrots, turnips or cauliflower, and for fruit (pears, cherries), use ¾ red wine vinegar to ¼ white vinegar.

*1 ear of corn*
*Sea salt*
*1½ cups red wine vinegar*
*Leaves from 1 stalk fresh*
*    tarragon*
*Peppercorns*
*1 whole clove*

## Oils

Oil was first used in cooking to fill the lamps to light the kitchens. Then for a long time olive oil and the fat of geese, pigs, etc., were the only cooking fats. Today we have a large selection of oils available to us; peanut, corn, safflower, walnut and olive oils are the most popular.

Oil is a basic ingredient in cooking, and I prefer it to butter when I need to cook food quickly. For me, peanut oil is the most neutral and holds up the best for cooking at high temperatures.

Olive oil is one of the most perfumed oils. It is marvelous for salads and cold sauces and to flavor raw fish and meat, but I do not like to cook with it. Olive oil reigns supreme in Provence, where there still remain working oil mills that produce a dark black elixir so concentrated that the entire region is almost intoxicated with its aroma.

My advice is to choose an oil to suit your taste and according to your cooking needs.

Create your own perfumed oil simply by adding to peanut or any other oil sprigs of fresh thyme, or a few peppercorns, or a small piece of red or green pepper, or 1–2 unpeeled garlic cloves, or a whole clove.

Or use oil to preserve the fresh herbs of summer, such as basil, tarragon, marjoram and thyme. Fill the bowl of a food processor with basil leaves. (Do not use the large stems of the basil, but the small ones are fine; do not worry if the leaves have begun to turn brown.) Process the leaves for about a minute, then scrape down the leaves left on the sides of the bowl with a rubber spatula and process again. Pour in ½ cup

olive oil with the processor still running. When thoroughly mixed, spoon the basil along the center of a rectangular piece of aluminum foil. Roll the foil up lengthwise, twist the ends to close, and freeze. Cut off portions as needed, for fish soup or for fresh herb sauce.

You can also keep meat, fish or poultry by covering it with any oil in a shallow plastic refrigerator box, carefully sealed. Keep in the refrigerator for up to 1 week, or much longer in the freezer. When you remove the meat, pat off all the oil, which will have kept the flesh moist. You can reuse the oil after straining, then boiling it, but be careful to keep fish oil and meat oil separate from each other.

# VINAIGRETTE

2 tablespoons finely diced
   carrots
2 tablespoons finely chopped
   fresh spinach leaves
1 generous pinch chopped
   shallots
1 pinch chopped garlic
1 pinch chopped fresh basil
2 teaspoons lemon juice
1 tablespoon seedless French
   mustard
1½ cups peanut oil
Salt, white pepper
¼ cup water

YIELD: approximately 1½
   cups

*This vinaigrette is for all sorts of salads, for cold meats, for vegetables served hot, cold or warm.*

Put all the ingredients except the oil, salt and pepper and water in the bowl of a food processor, and start processing. Pour the oil in through the feed tube with the processor running. Season with salt and pepper and add the water. Process briefly to incorporate.

# WALNUT SAUCE

*Sauce aux noix*

1 slice white bread
1 tablespoon lemon juice
2 teaspoons Amaretto liqueur
¾ cup walnuts
1½ cups walnut oil
¼ cup water
Salt, white pepper
Grated rind of 1 lime

YIELD: approximately 2 cups

*Serve this sauce with cold vegetables, green salad or potato salad.*

Cut the crusts off the bread and cut the slice into small cubes. Mix the bread, lemon juice and Amaretto in a small bowl. Chop the walnuts in the bowl of a food processor, then add the lemon juice mixture and process briefly. Pour the oil in through the feed tube with the processor running. Add the water, 2 pinches of salt and pepper, and the grated lime rind. Process briefly to incorporate.

This sauce will keep for a few days in the refrigerator.

# TRUFFLE VINAIGRETTE
## Vinaigrette truffée

*This is a delicate, aromatic vinaigrette that goes beautifully with a lobster or foie gras salad, or even with a warm chicken salad.*

Whisk generous pinches of salt and pepper into the truffle juice. Add the lemon juice, then whisk in the oil and finally the truffles. Serve fresh.

Salt, white pepper
2 teaspoons truffle juice
2 teaspoons lemon juice
¾ cup olive oil
1 tablespoon chopped truffles

YIELD: approximately 1 cup

# FRUIT VINAIGRETTE
## Vinaigrette aux fruits

*This lovely pink vinaigrette is nice with fruit salads, potato salad or cold chicken.*

Peel and core the apple and pear, and cut them into small pieces. Put the vinegar, lemon juice, apple and pear in the bowl of a food processor and, with the motor running, add the oil, then the water. Season with 2 pinches pepper, but no salt. Stir in the raspberries just before serving.

¼ apple
½ pear
1 tablespoon raspberry vinegar
1 teaspoon lemon juice
1 cup peanut oil
¼ cup water
White pepper
A handful of raspberries

YIELD: approximately 1½ cups

# LIGHT VINAIGRETTE
## Vinaigrette légère

*If you like to use a light oil in your vinaigrette, it is important to enhance the taste with fresh herbs and other seasonings. This vinaigrette goes nicely with poached fish, boiled meat, salads and vegetables.*

Put all the ingredients except the oil, water, salt and pepper in a food processor. Process, then add the oil in a steady stream, not all at once, but not too slowly. Finish with the water and salt and pepper to taste. Omit the salt if you are on a salt-free diet.

1 generous tablespoon seedless French mustard
4 teaspoons thyme vinegar
1 tablespoon chopped scallion
1 teaspoon fresh chopped herb, such as basil or tarragon
1 tablespoon chopped parsley
1½ cups light oil
¼ cup water
Salt, white pepper

YIELD: approximately 2 cups

2 teaspoons seedless French
    mustard
⅛ teaspoon curry powder
Pinch of ground cumin
A few drops Tabasco
1 tablespoon chopped scallion
1 teaspoon fresh chopped
    herb, such as basil or
    tarragon
1 tablespoon chopped parsley
1 tablespoon small diced
    pieces of green pepper
    (optional)
1 tablespoon small diced
    pieces of celery
1 egg
2 tablespoons thyme vinegar
1 cup water
Salt (optional)
White pepper

YIELD: approximately 1½
    cups

# VINAIGRETTE WITHOUT OIL
### Vinaigrette sans huile

*Although it is difficult to take the oil out of a vinaigrette and achieve a good result, I think this recipe will surprise you and make your diet less difficult.*

Process all the ingredients except the water, salt and pepper in the bowl of a food processor. When they are well mixed, pour in the water, process briefly and season with salt, if desired, and pepper.

### Butter

Culinary historians attribute the origin of butter to the Scythians (an ancient nomadic people who lived in the south of Russia), who evidently valued it more as a remedy than for its culinary properties.

Today butter plays a large part in our cooking and is present on almost every table. I like a pure, unsalted butter that has a light yellow color, a soft, delicate flavor and a smooth texture. In my cooking, I only use butter to finish a sauce (see Introduction) or in preparations that do not require high temperatures, because browned or blackened butter decomposes and becomes indigestible.

If you like to cook eggs or fish with butter, or wish to make hollandaise, try using clarified butter, that is, butter without its top froth and bottom white sediment of casein and salts. It is not hard to make clarified butter: melt ½ a pound of butter very, very slowly over very low heat. When it is all melted, skim off the froth on top and discard it. Pour the melted butter into a bowl very carefully so that you do not disturb the bottom white sediment, which you also discard. You will have about ¾ cup of clarified butter, which will keep in the refrigerator for 1–2 weeks.

You can enhance the taste of simply grilled or roasted meats, fish and chicken by topping them with a slice or two of one of the following delicious cold butters just before serving.

# GARLIC BUTTER
*Beurre à l'ail*

*The following butters are all made very quickly in the food processor and can then be shaped into a long roll and wrapped in aluminum foil for the freezer. When you need a piece, just cut off a slice and re-cover the end of the roll with a fresh piece of aluminum foil.*

½ *pound butter*
½ *teaspoon chopped garlic*
1 *tablespoon chopped parsley*
1 *teaspoon cognac*
3–5 *walnuts*
*Salt, white pepper*

Cut the butter into large pieces and mix it and the other ingredients briefly in the bowl of a food processor. Serve with escargots or on grilled fish, chicken or meat.

# ONION BUTTER
*Beurre aux oignons*

2 *large onions*
2 *tablespoons oil*
½ *pound butter*
*Freshly grated nutmeg*

Slice the onions and fry them in the oil until they are just brown, but not blackened. Strain out the oil. Cut the butter in pieces into the bowl of a food processor and process along with the onions. Season with nutmeg.

# ANCHOVY BUTTER
*Beurre d'anchois*

½ *pound butter*
12 *anchovy filets*
*Juice of* ½ *lemon*
⅛ *teaspoon chopped garlic*
  *(optional)*
*White pepper*

Follow directions for Garlic Butter (above); use 2 pinches pepper. Anchovy Butter will keep for 2 weeks in the refrigerator. It should not be seasoned with salt because the anchovies are already so salty. Serve with fish, meat or potatoes.

# GREEN BUTTER
*Beurre vert*

½ *pound butter*
½ *cup fresh spinach leaves*
1 *tablespoon chopped parsley*
2 *scallions, cut into large*
  *pieces*
1 *teaspoon fresh chopped*
  *basil*
½ *teaspoon chopped shallots*
⅛ *teaspoon chopped garlic*
  *(optional)*
*Juice of* ½ *lemon*
*Salt, white pepper*

Follow directions for Garlic Butter (above). Serve on grilled fish or meat or with baked potatoes.

# COLD BÉARNAISE BUTTER
### Beurre froid façon béarnaise

8 stalks fresh tarragon
2 shallots
½ clove garlic
¾ cup tarragon vinegar
1 tablespoon chopped parsley
A few peppercorns
½ pound butter
Salt, white pepper

*Here is an easy way to produce a béarnaise sauce without pain. It is particularly nice on grilled fish.*

Strip the leaves from the tarragon stalks. Peel and chop the shallots; peel, smash and chop the garlic clove. In a small saucepan, reduce the vinegar along with the tarragon leaves, shallots, parsley, peppercorns and the garlic until moist but no longer liquid. You should have 2 tablespoons of the mixture after the reduction. Cut the butter in pieces into the bowl of a food processor and process along with the tarragon mixture. Season with salt and pepper.

# SALTED BUTTER
### Beurre salé

½ pound butter
½ tablespoon sea salt
Seaweed (optional)

*Sea salt gives butter an intense flavor. If you are near the ocean, add a few pieces of seaweed.*

Follow directions for Garlic Butter (p. 177). Serve with grilled fish, meat or chicken.

# SPICY BUTTER
### Beurre aux épices

½ pound butter
1 pinch curry powder
1 pinch ground cumin
Freshly grated nutmeg
1 whole clove
1 clove garlic
1 teaspoon chopped basil
1 pinch saffron threads

Follow directions for Garlic Butter (p. 177). Serve with fish, meat or vegetables.

½ pound butter
1 tablespoon honey
½ teaspoon vanilla extract

# HONEY BUTTER
### Beurre au miel

Follow directions for Garlic Butter (p. 177). Serve on hot poached fruit or a hot brioche.

# *HERBS, SPICES AND FLOWERS*

*SPRING SALAD WITH
  NASTURTIUMS
CHICKEN
  FRICANDEAU WITH
  VIOLETS
CRÊPES WITH ROSE
  PETALS AND SYRUP
  OF POPPIES
BOUQUET GARNI*

$F$resh herbs play a prominent role in my cooking because I think they make food lively and interesting.

During the summertime, when fresh herbs are available and inexpensive, it is easy to freeze them in plastic bags for later use. Or store them in vinegar or in oil in the refrigerator, or dry them in the sun. If you can grow a few herbs yourself, even if only in a window box, you will find it easy to use fresh herbs in your cooking.

When I was very young on the farm, my grandparents grew early fruits and vegetables for the market and were proud of their reputation for supplying the first green beans of the season. I loved the days I did not have school and could wiggle my way through the large, fragrant plants and help pick tomatoes and other vegetables.

Gradually we gave up growing vegetables and specialized exclusively in flowers grown for their seed, a crop my mother still produces. As I was still very little, the flowers were often taller than I was and I grew up literally surrounded with them. So it is not surprising that when I marched into the kitchen as a small boy, I cooked with flowers; I still do. In other chapters, you will find recipes for Vinegar with Marigolds, Violet Wine and Syrup of Poppies.

Some other flower and food combinations you might enjoy are dandelions in an omelette (sauté the flowers in butter briefly, add them to the omelette and season with chervil); or a lemon flan flavored with rose petals. You can sauté veal filets mignons with chopped onion, parsley and the petals of a wild rose; deglaze the pan with white wine and finish the sauce with butter. Or stuff a duck with honeysuckle flowers, bread, cream, eggs, salt and pepper. And if you add more sugar to Syrup of Poppies (p. 215), you can make it into a sorbet.

Flowers could be called the herbs of paradise; use them to perfume your cooking. Here is a complete menu using flowers in every course.

Greens for salad: mache, red
  chicory, new dandelion
  leaves, arugula, etc.
Salt, white pepper
Lemon juice
Olive oil
Nasturtiums
Chervil leaves

# SPRING SALAD WITH NASTURTIUMS
*Salade de printemps aux capucines*

Combine the lettuces and the dandelion leaves. Mix salt and pepper into the lemon juice, and add a little olive oil.

In a salad bowl, mix the salad and dressing along with nasturtium flowers and some chervil leaves.

# CHICKEN FRICANDEAU WITH VIOLETS
*Fricandeau de coq aux violettes*

Carve off the breast, thighs and drumsticks of a chicken, and make a light brown stock with the rest of the carcass. Season the chicken pieces with salt and pepper, and brown them in a sauté pan in 1 tablespoon of the oil.

In another pan, sweat the chopped onion and carrot in the remaining tablespoon of oil. Add the chicken pieces, the flour and tomato paste, and stir until well mixed. Pour in the brown stock and cook over low heat for about 35 minutes. Halfway through the cooking time, add a bouquet of parsley sprigs, season with salt and pepper, and continue to cook slowly. Five minutes before the end of the cooking, add violet flowers and finish sauce with butter, if desired.

*Breast, thighs and drumsticks*
   *of 1 chicken*
*½ cup light brown stock (see*
   *Note p. 219) or chicken*
   *stock (p. 221)*
*Salt, white pepper*
*2 tablespoons oil*
*½ cup chopped onion*
*½ cup chopped carrot*
*1 teaspoon flour*
*1½ tablespoons tomato paste*
*Fresh parsley sprigs*
*Violet flowers*
*Butter, softened (optional)*

# CRÊPES WITH ROSE PETALS AND SYRUP OF POPPIES
*Crêpes aux pétales de roses et sirop de fleurs de coquelicots*

*Butter*
*Crêpes (p. 184)*
*Rose petals*
*Syrup of Poppies (p. 215)*

In a lightly buttered pan, cook a crêpe until it is just brown on one side. Turn it over and sprinkle rose petals on the cooked side. When crêpe is cooked on the second side, roll it up with the rose petals inside and serve with Syrup of Poppies.

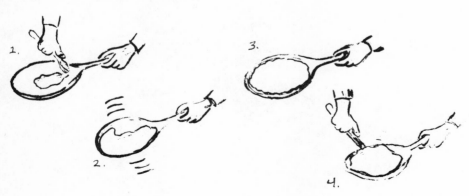

### Bouquet Garni

Bunches of mixed fresh herbs add flavor to foods that need to simmer for a long time, such as stocks, sauces and stews. Stalks of fresh herbs can be mixed together, or any one or two of them can be combined with a carrot and/or leek. Cut the carrot and leek in half lengthwise and tie the herbs to them with string. (If you wish, leave a length of string to attach to the handle of the pot to facilitate removing the bouquet garni at the end of the cooking.) Here are a handful of bouquets garnis that will add taste to your cooking.

1. For stock, bouillon, poached chicken: 2–3 stalks of fresh parsley, thyme, basil or rosemary, mixed together; or any one or two of them combined with a carrot and/or leek.

2. For consommé, stock (especially fish stock), lobster sauce: 6 peeled whole shallots, 4–5 stalks of basil or parsley and 1–2 stalks of rosemary or thyme. In this case wrap the shallots and herbs in a square of fine cheesecloth and tie with a string.

3. For stock, game dishes, bordelaise sauce: 5 peeled whole shallots, 2–3 basil leaves, 1 teaspoon dried thyme and ¼ teaspoon whole cloves. Wrap in cheesecloth.

4. For sugar syrup or poaching fruit: 3 cinnamon sticks and 1 teaspoon whole cloves, wrapped in cheesecloth.

*Freezing:* It is easy to freeze bouquets garnis in the summer when fresh herbs are readily available. Tie the herbs to the carrot and/or leek, or wrap them in cheesecloth. Tightly wrap with plastic wrap and freeze until needed.

*Dried herbs:* Substitute dried herbs for fresh in the winter or at other times when it is impossible to get fresh herbs, especially dried thyme. Use only ¼–½ teaspoon of the dried herb. Enclose the dried herb with the shallots, carrot, leek, other fresh herbs, etc., in a cheesecloth square.

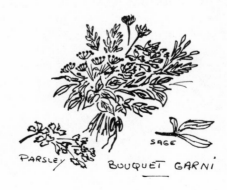

PARSLEY     SAGE

BOUQUET GARNI

# DESSERTS

EGG WHITES IN THE
   STEAMER
CRÊPES IN THE
   PROCESSOR
SHORT PASTRY

ORANGE TART
CARAMELIZED APPLE
   TART
VALENTINE TARTS
CHOCOLATE TART
   WITH PINE NUTS
PECAN PIE

CHOCOLATE
   COBBLESTONES

CHOCOLATE
   NAPOLEONS

RICE PUDDING
APPLE COMPOTE
APPLE AND PLUM
   COMPOTE
APPLES IN THE OVEN,
   FARM STYLE

CARAMEL CUSTARD
   WITH BROWN SUGAR
MAPLE SYRUP ICE
   CREAM WITH
   PECANS

TULIPS
CRISPY COOKIES
A SMALL SWEET

**DESSERTS WITHOUT
   SUGAR**
HOT GRAPEFRUIT
FRUIT COMPOTE
APPLE TART WITH
   PLUM SAUCE
CRÊPES WITH ROSE
   PETALS AND SYRUP
   OF POPPIES (p. 181)

# EGG WHITES IN THE STEAMER
*Oeufs à la neige à la vapeur*

*You will need a large ice-cream scoop to form the egg whites into perfectly shaped balls.*

¾ cup egg whites
½ cup sugar
4 tablespoons honey
1 lemon

Caramelized Sugar
3 tablespoons sugar
2 tablespoons water

SERVES 6

Beat the egg whites until they take shape, add the ½ cup sugar and continue beating until shiny. In the bottom of a steamer, bring the water, honey and lemon to a boil. (That is, the juice of the lemon and the 2 squeezed halves.) When it is boiling, bring the egg whites, a large ice-cream scoop and a bowl of very hot water to the stove. Dip the scoop first into the hot water, then into the egg whites to form the balls. Place the formed egg whites in the perforated top section of the steamer and immediately turn the heat under the steamer to very, very low. The egg whites cook in half a minute or less. They are done when their surface is glossy and you can feel a little resistance when you press your finger on them lightly. Remove the egg whites to a plate, cool them and chill in the refrigerator until ready to serve.

Repeat with the remainder of the egg whites. No more than 4 large egg white balls will fit in the steamer at one time; if there is even a short delay before forming the second batch, keep egg whites in the refrigerator.

Mix the 3 tablespoons sugar and 2 tablespoons water together in a small pot over high heat. Be very careful; this hot sugar can give you a bad burn. If it cooks a little too long, add a bit of cold water, but hold the pot at arm's length. Just before serving, dribble the hot caramel onto the cold egg whites.

1⅓ cups flour
1 tablespoon oil
1 egg
1½ cups milk
Salt
Oil or butter

YIELD: 12 crêpes

# CRÊPES IN THE PROCESSOR

*You will notice these crêpes have no sugar and so can be used for appetizers like Asparagus Crêpes. For desserts, fill them with jam, confectioners' sugar, liqueurs or whipped chestnut cream with melted chocolate sauce.*

Mix the flour, oil and egg in the processor briefly, pulsing it on and off. Pour in the milk, add a pinch of salt and blend well. Let the batter rest in the refrigerator for 30 minutes.

Heat 2–3 tablespoons oil or butter in a 6–7-inch pan. Pour in 1½ generous tablespoons of batter and let it run to the edges of the pan. Cook over medium-high heat until crêpe is lightly browned on each side, about 1 minute a side. Repeat until all the batter is used. Crêpes will keep up to 2–3 days in the refrigerator, stacked on a plate and covered with plastic wrap, or longer in the freezer. Reheat them in a 350° oven for a few minutes.

# SHORT PASTRY
### *Pâte brisée*

4 cups flour
½ pound butter, at room
  temperature
Salt
3–4 tablespoons sugar
  (optional)
1 egg
3–4 tablespoons cold water

YIELD: Pastry for 2–3 8-inch
  tarts

Dump the flour in a pile on your work surface. Cut the softened butter into large pieces and distribute it over the flour. Add a pinch of salt; if you want sweet pastry, add the sugar. Squeeze the butter and flour together in your hands, very lightly, until it is well mixed and is the consistency of rough cornmeal. It is important to do this quickly and with a delicate touch.

Beat the egg and 3 tablespoons of the cold water together in a small bowl, then stir it into the center of the flour-butter mixture and lightly squeeze the pastry together with a few quick movements. If necessary, add the remaining tablespoon of cold water to the pastry to hold it together. Form it into a ball. Let the pastry rest 1 hour at room temperature before rolling it out, or keep it overnight in the refrigerator.

*Note:* Uncooked, frozen puff pastry is available in many cities. If you cannot find it and do not wish to make your own puff pastry, in recipes where a choice is indicated, you may substitute this Short Pastry, although the result will not be as light. I do not recommend this Short Pastry as a substitute for puff pastry for Turnover with Truffles (p. 32), Bass in Puff Pastry (p. 70), Quick Rabbit Pie (p. 148) or Chocolate Napoleons (p. 189).

3 oranges (navel type)
2 eggs
1 cup sugar
2 tablespoons butter plus a
    little extra
2 tablespoons Grand Marnier
Puff pastry or Short Pastry
    (p. 185)

**SERVES 6**

# ORANGE TART
### Tarte à l'orange

Preheat oven to 350°–400°. Grate the rind of 1 orange and cut it in half. Very thinly slice the other 2 oranges so that you have 12–15 perfect slices. Throw out any slices that are too thick or uneven. Beat the eggs and ½ cup of the sugar in the bowl of an electric mixer until they are light and fluffy. Melt the 2 tablespoons butter very, very slowly so that it remains creamy-looking. (Start with the pan over very low heat, then remove the pan from the heat and shake it until the butter is melted.) Add the Grand Marnier and grated orange rind to the melted butter.

Roll out the pastry until it is thin, and fit it into a buttered tart pan (9–10 inches in diameter); prick the pastry with a fork. Mix the butter-liqueur mixture into the eggs and sugar, and pour into the tart shell. Bake the tart for 30–40 minutes.

Put the orange slices in a small pan with the remaining ½ cup sugar and 1 cup boiling water. Bring to a boil, turn down the heat to low and poach the slices in the syrup for 10–15 minutes. Remove the slices to a plate and reduce the sauce still further over very low heat. If it gets away from you and reduces too much, add a little water.

Remove the pastry from the pan and arrange the orange slices in a circular pattern on top of the tart. Paint the syrup on the slices. Cool the tart and chill.

3 large apples (firm)
3 tablespoons butter plus a
    little extra
1 cup sugar
1 tablespoon vanilla extract
Juice of 1 lemon
Puff pastry or Short Pastry
    (p. 185)
2 tablespoons sour cream

**SERVES 4**

# CARAMELIZED APPLE TART
### Tarte aux pommes caramélisées

Preheat oven to 350°–400°. Peel and core the apples, and cut them lengthwise into 3–4 large pieces. Cut the pieces crosswise into thick slices or wedges. Melt the 3 tablespoons butter and add the apples, ¾ cup of the sugar, the vanilla and lemon juice. The best pan for this is a medium-size frying pan with sloping sides. Cook the apples over medium-high heat for about 15–20 minutes until they are brown. Shake the pan every few minutes to mix the apples about and turn them over.

Roll out the pastry and cut out 2 6-inch circles (use a saucer to outline the circle). Crimp the edges of the pastry to create a slightly raised edge and put tarts on a buttered baking sheet. Arrange the apple slices in a wheel on each of the pastry circles and sprinkle them with the remaining sugar. Bake tarts for 15–20 minutes and serve warm with sour cream on the side.

# VALENTINE TARTS
### Tarte de la St-Valentin

Preheat oven to 350°–400°. Roll out pastry until it is very thin. Using a heart-shaped cookie cutter about 3½ inches wide, cut out 4 hearts. Cut 4 thin strips about 4 inches long from the extra pastry; a pastry wheel is the best tool for this, otherwise use a sharp knife.

Brush the hearts with egg wash. Make a bow on each tart with the strips of pastry; brush the bows with egg wash. Butter a baking sheet or metal plate and bake the tarts for 15 minutes. Let them cool.

Slice the tarts horizontally so that you have upper and lower halves: remove the insides of the pastry. Spoon 1½ tablespoons whipped cream onto each of the 4 bottom pieces and arrange 6 raspberries (or 6 strawberry halves) on top of the whipped cream. Cover the berries with the remaining whipped cream. Place the pastry tops on the whipped cream.

Puree 1 cup fresh or frozen raspberries in the bowl of a food processor or blender along with the sugar and lime juice. (If the raspberries are frozen in a sweet syrup, omit the sugar.) Strain if you wish to eliminate the seeds. To serve, ladle 2 tablespoons raspberry puree on each plate. Place 2 tarts on each plate. Sprinkle with confectioners' sugar and grated lime rind.

**Puff pastry or Short Pastry (p. 185)**
**Egg wash (p. 13)**
**Butter**
**1 cup whipped cream**
**24 raspberries or 12 strawberries**

**Raspberry puree**
**1 cup raspberries**
**3 tablespoons sugar**
**1 tablespoon lime juice**

**Garniture: confectioners' sugar, grated lime rind**

**SERVES 2**

# CHOCOLATE TART WITH PINE NUTS
### Tarte au chocolat et pignons

Preheat oven to 350°–400°. Butter a tart mold, line it with the pastry and prick the pastry all over with a fork. Break the chocolate into squares and spread it over the pastry; sprinkle with grated orange rind. Beat the egg and cream together, add the sugar and mix in the Grand Marnier. When the mixture is well blended, pour it into the tart shell and sprinkle the pine nuts on top. Bake 30–35 minutes.

Paint the top of the tart with melted apricot jam and return to the oven for 2–3 minutes. Decorate tart with thin strips of the candied orange and mint leaves. Serve warm.

**Butter**
**Puff pastry or Short Pastry (p. 185)**
**5 ounces dark semisweet chocolate**
**Grated rind of 1 orange**
**1 egg**
**½ cup heavy cream**
**5⅓ teaspoons sugar**
**2 tablespoons Grand Marnier**
**1 cup pine nuts**
**3 tablespoons apricot jam**
**Garniture: candied orange peel, fresh mint leaves**

**SERVES 6**

1 cup maple syrup
1 cup water
2 eggs
1 tablespoon cornmeal
Puff pastry or Short Pastry
    (p. 185)
1 cup pecans
3 tablespoons apricot jam
½ cup whipped cream
1 tablespoon sour cream

SERVES 6

# PECAN PIE
## Tarte aux noix de pecan

Preheat oven to 350°–400°. Bring the maple syrup and water to a boil. Beat the eggs together with the cornmeal. Slowly pour the maple syrup and water onto the egg-cornmeal mixture, beating constantly. Return the mixture to the syrup pan and bring it to a boil. Boil for 1 minute, stirring all the time. Push mixture through a sieve; let it cool.

Butter a tart mold, line it with the pastry and prick all over with a fork. Pour the filling mixture into the pastry. Roast the pecans in the oven and distribute them over the filling. Bake for about 15 minutes. Coat with melted apricot jam and return to the oven for 2–3 minutes. Serve with whipped cream mixed with sour cream.

1 pound semisweet chocolate
½ pound unsalted butter plus
    a little extra
¼ cup almonds, peeled
½ cup sifted flour
6 eggs
4 tablespoons granulated
    sugar

Icing
½ pound bittersweet
    chocolate
2 tablespoons butter

Confectioners' sugar

SERVES 8–12

# CHOCOLATE COBBLESTONES
## Pavé au chocolat

*I like to serve this cake in small individual servings, the size of petits fours, and that is why I call it "chocolate cobblestones."*

Preheat oven to 325°. Melt the semisweet chocolate and ½ pound butter in a double boiler. Pulverize the almonds in a food processor. (You should have 2 tablespoons powdered almonds.) Sift the flour and powdered almonds together, and mix them into the chocolate.

Separate the eggs. Beat the egg yolks and 2 tablespoons of the granulated sugar until yolks are light in color. In a separate bowl, whip the egg whites along with the remaining 2 tablespoons granulated sugar until they are firm. Mix the egg yolks into the chocolate mixture, then fold in the egg whites. Butter and flour a 8-inch cake mold and pour the batter into it. Bake for 45 minutes.

Let the cake cool at room temperature for 1 hour, then chill it (still in the mold) for at least 2–3 hours (or overnight). The cake must be cold and firm.

Using a rolling pin, tamp the cake down several times, then remove it from the mold. With a long, sharp knife, cut the cake across horizontally to create 2 layers.

Melt the bittersweet chocolate and 2 tablespoons butter in a double boiler. Spread the chocolate on one layer, then place the other one on top. Continue icing until the cake is completely covered on the top and the sides. Refrigerate the cake for 10–15 minutes.

Cut the cake into little rounds with a cookie cutter no more than 1 inch in diameter. Sprinkle the rounds with confectioners' sugar and place in paper pastry cups. (Or top the cake with confectioners' sugar and serve wedges from it in the more traditional manner.)

# CHOCOLATE NAPOLEONS
## Mille-feuilles aux deux chocolats

*There are four parts to this procedure. You can make the mousses as much as 24 hours ahead of time, the puff pastry an hour ahead. Just before serving, assemble the napoleons and finish them with melted chocolate. They must be served within 15 minutes of completion, otherwise they will become soggy.*

Make the chocolate mousse: melt the chocolate and butter in a double boiler and mix them well. Remove from the heat and cool. In a small saucepan, cook the sugar with the water for approximately 10–15 minutes. Beat 4 tablespoons of this syrup into the beaten egg yolks to make a thick sauce; the syrup should be warm but not hot. Fold into the melted chocolate and let cool completely. Reserve remaining 4 table-spoons syrup for the white chocolate mousse.

Whip the cream and fold it into the chocolate mixture. Whip the 4 egg whites until firm but not dry, and incorporate them into the choco-late. Refrigerate the mousse for 6–24 hours.

Make the white chocolate mousse: melt the white chocolate in a double boiler. Remove it from the heat and let cool. Whip the 5 egg whites, add the 4 tablespoons of sugar syrup and fold into the melted white chocolate. Refrigerate the mousse for 6–24 hours.

Preheat oven to 350°–400°. Roll out the puff pastry on a floured surface until it is an 8 × 10-inch rectangle. Place it on a lightly oiled pan, prick it all over with a fork, sprinkle with 1 tablespoon sugar and bake in the oven for only 4–5 minutes. The pastry must be soft, not crumbly.

Remove the pastry to your work surface and cut it into small rect-angles, about 1½ × 3 inches. Then cut each rectangle in half horizon-tally to create double the number of pastry rectangles. Place these back on the baking sheet cut side up. Sprinkle them with the remaining 1 tablespoon sugar and return them to the oven for another 5 minutes until they are dry and crispy.

Fill 2 pastry bags, one with chocolate mousse and one with white chocolate mousse. Cover one pastry rectangle with white chocolate mousse piped from its pastry bag, place another pastry rectangle on top of it and pipe chocolate mousse on it. Add another piece of pastry and cover this one with melted white chocolate. Continue building the napoleons in this manner until you have used all the mousse and the pastry.

Finish the napoleons by dipping a knife into the melted dark choco-late and with it drawing a straight line the length of the napoleons on top of the white chocolate, then draw a curvy line back and forth across the straight line.

**Chocolate mousse**
*1 pound semisweet chocolate*
*¼ pound unsalted butter*
*½ cup sugar*
*1 cup water*
*10 egg yolks*
*2 cups heavy cream*
*4 egg whites*

**White chocolate mousse**
*1 pound white chocolate*
*5 egg whites*
*4 tablespoons sugar syrup*
*(reserved from chocolate mousse above)*

*Puff pastry (see* **Note** *p. 185)*
*2 tablespoons sugar*
*3 ounces white chocolate, melted*
*2 ounces dark chocolate, melted*

***SERVES 8–10***

**1 cup Uncle Ben's Converted
   Rice**
**1⅓ cups sugar**
**4 tablespoons water**
**3½ cups milk**
**1 vanilla bean, cut in half
   lengthwise**
**3 eggs**

**SERVES 6**

# RICE PUDDING
### Riz au caramel

Blanch the rice in boiling water for 5 minutes. Drain. Melt 5 table-spoons of the sugar into the 4 tablespoons water over high heat. Let it turn brown, but it should stay soft. If it goes too far and gets hard, very carefully add a little water (at arm's length to prevent burns). Ladle the caramel into 3–4½-inch individual soufflé molds and roll it around so that the sides and bottoms of the molds are completely covered. After the first layer of caramel has firmed up, pour any leftover caramel into the molds.

Bring the rice, milk, the remaining 1 cup of sugar and the vanilla bean to boil in a large pot over medium-high heat. Reduce the heat and cook over medium-low heat for about 30 minutes until the rice is *al dente* and has absorbed the milk but is not gluey.

Preheat oven to 350°. Remove the pot from the heat and beat in the eggs, one at a time. Ladle the pudding into the molds and cook them in a bain-marie in the oven for 15 minutes. Cool and refrigerate; serve cold. Custards will keep for 2 days in refrigerator.

**6 tart apples (Granny Smith
   or similar yellow or green
   apples)**
**2 cups sugar**
**1½ cups water**
**1 vanilla bean, cut in half
   lengthwise (see Note
   below)**
**½ lemon**

**SERVES 4–6**

# APPLE COMPOTE
### Compote de pommes

Peel and core the apples and cut them into small dice. Heat the sugar, water and the vanilla bean. Squeeze the juice from the ½ lemon into the pan and add the squeezed lemon half. When the syrup is hot, add the apples; putting the apples in the hot syrup ensures that they will retain their fresh blond color and not darken.

Cook for about 5–6 minutes, or until the apples are translucent. Skim off any scum, remove the half squeezed lemon, and transfer apples into a bowl. Let cool, then chill. Compote will keep for up to 1 week, covered, in the refrigerator. Serve cold.

*Note:* If you do not have a vanilla bean, you can substitute ⅛ teaspoon vanilla extract.

*Variatons:* Peel a kiwi fruit, cut it into half-moon slices (slice it length-wise, then across) and add it to the compote while it is still hot. Or add sliced strawberries or whole raspberries or any fresh fruit cut into small pieces to the compote while it is still hot. (Peaches and plums must be peeled.) Or substitute 3 pears for 3 of the apples.

# APPLE AND PLUM COMPOTE
*Compote de pommes et prunes*

Cut 1 apple in half lengthwise and scoop out the inside, discarding the core and seeds, but reserving the scooped-out apple. You should have 2 complete shells about ½ inch thick. Squeeze a little lemon juice on the apple shells. Cook them briefly in a steamer, 2 minutes, then refrigerate.

Chop up the scooped-out apple pieces. Peel, core and chop the remaining apple. Peel and chop the plums. In a large saucepan, cook the chopped apples and plums, 4 tablespoons of the sugar, the ½ cup water and all but ½ teaspoon of the remaining lemon juice, for 15 minutes over medium-high heat.

While the fruit is cooking, make a caramel with 3 tablespoons of the sugar and 3 tablespoons of the hot water, flavored with the ½ teaspoon lemon juice. Melt sugar and let it froth; when it is a nice brown color, add remaining 3 tablespoons hot water, agitating continuously. Scrape the fruit and the caramel into a food processor and puree. Chill in the refrigerator.

Just before you are ready to serve, whisk the heavy cream and sour cream together; add 3 tablespoons sugar at the end. Spoon the cream into a pastry bag. Fill the apple cups with the puree and pipe cream rosettes around on the top. Serve cold. The puree will keep for 1 day in the refrigerator.

*2 large red apples*
*Juice of 1 lemon*
*4 red plums*
*10 tablespoons sugar*
*½ cup water*
*6 tablespoons hot water*
*½ cup heavy cream*
*1 tablespoon sour cream*

**SERVES 2**

# APPLES IN THE OVEN, FARM STYLE
*Pommes au four comme à la ferme*

Preheat oven to 350°–400°. With a vegetable peeler, cut straight through the apples to remove the core. The hole should be small, less than 1 inch in diameter. Butter a pan with 3 tablespoons of the butter. Arrange the apples in the pan, sprinkle the sugar on top of the apples so that some goes into the holes, and dot with the remaining 1 teaspoon of butter. Add the white wine and water to the pan, and bake the apples in the oven for 15 minutes. Remove the apples to plates, reheat the juice briefly and pour it over the apples. Serve with sour cream on top.

*2 apples*
*4 teaspoons butter*
*2 teaspoons sugar*
*2 tablespoons white wine*
*2 tablespoons hot water*
*Sour cream*

**SERVES 2**

## CARAMEL CUSTARD WITH BROWN SUGAR
*Crème caramel au sucre brun*

8 tablespoons brown sugar
5 tablespoons hot water
2 teaspoons lemon juice
6 eggs
2 cups milk
1 cup heavy cream

SERVES 5

Preheat oven to 350°–400°. In a small pan, heat 4 tablespoons of the brown sugar, the hot water and lemon juice until it melts and bubbles. Pour the caramel into 5 individual soufflé molds 4 inches in diameter. There will be enough caramel to just cover the bottoms, but not the sides, of the molds.

Beat the remaining 4 tablespoons brown sugar and the eggs together with a wire whisk until they are very well blended. Add the milk and cream, and continue beating. Skim off all the froth from the top. Ladle the liquid into the molds and place them in a bain-marie of hot water in which you have placed a piece of paper to prevent spattering. Bake in the oven for about 25 minutes.

Cool to room temperature, then chill in the refrigerator. Serve cold in the molds. They will keep 1 day in the refrigerator.

## MAPLE SYRUP ICE CREAM WITH PECANS
*Crème glacée au sirop d'érable et noix de pecan*

8 egg yolks
¾ cup sugar (generous)
1 quart milk
10–12 whole pecans
½ cup maple syrup
1 tablespoon sour cream

SERVES 4–6

Whip the egg yolks and sugar together until the mixture is a pale lemon color. (An electric mixer is good for this.) Heat the milk in a saucepan to which you have first added 1 tablespoon water to prevent the milk from burning. Bring to just under a boil over medium heat. Remove the milk from the heat and whip a small amount of the milk into the egg-yolk mixture very slowly. Add the remainder of the milk and whip it slowly into the egg mixture.

Return all to the saucepan and cook until the mixture thickens enough to coat a spatula or spoon, about 5–8 minutes. Strain the mixture into a clean bowl and let it cool. Aerate it and stop the cooking process by whisking it several times while it is cooling. You have made a *crème anglaise*, a good base for many ice creams. Sometimes it is a little tricky to prepare. If you overcook it and the eggs and the milk separate, you can save it by pouring it into a bottle and shaking it very hard.

Roast the pecans and chop them into fine pieces. Pour the *crème anglaise*, pecans and maple syrup into an ice-cream maker and run it for 20–30 minutes. About 5–10 minutes before it is finished, add the sour cream.

# TULIPS
## Tulipes

*These attractive thin cookie shells formed into the shape of a tulip are a lovely way to serve ice cream, chocolate mousse or fruit with whipped cream.*

⅔ cup sugar
3 egg whites
½ cup flour
1 teaspoon vanilla extract
3 tablespoons milk
Zest of ¼ of an orange
Butter

Briefly beat the sugar and egg whites together with a whisk; sift the flour into the egg whites and mix it in. Add the vanilla, milk and orange zest, and mix quickly with the whisk. Refrigerate for at least 1 hour.

Preheat oven to 325°–350°. Butter heavy waxed paper or parchment paper the size of a baking pan. With a rubber spatula, spoon a small amount of the batter onto the paper and smooth it out to a very thin circle about 4 inches or larger in diameter. You can probably fit 2 circles on the sheet. Bake the circles for 5–6 minutes. When they are cooked, the outside rim of the cookies will be brown and the center white.

Using a cup or any other round form about 3½ inches in diameter, cut out perfect rounds. Immediately transfer each hot, soft cookie into a cup; lightly push the cookie down into the cup so that it falls into a tulip shape. Repeat until all batter is used.

You can make these shells 1–2 days ahead of time. Keep them in a dry place until you are ready to fill and serve; humidity will destroy the shape.

# CRISPY COOKIES
## Croustillants

4 egg whites
¾ cup sweetened coconut
3 tablespoons flour
½ cup sugar
1 teaspoon vanilla
½ cup blanched, slivered almonds

Whisk the egg whites, coconut, flour and sugar together in a bowl. Add the vanilla and almonds. Let the batter rest at least 1 hour (or overnight) in the refrigerator.

Preheat oven to 300°–350°. Spoon 1 tablespoon batter onto a buttered baking sheet and spread it into a large, thin circle with a fork. Repeat until all batter is used. The average baking sheet will probably hold about 5 cookies.

Bake cookies 5–10 minutes. They will brown at the edges first: take them out while the center is still soft and light yellow. Immediately form them by wrapping them around a thin rolling pin.

2 cups flour plus a little extra
¼ cup butter plus a little
    extra
½ cup granulated sugar
1 egg
½ teaspoon vanilla
3 tablespoons water
Egg wash (p. 13)
Confectioners' sugar

# A SMALL SWEET
*Petit sucré*

Dump the 2 cups flour onto your work surface and make a hole in the middle. Cut the butter into pieces—it should be moist but not soft—and add it to the center of the flour along with the granulated sugar. Squeeze the flour, butter and sugar together with your hands and fingers until it has the consistency of cornmeal. In a small bowl, beat the egg, vanilla and water with a fork. Make a hole in the center of the pastry and pour in the egg mixture. Stir it all together with the fork.

Preheat oven to 300°. Flour your hands and form the pastry into a ball; cut the ball in half. Flour your work surface and roll out the pastry about ½ inch thick. It should not be thin. Cut out the cookies with a small, round cookie cutter. I like to use a fluted tartlet mold 1¾ inches in diameter. Put the cookies on a buttered baking pan, paint with egg wash and sprinkle with confectioners' sugar. Put the pan in the refrigerator for 5–10 minutes. You can incorporate the leftover pastry into the other ball and use it for the next batch, but be careful not to handle dough too much.

Bake the cookies for 10 minutes. Sprinkle them with confectioners' sugar when you take them out.

*Note:* The pastry may be frozen or kept for up to 2–3 days in the refrigerator.

### Desserts Without Sugar

Sugar is an important ingredient in many desserts, the very base of the art of confectionery. But in our society today, we consume too much sugar in all sorts of drinks, candies and cakes. So I thought it would be interesting to give you a few recipes for desserts without sugar that utilize instead the natural sugars of fruits.

The three following recipes are not medically tested, but simply the result of my experience and imagination. I hope you will enjoy their simplicity.

4 grapefruit
4 ounces butter

SERVES 2

# HOT GRAPEFRUIT
*Pamplemousse chaud*

Preheat broiler. Cut the peel off 2 grapefruit and section out the pieces from between the white membranes. Reserve the pieces on a metal plate; squeeze out the juice from the remaining grapefruit cores into a measuring cup.

Cut a shallow slice off the top of each of the other 2 grapefruit; reserve. Using a curved grapefruit knife, cut the meat out of the grapefruit, leaving 2 grapefruit shells. Reserve the shells. Section out the meat as before and chop it into small pieces; squeeze juice from leftover cores into the measuring cup. Add the chopped grapefruit to the juice; you should have about 1 cup.

Run the grapefruit sections from the first 2 grapefruit under the broiler for about 5 minutes until they are lightly browned on top.

In a small saucepan, reduce the juice and chopped grapefruit pieces by more than half over a hot flame. Then turn the heat to very low and add the butter, a small piece at a time, whisking vigorously with each addition.

Pile the broiled grapefruit sections into the 2 grapefruit shells, reserving 4 sections for garnish. Pour the juice and butter sauce into the shells, garnish with the reserved sections and top with the 2 reserved top pieces cut off the grapefruit shells, as little hats.

Serve hot as an appetizer or dessert.

# FRUIT COMPOTE

## Compote de fruits

Put the tea bags and hot water in a large saucepan over medium-high heat. Cut the lemon in quarters and squeeze slightly into the pan, then add squeezed lemon quarters. Cut the vanilla bean in half lengthwise and add it. Cook for 5 minutes after liquid comes to a boil, then remove the tea bags and lemon. (If you leave the tea bags in too long, the taste will be too strong and bitter.) Cook the tea another 5 minutes after you remove the tea bags.

Prepare the fruit: peel, slice and dice the apple and the pear. Peel and slice the peach (do not dice). Slice the plums and cut into pieces (do not peel). Cut the strawberries into quarters or halves, depending on their size. If using kiwi, peel and slice it thinly.

Add the cut-up apple, pear, peach and plums to the tea, bring to a boil and let cook for 1–2 minutes. Add the cinnamon, then the blueberries and strawberries (and raspberries or kiwi, if using). Instantly remove the pan from the heat, place the fruit in a bowl and let it cool to room temperature, then chill in the refrigerator. (It will keep up to 1 week.)

I like to serve this fruit arranged in a circular pattern on a flat plate, with the juice spooned over it. You may wish to add a spoonful of mixed sour cream and whipped cream on the side of the plate.

*6 tea bags*
*6 cups hot water*
*1 lemon*
*1 vanilla bean*
*1 cooking apple*
*1 pear*
*1 peach*
*2 plums*
*5 strawberries*
*A handful of raspberries or a*
*    kiwi fruit (optional)*
*¼ teaspoon cinnamon*
*A handful of blueberries*

*SERVES 2*

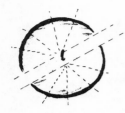

**Puff pastry or Short Pastry**
   **(p. 185)**
**2 large apples**
**A few drops of vanilla**
**4 tablespoons water**
**½ teaspoon lemon juice**
**The juice of 1 orange (2**
   **tablespoons)**
**2 limes**
**1 teaspoon butter**
**6 red plums or 4 purple**
   **plums**
**3 tablespoons water**

**SERVES 4**

# APPLE TART WITH PLUM SAUCE
*Tarte aux pommes et coulis de prunes*

Preheat oven to 350°–400°. Roll out a piece of pastry until it is thin; cut out 4 circles (3–4 inches) for the individual tarts. Place the pastries on a lightly greased baking sheet; crimp the edges of the circles to make a shallow lip and prick the pastry with a fork in many places.

Peel the apples. Cut each apple vertically in two places on either side of the core. (See illustration.) Cut each apple half into thin slices and reserve. Cut the remaining pieces of apple away from the core and chop into small pieces. Put these pieces into a small pot with the vanilla, 4 tablespoons water and the lemon juice, and cook over medium-high heat for 5 minutes. Remove from the heat, add the orange juice and mash the apple with a fork. (This can also be done in a food processor.)

Spread the mashed apple onto each of the 4 pastry circles so that the pastry is completely covered. Arrange the apple slices on the mashed apple so that the pieces overlap slightly in a circular pattern. (You will have slices from half an apple for each tart.)

Grate the lime rinds onto a piece of waxed paper and reserve. Cut the limes in half; squeeze the juice of 1 lime onto the apple slices. Cut the butter into very small pieces and distribute over the apple slices. Bake the tarts in the oven for 30 minutes.

Peel the plums and cut them into pieces into the bowl of a food processor. Squeeze the juice of the remaining lime over the plums and add the 3 tablespoons water. Process in the food processor for about 1½ minutes until the plums have become a thick, liquid sauce.

To serve the tarts, ladle 2 large spoonfuls of plum sauce onto each plate. Place the tarts on the plates and sprinkle each one with some of the grated lime rind.

# *BREAD*

*MY BREAD (BASIC RECIPE)*
*ONION BREAD*
*BASIL BREAD*
*GARLIC BREAD*
*WALNUT BREAD*
*ANISE BREAD*
*MARBLED BREAD WITH ORANGE*
*MUFFINS*

"It is our daily bread" proclaims the importance of this basic food, which is as old as civilization. In the old days, in France, a piece of blessed bread held in one's mouth was believed to be a protection against evil and illness.

The Egyptians made bread with millet and barley or wheat; the Pharaohs ate bread made of roots and the seeds of white lotus flowers. The Greeks knew about wheat, but preferred rye and oats for their bread.

For thousands of years, of course, bread was made at home. I remember knowing people in Provence twenty years ago who baked bread in old ovens made of cut stone. Although these ovens are no longer used for baking, they can still be found in some of the oldest houses, where they are treasured for their decorative beauty.

When I was little, my mother would send me on my bicycle to a little bakery to buy our bread. I will always remember the divine odor of baking bread in that bakery.

Although there are some bakeries today where bread is made by hand, factory-made bread has become the rule. You will give great enjoyment to yourself and your family if you make bread at home. It is easy to do and the bread will keep well in the refrigerator or freezer. Besides, when you make your own bread, there are infinite taste possibilities open to you—bread with herbs, bran, onion, garlic, etc.

### A Few Tips on Bread

• To easily cut very fresh bread, pass the blade of the bread knife under very hot water.

• To reheat bread, dampen it with a little water before putting it in the oven.

• When cooking cauliflower or cabbage, put a piece of bread in the pot to absorb the odor. In the same way, if you do not want to cry when cutting onions, put a piece of bread at the end of your knife.

• Stale bread can always be made into bread crumbs.

# MY BREAD (BASIC RECIPE)
## Mon pain

Dump the yeast, sugar and warm water into a small bowl and put it in the warmest place in your kitchen. Cover with a saucer and let the yeast work with the sugar and water for about 5–8 minutes. (If there is no visible change after that time, if the liquid seems lifeless, throw the mixture out and start over with fresh yeast.)

Mix the flour, salt and wheat germ in a large bowl, and add the 3 tablespoons melted butter. Add the yeast mixture, then the cold water, and mix all this together with your hands. If the mixture seems too dry, add a small amount of water; if it seems too wet, add some flour. Turn dough out onto a floured surface and knead it hard with your hands for 4–5 minutes.

Butter a large bowl and put the dough in the bowl; make a large X in the top of the dough with a knife; brush the top with a little melted butter. Cover the bowl with a clean napkin or dish towel and let dough rest in a warm place for about 1 hour.

Turn the dough out and form it with your hands into a round, flat ball. Place it on a buttered baking pan and make 3 vertical slashes across the top. Cover with the towel and put back in its warm place for another 10–20 minutes. During this time it will spread and expand.

Preheat oven to 350°. Brush the top of the dough with egg wash and bake it for 30–40 minutes.

*Variations:* You can mix this bread in a food processor. Ferment the yeast in warm water in a small bowl as above. Using the plastic blade, mix the flour, salt, wheat germ, sugar and 1 tablespoon baking powder in the bowl of the processor. Mix the melted butter, cold water and yeast mixture together, and add to the dry ingredients. Process until dough forms a ball.

*1 generous tablespoon dry yeast*
*1 teaspoon sugar*
*6 tablespoons warm water*
*5 cups flour, approximately*
*2 teaspoons salt*
*1 generous cup wheat germ*
*3 tablespoon melted butter plus 1 tablespoon*
*1¾ cups cold water*
*Egg wash (p. 13)*

*YIELD: 2 large loaves or 3 small loaves*

# ONION BREAD
## Pain aux oignons

Follow the basic recipe (above) but omit the wheat germ and reduce the water to 1½ cups. Dice a large onion into small pieces and cook it (uncovered) in 2 tablespoons butter over medium heat for about 5 minutes, or until it is soft. Add the onion and ½ teaspoon ground cumin to the dough before kneading. Place the bread in buttered pans for the second rising.

# BASIL BREAD
*Pain au basilic*

Follow the basic recipe (p. 199), but omit the wheat germ and reduce the water to 1½ cups. Add 2 tablespoons chopped, fresh basil or other herbs such as thyme or coriander (use only 1 tablespoon coriander) to the dough before kneading.

# GARLIC BREAD
*Pain a l'ail*

Follow the basic recipe (p. 199), but omit the wheat germ and reduce the water to 1½ cups. Add 3 cloves peeled, finely chopped garlic to the dough before kneading.

# WALNUT BREAD
*Pain aux noix*

Follow the basic recipe (p. 199), but omit the wheat germ and reduce the water to 1½ cups. Add 1 cup coarsely chopped walnuts to the dough before kneading.

# ANISE BREAD
*Pain d'anis*

*3 whole eggs*
*3 egg yolks*
*1⅓ cups sugar*
*1 cup sifted flour*
*1 tablespoon baking
    powder*
*1 tablespoon Pastis (anise
    liqueur)*
*4 egg whites*
*Butter*

*YIELD: 2 small or 1 large
    loaf*

*This and the following recipe are for cakelike breads that are delicious for breakfast or tea or served with ice cream. They are easy and quick to make, especially if you have an electric mixer.*

Preheat oven to 350°–400°. Beat the whole eggs, egg yolks and 1 cup of the sugar together until they are light and fluffy. (If using an electric mixer, use the whisk attachment.) Add the flour and baking powder to the eggs and mix thoroughly. After mixture is well blended, add the anise and mix well.

Beat the egg whites, and when they are well formed, add the remaining ⅓ cup of sugar and continue beating until they are firm. Fold the egg whites into the batter in 3 batches, mixing well after each addition.

Butter 2 round charlotte molds or a rectangular bread tin, then sprinkle with flour or sugar; fill ¾ of the way to the top and bake for 35–40 minutes.

# MARBLED BREAD WITH ORANGE

*Marbré à l'orange*

2 whole eggs
2 egg yolks
1 cup plus 1 tablespoon sugar
3½ tablespoons butter
Grated rind of 1 orange
¾ cup flour
1 tablespoon baking powder
6 egg whites
2 tablespoons Baker's
    unsweetened cocoa

YIELD: 1 loaf

Preheat oven to 350°–400°. Beat the whole eggs, egg yolks and ¾ cup of the sugar together until they are light and fluffy. (If using an electric mixer, use the whisk attachment.) Melt 3 tablespoons of the butter very, very slowly; you want to keep it creamy rather than let it become greasy and separated. Start the butter over low heat, then remove it from the stove and shake the pan around until the last bits are melted. Add the grated orange rind to the butter.

Add the flour and baking powder to the beaten eggs. After they are well blended with the batter, slowly mix in the butter and orange rind. Divide the batter into 2 bowls (one bowl should have slightly more batter than the other). In a clean bowl, beat the egg whites, and when they are well formed, add the remaining ⅓ cup of sugar and beat until they are firm. Mix the cocoa into the bowl with the smaller amount of batter.

Divide the egg whites in half and fold them into the 2 separate batters, using a clean rubber spatula each time. Butter and sugar a bread pan and pour the white batter into the pan. Now scrape the chocolate batter into the center of the pan so that the white batter is on the outside all the way around. Bake the bread for 35–40 minutes.

# MUFFINS

*These nonsweet muffins are light and fresh, a nice accompaniment to game, meat, etc. Use a mixture of green, yellow and red peppers for a colorful effect.*

4 whole eggs
A pinch of ground cumin
Salt
1 tablespoon olive oil
1 cup flour
1 tablespoon baking powder
4 tablespoons chopped bell
    peppers
½ teaspoon chopped garlic
    (optional)
½ teaspoon chopped basil
4 egg whites
Butter

YIELD: 8 muffins

Preheat oven to 350°–400°. Beat the eggs for a few minutes. (If using an electric mixer, use the whisk attachment.) Season with a pinch of cumin and a little salt. Beat in the olive oil. Add the flour and baking powder, and mix briefly. Stir in the peppers, garlic and basil.

In a clean bowl, beat the egg whites until they hold their shape. Fold them into the batter with a rubber spatula. Bake the muffins in buttered tins for about 10 minutes. (Ten minutes is fine for the very small muffin tins, larger ones will take a little longer.)

# JAMS

PEACH JAM
MELON JAM
PINEAPPLE JAM
WATERMELON JAM
PLUM AND PEAR JAM
BLACK FRUIT JAM
ORANGE MARMALADE
FROSTY MARMALADE
GREEN TOMATO JAM
VEGETABLE JAM

To round out your culinary knowledge, I hope you will learn to make your own jams. The process is a simple one that, once mastered, allows you to blend different fruits into any number of clever combinations. You will be able to give yourself the pleasure of serving your family and friends jams of your own creation.

These jams are fresh-tasting, intense in color and easy to make. Since they are not meant to keep a long time, they do not have to be vacuum sealed. They will keep for 2–3 weeks in the refrigerator.

I like jam with large fruit pieces; it seems more homemade to me and less like standard commercial jams. But if you prefer smoother jams, cut the larger chunks of fruit into smaller pieces after the cooking. A heavy copper pot lined with tin helps ensure slow, even cooking, but any large, heavy pot is appropriate. Lemon juice preserves the color and texture of the fruit and adds a little acidity to the jam. The squeezed lemon half should be removed after the cooking.

Create your own labels for the jars. Cut a piece of white or colored paper, glossy if possible, into a 3 × 4-inch rectangle. Draw a design on the edges with ink or paint; write the date of preparation and the name of the jam in the middle of the label. Coat the interior circumference of the label with glue, position it on the jar and rub it with a cloth to get rid of any air bubbles.

Cover the jam jar with a piece of attractive fabric, such as a Provençal country-type pattern. Cut the fabric in a circle about 6 inches in diameter. Place it over the top of the jar and secure it with an 8-inch piece of brightly colored wool.

# PEACH JAM
## Confiture de pêches

6 peaches
2½ cups sugar
3 tablespoons water
Juice of ½ lemon and the
    squeezed lemon half

YIELD: 2½ cups

Peel the peaches and cut them into large pieces. (It is not necessary to peel the peaches if you can pick them from your own trees or in a local orchard.) Place them in a large, heavy saucepan with the sugar, water and lemon juice. Add the peach pits and the squeezed lemon half.

Mixing the ingredients with a wooden spoon, cook over medium-high heat until jam just comes to a boil. Be careful not to let the sugar caramelize due to excessively high heat. Lower the heat and cook the jam very slowly, uncovered, for 1–1½ hours until it reaches the consistency you want. With a ladle, skim off the froth 5–6 times during the cooking period and just at the end. Stir with the wooden spoon after each skimming. Remove the lemon half and peach pits, and pour the jam into hot, clean jars. Cool to room temperature, cover the jars and store in the refrigerator.

*Variation:* Add 1 pint strawberries or raspberries halfway through the cooking.

# MELON JAM
### Confiture de melon

*This unusual jam takes on a lovely golden color.*

Peel the melon and cut it into large pieces. Cook with the sugar, water, lemon juice and squeezed lemon half as directed for Peach Jam (p. 204), for about 1½ hours.

*Variation:* Substitute 1 whole cantaloupe if Cranshaw melon is not available; or add 6 whole green figs, quartered, with the melon pieces; or add 10 green pistachio nuts at the very end of the cooking.

½ a Cranshaw melon
2½ cups sugar
1 tablespoon water
Juice of ½ lemon and the
    squeezed lemon half

**YIELD: 2½ cups**

# PINEAPPLE JAM
### Confiture d'ananas

Cut off the top and bottom ends of a pineapple. Cut off the rind and any remaining brown spots. Remove the hard center core, cut the pineapple into pieces and cook with the sugar and water as directed for Peach Jam (p. 204), for about 1 hour.

*Note:* It is not necessary to add lemon juice to this jam because pineapple is an acidic fruit.

1 pineapple
2½ cups sugar
2 tablespoons water

**YIELD: 2½ cups**

## WATERMELON JAM
*Confiture de pastèque*

*The shiny pink pieces of watermelon make this jam very appetizing.*

2 pounds watermelon
5 cups water, approximately
1 teaspoon sea salt
2½ cups sugar
2 tablespoons water
Juice of ½ lemon and the
    squeezed lemon half

YIELD: approximately 3 cups

After removing seeds from watermelon, cut into pieces. Add the sea salt to the 5 cups water, bring to a boil and add the watermelon pieces just long enough for the water to return to a boil. Remove from the heat and drain off the water. This brief cooking in salted water firms up the watermelon pieces so they will not fall apart during the cooking.

Cook melon with the sugar, 2 tablespoons water, lemon juice and squeezed lemon half as directed for Peach Jam (p. 204), for about 1½ hours.

## PLUM AND PEAR JAM
*Confiture de prunes et poires*

4 pears
4–5 large purple plums
2½ cups sugar
3 tablespoons water
Juice of ½ lemon and the
    squeezed lemon half

YIELD: 2½ cups

Peel plums and pears, and cut them into large pieces. Cook with the sugar, water, lemon juice and squeezed lemon half as directed for Peach Jam (p. 204), for about 1 hour. I like to add the plum pits to the pot while the fruit is cooking, but remember to remove them before transferring the fruit into a jar.

## BLACK FRUIT JAM
*Confiture de fruits noirs*

4 black plums
1 pint blackberries
1 pint blueberries
1½ cups sugar
3 tablespoons water
Juice of ½ lemon and the
    squeezed lemon half

YIELD: 2½ cups

*During the hot summers of my childhood in Provence, the blackberries became plump and bursting with sunshine. My sister and I were sent to pick the berries for jam making, and of course we never forgot to eat quite a lot and would come home covered with the sweet brown juice.*

Cut the plums into thin wedges; do not peel them. Cook the fruit with the sugar, water, lemon juice and squeezed lemon half as directed for Peach Jam (p. 204), for 1½ hours.

# ORANGE MARMALADE
## Marmelade d'orange

*Orange marmalade is probably the most popular of all jams, and it is one of my favorites on the breakfast table.*

Wash oranges, cut a small piece off each end, then cut each orange in half. Cut the halves into slices, then into pieces. Cook with the sugar and water as directed for Peach Jam (p. 204), for about 1½ hours.

*Variations: Lemon Marmalade:* substitute 8 lemons for the oranges; *Grapefruit Marmalade:* substitute 4 grapefruit for the oranges; *Mixed Citrus Marmalade:* use 3 oranges, 1 grapefruit, 3 lemons.

6 navel oranges
3 cups sugar
1 cup water

**YIELD: 3 cups**

# FROSTY MARMALADE
## Marmelade givrée

*I particularly like the texture of this jam made with a raw egg, it resembles English lemon curd. The Grand Marnier is optional, but it adds a nice flavor.*

Place the marmalade, egg and Grand Marnier in the bowl of a food processor and blend for 1 minute. Store in the refrigerator for 4–5 hours before serving.

2 cups Orange Marmalade
   (above)
1 egg
1 tablespoon Grand Marnier

**YIELD: 2 cups**

# GREEN TOMATO JAM
## Confiture de tomates vertes

*My grandmother Marguerite made this jam every October. I loved it when I was young and now think of her every time I make it. Serve it on toast.*

Cut out the tomatoes' hard center cores and discard along with the stems. If the tomatoes are very watery, squeeze out some of the seeds and water; it is not necessary to completely remove the tomato seeds. Cook the tomatoes with the sugar, water, lemon juice and squeezed lemon as directed for Peach Jam (p. 204), for about 1½ hours.

2 generous pounds green
   tomatoes
1½ cups sugar
1 cup water
Juice of ⅓ lemon and the
   squeezed lemon third

**YIELD: 2 cups**

# VEGETABLE JAM
## Confiture de légumes

1 medium zucchini
½ cucumber
1 carrot
1 leek
10 snow peas
1 Belgian endive
½ fennel root
4–5 small new potatoes
½ small celery root
3 stalks asparagus
4 cups sugar
1½ cups water
Juice of ⅓ lemon and the
    squeezed lemon third

YIELD: 2½ cups

*Here is an unusual jam made from a mixture of fresh vegetables. The perceptible, delicate taste of each vegetable merged and yet drowned into the sweetness of the whole will astonish and please you.*

Prepare the vegetables so that they are all in small pieces or dice: cut the zucchini into julienne strips, then dice. Peel the cucumber and carrot and cut into dice. Wash the leek well, remove most of the green top and cut remaining leek into small pieces. Remove ends of snow peas and cut into small pieces. Cut the endive and fennel root into small pieces. Peel and dice the potatoes, celery root and asparagus, and cut each into dice.

Cook the cut-up vegetables with the sugar, water, lemon juice and squeezed lemon as directed for Peach Jam (p. 204), for about 1½–2 hours.

*Note:* If you are using truly garden-fresh vegetables, you may wish to cut the sugar to 3½ cups.

# WINES AND OTHER DRINKS

ORANGE WINE
PEACH WINE
VIOLET WINE
STRAWBERRY OR RASPBERRY WINE
HOT WINE

*NONALCOHOLIC DRINKS*
*INFUSION*
*PIERRE'S COCKTAIL*
*VEGETABLE WINE WITHOUT ALCOHOL*
*SYRUP OF POPPIES*

 ine has played a key role in the history of cooking since ancient times; it is fair to say that one cannot exist without the other. Because wine holds this indisputable place in our cuisine, I want to discuss it with you briefly.

In antiquity wines were used in religious services as well as for man's pleasure. Even today wine is an elixir of God closely tied to our past. Over the years wines have acquired personality, elegance and refinement. Certain vineyards have produced great vintages, *les grands crus*, in France particularly in Bordeaux and Burgundy, and in California in the Napa Valley.

France enjoys a wide range of wines. Nearly every region has its own vintage—Burgundy, Bordeaux, Alsace, Provence, Languedoc, the Roussillon, the Loire and many others. In the United States wine is grown mainly in California; some great vintages have come from the Napa Valley, such as Chardonnay, Cabernet Sauvignon, Sauvignon and Pinot Noir.

Autumn, the time of the grape harvest, is a happy time in the wine country. The workers sing and tell stories as they move among the vines. I can remember damp mornings during the harvest in Provence, when the sweet smell of the grapes pervaded the air. Many mosquitoes swarmed around us as we worked, and our hands became sticky from the sweet clusters of grapes. The grapes look so good that everyone picks and eats them during the long day so that by evening, when the baskets are full of grapes on their way to the wine cooperative, the stomachs of the workers are full also.

I think wine should play the role of an elegant knight accompanying Dame Cuisine; for the discerning diner, wine gives the palate the tasting ability to appreciate fine cooking. The marriage of wine and cuisine creates gastronomy.

I am not enthusiastic about a great assortment of wines at a dinner and usually content myself with one, be it a dry white or a light Bordeaux. It is not my personal taste that counts, however, or strict rules; everyone should feel comfortable serving wines of his or her own choice. All the same, a certain amount of education will help you choose wines that marry well with your food.

*White Wines*: Sancerre, Muscadet, Chablis, Sylvaner, Sauvignon Blanc, etc., go excellently with shellfish, smoked salmon and raw fish.

Bordeaux (Graves, Médoc), Burgundy (Côte de Nuits), Chardonnay (Napa Valley) go very well with any dish made with fish.

*Rosés* of Provence or Italy go nicely with a light meal or with pasta.

*Red Wines* like Burgundies (Côte de Beaune, Côte de Nuits, Côte Rôtie) or Bordeaux (Médoc, Graves, St-Emilion), Châteauneuf-du-Pape, and Cabernet Sauvignon and Pinot Noir (both from the Napa Valley) all complement meats, game or fowl. A few great Burgundies go very well with cheese.

*Champagne and Sauternes* are dessert wines; sauterne is also excellent with foie gras. Of course, champagne is a lovely wine to drink with all foods. A dinner where champagne is the only wine served seems to me most elegant and harmonious.

This is only a brief guideline for choosing wines for your meals. For the great years of famous vintages (which are unfortunately becoming increasingly rare), it is rewarding and pleasurable to learn from a good wine encyclopedia. If you have occasion to taste one of these great wines, save the label from the bottle. It will bring back memories of the wine and increase your love for this nectar of Dame Nature.

### The Labels

*Why save wine labels?* Their beauty, diversity and the stories they tell can become a fascinating study. Also, wine labels contain information that will be helpful to you, such as the following:

- The year the wine was made (very important)
- The origin—the different areas and the vines: for example, Médoc and Graves from Bordeaux; Côte de Beaune and Côte de Nuits from Burgundy; Sauvignon and Cabernet from the Napa Valley
- The name of the proprietor or *négociant* (a merchant who buys wine from a grower to mature, bottle and sell)
- The place of origin, that is, the château, or the city or town
- The years of the great vintages

You may wish to keep your labels in a loose-leaf file or in a photograph album; some of the more beautiful specimens can be put in a glass frame to decorate a dining room or kitchen.

These labels will bring back memories of wines and meals you have enjoyed with a lover, with family or with friends. Happy Collection.

### Wines with Fruit

These light, colorful wines are meant to be drunk soon after you make them; they only keep for about 2 weeks in the refrigerator. Therefore, you need not worry about fermentation.

You do not have to use expensive wines to make these refreshing drinks. When the recipe calls for a white wine, use a dry white like a California chablis; never use a sweet white wine.

You may omit the eau-de-vie or applejack if you wish; the function of the brandy is to help preserve the wine. If you with to substitute another eau-de-vie for applejack, try kirsch, raspberry, pear or prune brandy.

In hot weather, the marination should take place in the refrigerator. This is not necessary during the cooler months.

The wines should be served very cold.

## ORANGE WINE
### Vin d'orange

3 navel-type oranges
20 whole cloves
½ vanilla bean
6 cups dry white wine
¼ cup applejack or any eau-
  de-vie (optional)
½ cup sugar
4 tablespoons Grand Marnier
  (optional)

YIELD: approximately 1
  quart

Choose small- or medium-size oranges with bright-colored skin for this wine. Wash but do not peel them. Stick the cloves into 1 orange. Cut the other 2 oranges in half and then into slices. Cut the vanilla bean in half lengthwise.

Combine all the ingredients in a glass, china, porcelain or stainless-steel bowl and marinate overnight. Do not use an aluminum pot.

Bring the wine, oranges and other ingredients to a boil in a tall pot over high heat. Let cook for 15 minutes. Remove the clove-studded orange and place it in a glass jar. Strain the wine into the jar. Refrigerate the wine and serve chilled.

*Note:* If you have a particularly attractive bottle or decanter in which you wish to serve the wine, put a handful of cloves and a few pieces of the cooked orange peel into the bottle, then strain the wine into it.

## PEACH WINE
### Vin de pêche

3 peaches
½ vanilla bean
6 cups white wine
½ cup sugar
½ cup eau-de-vie (optional)
½ lemon

YIELD: approximately 1
  quart

*If you are fortunate and have fresh peaches that have not been overly sulfated by commercial methods, add a few peach leaves to the bottle as an attractive garniture.*

Wash and slice the peaches; save the pits. Cut the vanilla bean in half lengthwise. Marinate all the ingredients together overnight. Cook as directed for Orange Wine (above); include the pits for both the marination and the cooking. Strain and chill.

# VIOLET WINE
## Vin de violettes

*My aunt makes this wine in Provence in March when the first violets appear. The wine takes on a soft, light purple color and becomes even more beautiful if you put a few violets in the jar or bottle before chilling.*

Marinate the ingredients together overnight and cook as directed for Orange Wine (p. 212). Strain and chill.

*25 violet petals (dark colors are the best)*
*3 cups white wine*
*1 cup sugar*
*½ cup eau-de-vie (optional)*
*½ lemon*

**YIELD: approximately 3 cups**

# STRAWBERRY OR RASPBERRY WINE
## Vin de fraises ou framboises

*This sweet wine has a deep red color.*

Remove stems and leaves from the berries. Marinate the ingredients together overnight and cook as directed for Orange Wine (p. 212). Strain into a jar or bottle and chill. If you use raspberries, they may stay in the bottle. Strawberries will become mushy and should be strained out before chilling.

*3 cups strawberries or raspberries or 1½ cups of each*
*2 bottles rosé wine*
*½ cup applejack (optional)*
*½ cup strawberry or raspberry liqueur (optional)*
*½ cup sugar*
*½ lemon*

**YIELD: approximately 1½ quarts**

# HOT WINE
## Vin chaud

*This is a warming drink for cold winter ski weekends.*

Slice the orange and lemon. Chop the half apple into dice; it is not necessary to peel it. Bring all the ingredients to a boil and boil for 3–5 minutes to marry the flavors together. Strain and serve in cups or mugs.

*1 orange*
*1 lemon*
*½ apple*
*3 cups red wine*
*3 tablespoons sugar*
*2 whole cloves*
*1 stick cinnamon*

**SERVES 4**

*Nonalcoholic Drinks*

# INFUSION

1 orange
1 lemon
1½ cups sugar
12 cups water
1 stalk fresh mint
1 branch fresh thyme
1 stalk fresh rosemary
1 stick cinnamon

YIELD: approximately 2½
    quarts

*This herb-scented drink is refreshing and healthful. It is especially good served very cold on hot summer days.*

Wash orange and lemon, and cut them into quarters. Bring sugar and water to a boil. Add the orange and lemon, and cook for about 2 minutes over high heat. Add the mint, thyme, rosemary and cinnamon. Remove from heat and let steep until cold.

Strain the infusion into a glass jar. Store it in the refrigerator, where it will keep for 3–4 days. Serve hot or cold; if you add rum to the hot infusion, it becomes grog.

3 tablespoons lemon juice
    that has been mixed with
    egg white (see Note)
1 teaspoon confectioners'
    sugar (optional)
20–30 drops grenadine syrup
    (for color)
½ cup fresh grapefruit juice
½ cup fresh orange juice

SERVES 1

# PIERRE'S COCKTAIL
## A Refreshing Drink Without Alcohol

*This light and beautiful-looking drink is for those who do not wish to drink alcohol.*

Shake the above ingredients in a cocktail shaker and serve in a large, tall wine glass.

*Note:* Mixing lemon juice with egg white gives body and froth to the drink. The proportions are 1 egg white to 1¼ cups lemon juice. This mixture will keep in a covered glass jar in the refrigerator for up to 1 week.

# VEGETABLE WINE WITHOUT ALCOHOL

## Vin de légumes sans alcool

*Serve this vegetable wine with an outdoor barbecue in the summer.*

Peel the carrot and wash the leek thoroughly. Cut the carrot, leek, zucchini and celery into large pieces. Mash the garlic clove. Pour the tomato juice into a saucepan, add the water or chicken stock and all other ingredients except the lemon. Cut the lemon in half and squeeze the juice into the saucepan, then add the squeezed halves. Cook over medium heat until the liquid begins to shiver, just below a quiet boil. Cook another 6–8 minutes without letting it boil.

Remove the mixture from the heat and let it cool so that the vegetables can marinate in the tomato juice. When it is cold, strain the liquid through a fine sieve into a bottle or jar and discard the vegetables. Refrigerate; it will keep for 3–4 days.

*1 carrot*
*1 leek*
*1 zucchini*
*1 stalk celery*
*1 clove garlic*
*1 large can tomato juice (46 fluid ounces)*
*½ cup water or chicken stock (p. 221)*
*3 drops Tabasco*
*A pinch of celery salt*
*1 sprig parsley*
*1 teaspoon fresh chopped basil*
*1 lemon*

*YIELD: approximately 6 cups*

# SYRUP OF POPPIES

## Sirop de coquelicots

Bring the sugar and water to a boil, reduce the heat to medium and cook for about 20 minutes. Add the poppy petals and boil for another 10–15 minutes. Pour the syrup into a pitcher or bottle, let it come to room temperature, then chill, covered, in the refrigerator.

Mix the syrup with club soda or ice water for a cooling summer drink. Or use it as a topping for cold fruit, fruit salad, poached pears, etc. It will keep 1 week in the refrigerator.

*1 cup sugar*
*2 cups water*
*5–6 red poppies*

*YIELD: approximately 1 cup*

# STOCKS

**BROWN**     **WHITE**
VEAL         CHICKEN
DUCK        RABBIT
LAMB        FISH

VEGETABLE

To many home cooks a discussion of stocks *(les fonds)* sounds a little like the talk of a magician. In professional cooking, stocks are the foundation of cuisine, the building blocks for elegant sauces, for poaching food, for ragoûts, fricassees, sautés, etc., that can be prepared quickly. Please be reassured, however, if you do not have the time or the inclination to make stock, I have given you many recipes in this book that do not require a stock base.

I realize that it is not easy to prepare stocks in small quantities as part of your kitchen routine, but the following seven recipes are not hard, and I think you will find them interesting. They will open up a world of possibilities in your cooking, because to have a little stock in your refrigerator is like money in the bank.

With a stock base, you can improvise and create. When a brown stock is reduced and finished with butter, it becomes a brown sauce. I often combine a meat stock or chicken stock with fish, or a fish stock with meat, and I find these taste combinations are happy ones. Many cooks in the olden days created similar marriages of taste.

There are two kinds of stock, brown and white; I have given you several recipes for both. Stock keeps well in the refrigerator or freezer, so it makes great sense to take a little time and make some for the future. You should, however, store it in small portions so you do not take the risk of subjecting a large quantity to temperature changes by taking it in and out of the freezer.

Stocks may not play a large part in your everyday home cooking, where time is short and the price of ingredients important. I too like family cooking and respect its place in our lives. But I very much hope you will vary your menus with some of the more original recipes that call for a stock. Of course bouillon cubes are easy to use, but with just a small amount of time you can create a more savory cuisine and a more healthful one, without in any way falling into excess, by making a little chicken or fish stock, neither of which is in the least bit difficult to prepare.

# VEAL STOCK
*Fond de veau*

*A brown stock. Veal stock is one of the most important building blocks of professional cooking. In order to make your job easier, this recipe is very simplified; it is really more a juice than a stock.*

*If you want to give it a more concentrated taste, add a half a ham and some veal trimmings. Veal stock goes well with meat dishes and also with fish and vegetable recipes. It is lighter than beef stock, which is very strong. (See Note at end of recipe.)*

*6–7 pieces meaty veal bones*
  *(leg and rib, 3–4 pounds)*
*1 onion*
*1 carrot*
*2 tablespoons oil*
*1 tablespoon tomato paste*
*1½ tablespoons flour*
*1 cup white wine*
*Bouquet garni (p. 182)*
*Water*

*YIELD: 1 quart*

Ask your butcher to split the veal bones for you. It is important to get bones that have marrow; leg and rib bones are the best. Preheat oven to 450°–500°. Peel the onion; it is not necessary to peel the carrot. Cut the onion and carrot into large pieces. Place the oil, bones, onion and carrot pieces in a shallow baking pan. Brown the meat and vegetables over high heat for about 5–10 minutes, turning them several times with tongs. Just before they begin to burn, remove the pan to a hot oven for 20 minutes. Add the tomato paste and flour to the pan and stir them in with a wooden spoon; return the pan to the oven for another 10 minutes.

Remove the bones and vegetables to a large, heavy pot and pour out any extra fat that may remain in the pan. Deglaze the pan by pouring the white wine into it and stirring vigorously over high heat. (See *Note* at end of recipe.)

Pour the wine into the pot with the bones and vegetables, and add the bouquet garni. Cover the bones with water (about 10 cups). Let it come to a boil, skim off any scum, reduce the heat and simmer for 1–1½ hours over low heat.

Strain the stock into a bowl or container and let it cool to room temperature. Store it in the refrigerator; the fat will rise to the top and harden and can easily be removed before using the stock. It will keep 1–2 weeks in the refrigerator, or for months in the freezer.

*Note:* When veal stock is totally reduced to a gluelike consistency, it is *glacé de viande*, the essence of the stock.

If you do not have the time to make a true stock, you may prefer to make a light stock of bouillon (of veal, duck or lamb) by eliminating the first two steps of this recipe. Simply boil the bones, vegetables, bouquet garni and white wine with water for 1–1½ hours, skimming off scum and fat.

1 duck minus the breast, legs
  and thighs (not cooked)
1 leek
2 large onions
1 carrot
3 tablespoons oil
2 tablespoons flour
1 tablespoon tomato paste
2 cups wine
8 cups water
A fresh bouquet of basil,
  scallion and parsley
  (p. 182)

YIELD: 2–2½ cups

# DUCK STOCK
### Fond de canard

*A brown stock. Duck stock serves as the base for duck dishes.
Reduced, it becomes a delicious sauce for roast duck or for some fish
dishes.*

*This is an easy recipe; the most delicate pieces of the duck are
removed for use with other recipes, such as grilled duck breast and
confit of duck. (You can, of course, use the whole duck for the stock
if you wish.)*

Remove all the heavy fat from the duck carcass. With a large cleaver,
chop the duck into pieces. Wash the leek well. Peel the onions and
carrot. Chop onions, carrot and leek into large pieces. Brown the vegetables in oil over high heat. Add the duck pieces and brown them,
turning them with tongs. Add the flour, stir it in vigorously, then add
the tomato paste. A crust will form on the bottom of the pot. Add the
wine, water and the bouquet garni. Scrape the bottom of the pot so that
the crust comes up. Let liquid come to a boil over medium-high heat.
Skim off any scum, reduce the heat and let cook slowly for 1–1½ hours.

Strain the stock into a bowl or other container. Cool to room temperature, then store in the refrigerator. It will keep for 1 week. Remove
the fat before using.

*Glacé de canard* (the stock reduced all the way down to a gluelike
consistency) will keep up to 3 months in the refrigerator.

2 pounds lamb bones (not
  cooked)
1 large onion
1 large carrot
3–4 cloves garlic
2 tablespoons oil
2 tablespoons flour
1 tablespoon tomato paste
1 cup white wine
6 cups water
1 bouquet garni of leek leaves,
  parsley sprigs and basil
  leaves (p. 182)

YIELD: 1½–2 cups

# LAMB STOCK
### Fond d'agneau

*A brown stock.*

Cut the lamb bones to separate them. There should be small pieces
of meat on them. Peel the onion and carrot, and cut into large pieces;
mash the garlic cloves. It is not necessary to peel the carrot or the garlic.

Heat the oil in a medium-size saucepan, and when it is hot, add the
lamb, onion, carrot and garlic. Cook over high heat for about 4 minutes
until everything is brown; turn once or twice with a wooden spoon. Add
the flour and tomato paste, and mix well with the wooden spoon until
dry; a crust will form on the bottom of the pan. Pour in the wine and
water and bouquet garni, stir and bring to a boil over high heat. Then
lower the heat and cook for about 1 hour, skimming off the scum
occasionally.

Strain the stock through a fine-meshed sieve. Cool to room temperature, then refrigerate. Stock will keep for 1 week in the refrigerator.
Or put it in the freezer in small portions for future use.

# CHICKEN STOCK
## Fond de volaille

*A white stock. Chicken stock is one of the pure wonders of cooking. If you have a cold, it is very nice to warm yourself with a cup of this delicious bouillon. Moreover, it is extremely useful in cooking. (You can also make a brown chicken stock, if you wish; use the same method as for duck stock.)*

*I do not recommend making chicken stock from the bones of an already cooked chicken, the taste is too diminished. You may, however, when making stock from an uncooked chicken, remove the breast after the first 45 minutes of cooking to serve as poached chicken. Return the breast bones to the stock.*

**1 whole chicken**
**Salt, pepper**
**1 carrot**
**1 turnip**
**1 onion**
**1 stalk celery**
**10 whole cloves**
**A little oil**
**Bouquet garni (p. 182)**
**Sea salt**
**Water**

**YIELD: 1 quart**

Remove the liver, heart and kidneys from the chicken, and sprinkle the body cavity with salt and pepper. (I suggest you look carefully at the inside of the chicken and scrape out any remaining innards; modern chicken factories do not clean chickens well, and any liver scraps will mess up the stock.) Truss the chicken by tying the legs together, the wings to the body and the pope's nose to the drumsticks.

Peel the carrot, turnip and onion, and cut them into large pieces. (This is important because here you are making a white stock whereas the veal stock is a brown stock that does not require the carrot to be peeled.) Cut the celery stalk into large pieces; cut the onion in half and stick the cloves into the halves.

Brown the onion halves quickly on the cut sides in a very little bit of oil over high heat. Put the onion, carrot, celery, turnip and trussed chicken into a large pot with a fresh bouquet garni. Add ½ tablespoon of sea salt and water to cover, about 1 quart.

Bring the water to a boil, skim off any scum and cook over medium heat for 45 minutes. If desired, carve the breast off the chicken and reserve it with several spoonfuls of the stock. Return the rest of the chicken to the stock and continue cooking for another 30–45 minutes.

Strain stock into a bowl or container. If you need it immediately, you can remove the fat by letting the stock rest in the bowl for a few minutes, then floating a paper towel on top. The paper will absorb the fat. Or let cool to room temperature, then store in the refrigerator and remove fat just before using.

*Variation: Chicken Stock II.* Cut the chicken into parts, reserving the breasts, legs and thighs for other uses. Add 1 cup wine to the water to help intensify the taste. Otherwise, prepare as above.

# *RABBIT STOCK*
## Fond de lapin

*1 rabbit minus the breast and*
*hind legs (not cooked)*
*1 onion*
*1 carrot*
*A bouquet garni (p. 182)*
*10 cups water*
*2 cups white wine (optional)*

*YIELD: 3 cups*

*A white stock. This is prepared by the same method as Duck Stock and Chicken Stock II. The breast and hind legs of the rabbit are not used for the stock but are saved for other recipes. The chief use of rabbit stock is for recipes based on rabbit, but I also like to use it as the base of a white wine sauce with cream for fish.*

Chop the rabbit into large pieces with a cleaver. (If you are using a whole rabbit, discard the head; remove the liver and kidneys and save for other recipes, they never go into a stock.) Peel the onion and carrot, and cut into large pieces. Put all the ingredients into a large, heavy pot and bring to a boil over high heat. Skim off any scum, reduce the heat and cook slowly for 1 hour.

Strain through a sieve lined with cheesecloth or a damp tea towel into a bowl or other container. Let cool to room temperature and store in the refrigerator.

# *FISH STOCK*
## Fumet de poisson

*Bones from 2 sole or flounder*
*1 onion*
*2 pieces carrot (about ⅓ of a*
*carrot)*
*2 leek leaves (green part only)*
*1½ tablespoons peanut oil*
*A bouquet garni (p. 182)*
*2 cups white wine*
*4 cups water*

*YIELD: 1½ quarts*

*A white stock. A good fish stock is silver gray in color and translucent. When kept in the refrigerator, it should become gelatinous. It is used to poach fish and as a base for velouté and other light sauces.*

*Fish bones are the key to making fumet because they are the source of the gel. The best choices are bones of the sole family, especially Dover sole, flounder, monkfish and red snapper. Turbot bones are excellent, but turbot is very expensive.*

*Although making fish stock may sound intimidating if you have never done it, it is one of the fastest and easiest to prepare of all stocks.*

Chop the bones from the fish crosswise into large pieces; a cleaver is good for this. Peel the onion and cut into large pieces. Peel about a third of a carrot and cut it into 2 pieces. (Do not use a whole carrot; it will make the stock too sweet.) Cut the leek leaves into 4–6 pieces.

Put the oil, bones, onion, carrot and leek into a large, heavy pot. Place over high heat for about 5 minutes until the fish bones turn white. Do not let the onion brown.

Add the bouquet garni, white wine and water, and let come to a boil over high heat. Skim off any scum that rises to the top. Lower the heat and continue cooking at a gentle boil for 5 minutes.

Remove from the heat and let the stock settle for a minute. Strain through a sieve lined with cheesecloth or a damp tea towel. Let cool to room temperature, then store in the refrigerator or freezer.

*Note:* You could substitute the green leaves of 4 scallions if leeks are not available. Corn or safflower oil is good for this, but do not use olive oil.

# VEGETABLE STOCK

*This stock can serve as the base for a diet cuisine or for vegetarian dishes.*

Peel the onion and cut into large pieces and sweat in the oil in a large saucepan. Wash the leek well. Cut the carrot, celery, leek, tomato and zucchini into large pieces. Add all ingredients, except the water, to the saucepan and continue cooking for a few minutes.

Add the water and bring to a boil; cook for about 30 minutes over medium-low heat. Strain. You now have the bouillon for vegetable stock and you can make the vegetables into a puree in a food processor.

*1 onion*
*2 tablespoons oil*
*1 stalk celery*
*1 carrot*
*1 leek*
*1 tomato*
*½ zucchini*
*3–4 lettuce leaves*
*2 cloves garlic*
*A fresh bouquet garni*
  *(p. 182)*
*2 whole cloves*
*1 teaspoon peppercorns*
*8 cups water*

*YIELD: 2 cups*

# SAUCES

VELOUTÉ

## HOT SAUCES

LEMON OR LIME
  BUTTER
RED BUTTER
HOLLANDAISE
HOLLANDAISE IN THE
  PROCESSOR
ZUCCHINI
FRESH HERB
ORANGE
MOREL
ASPARAGUS
SMOKED SALMON

PARSLEY
CHAMPAGNE
LOBSTER
MADRAS
CAVIAR

WARM SAUCE WITH
  HARD-BOILED EGGS

## COLD SAUCES

MAYONNAISE
MAYONNAISE IN THE
  PROCESSOR
GREEN
TARTARE

COCKTAIL
ROUILLE
CURRY
CAPER
MAYONNAISE
  WITHOUT EGGS
FRESH TOMATO
WHIPPED SOUR
  CREAM
SOUR CREAM WITH
  HORSERADISH AND
  SALMON ROE
SOUR CREAM AND
  VINEGAR

Long ago, sauces were mostly reductions or infusions of vinegar, wine, garlic, onion and *verjus* (juice of green raisins or acid plants like sorrel that served as the base of sauces in medieval times). Many sauces we know today were created in the eighteenth century in France, a time of great transformation in cooking. Often these sauces were dedicated to a great noble or personage, such as the Marquis de Béchameil, from whom we get the name for béchamel sauce.

We now have refrigerators and other ways to save food, but we must not forget that our ancestors did not have these useful appliances. Meat and fish often came to the table with a strong odor and taste. It was necessary to mask the food, to hide it with sauces, which therefore became indispensable in cooking. It is not surprising that sauced dishes played an important part in cooking.

Today it is the opposite. The sauce must be an accompaniment; it must never overwhelm or outshine the food with which it is married; they must be equals. If the food keeps its taste, freshness and flavor and the sauce is satiny and tasty, then the marriage is a success. A great cook is always a great saucier. I would rather have a dish of humble ingredients accompanied by a good sauce than the opposite.

The hot and cold sauces that follow are some of those that I have adapted to my cuisine. I am sure you know that there are an infinite variety of sauces, but for the most part these are easy and light.

It is entirely possible to add other ingredients than those listed in the recipes or to change the proportions. If you wish to make your sauce more liquid, add water, bouillon, stock or wine. If you like a somewhat thicker sauce, reduce it for a longer time. If you know you are serving people who like a lot of sauce, you can multiply the amounts to increase the yield. Here are a few general rules that may help you.

It is better to season a sauce at the end of a reduction, otherwise the salt and pepper will intensify too much. There is no hard-and-fast rule for seasoning; it depends on your taste. You must be the judge of how much salt and pepper you wish.

Finishing a sauce with butter is not obligatory, but simply a method of making the sauce more silken, satiny and smooth.

If you prepare a sauce in advance, keep it in a bain-marie until the moment of serving.

In order to avoid having a skin form on top of a sauce while it is waiting to be served, sprinkle little bits of butter on the sauce while it sits in the bain-marie. You can skim this off before serving if you wish.

If a sauce is too salty, you can save it by stirring half a lump of sugar into it. Hold the sugar lump in your fingers (being sure to have a small piece of paper wrapped around the top of the lump where you hold it) and mix it around in the sauce.

To make a fish sauce more tart, just add a little dry white wine or champagne.

Finally, you should be free to follow your own inspiration. Serve meat with a fish or shellfish sauce, filets of veal with lobster sauce, for example, or use a sauce with a meat base for fish, such as filet of sole with a sauce based on rabbit stock or salmon with a morel sauce based on brown stock.

In general hot sauces should be eaten directly after they are made, but there are some exceptions indicated throughout the recipes. Cold sauces are easier to keep for a short time in the refrigerator, but pay attention to their delicate nature and treat them carefully. Always serve them at the same temperature as the food.

In 1980, when I first came to the United States, I was asked to a very elegant dinner party in my honor in Texas. The long table was beautifully set with fine china and handsome silver *objets*. This was my first introduction to real American food, and I loved the ribs, red beans, sweet corn, the apple and pecan pies. But I especially remember the warm monkey bread served in a long basket and a wonderful spicy barbecue sauce that is a specialty of the family cook.

I hope you too will experiment a little and develop your own sauces.

# VELOUTÉ

*Velouté is a base for many sauces flavored with wine and herbs, especially sauces with cream.*

Melt the butter in a heavy pan over medium heat and stir in the flour with a whisk or wooden spoon until well blended and smooth. If this butter and flour combination, a roux, is to be reserved for future use, remove it from the heat and let it cool to room temperature, then cover and refrigerate. It will keep 2 weeks.

Add fish or chicken stock to the roux and bring it to a boil over medium heat. Reduce the heat and cook slowly for 30–45 minutes, stirring occasionally.

*Important note:* The roux and the liquid must be at different temperatures. If the roux is hot, the added stock must be cool. If the roux is cold from the refrigerator, heat the stock first.

The correct amount of liquid for a strong, fresh velouté that you intend to use immediately is 3 cups. If you are making velouté for future use, I suggest using 4 cups stock.

Pour the finished velouté into a bowl or container and let cool. Store in the refrigerator, covered. It will keep 1–2 weeks.

*3 tablespoons butter*
*4 tablespoons flour*
*3 cups liquid: fish stock*
   *(p. 222) for fish velouté,*
   *chicken stock (p. 221) for*
   *chicken velouté*

*YIELD: approximately 1 cup*

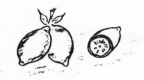

# LEMON OR LIME BUTTER SAUCE
*Beurre au citron ou citron vert*

3 tablespoons lemon or lime
juice
5 tablespoons water
½ pound butter, softened
Salt, white pepper

**SERVES 4**

*Lemon Butter Sauce is the most neutral of the sauces that can be married with fish, meat, vegetables, or even blended with another sauce. It must be used just after it is made because refrigeration solidifies it and it is not possible to reheat it without it becoming melted butter. On the other hand, you may prepare it just a little in advance of serving and keep it at room temperature in a bain-marie.*

Reduce the lemon or lime juice and water by half over medium-high heat. Cut the butter into pieces and begin energetically whisking the pieces into the juice. Season with 2 generous pinches salt and 1 pinch pepper, and keep whisking until every piece of butter is incorporated. Stop the cooking just before the sauce comes to a boil; if you let it boil, it will separate.

½ pound sweet butter
2 shallots
4 tablespoons red wine
3 tablespoons port
Salt, white pepper

**SERVES 4**

# RED BUTTER
*Beurre rouge*

*Red Butter is a marvelous companion for lightly grilled fresh salmon; you can also serve it with many other fish and shellfish, such as bass, red snapper, scallops, monkfish, flounder, etc. But, like Lemon Butter Sauce, it must not be refrigerated.*

Let the butter soften outside the refrigerator for about 30 minutes. Peel the shallots and chop them finely. Put them in a pan with the red wine and port, and reduce the liquid by more than half. (There will be very little juice left.)

Over high heat, start adding the butter to the sauce, piece by piece. Whisk the sauce vigorously while you are incorporating the butter.

When the sauce is finished, season it with salt and pepper, and either serve immediately or let it wait in a double boiler.

# HOLLANDAISE

1 pound butter
4 egg yolks
3 tablespoons water
1 teaspoon lemon juice
Salt, white pepper

**SERVES 4–8**

Melt the butter over very low heat. Remove the pan from the heat before the butter is completely melted, and swirl the pan around so that the remaining pieces melt in slowly and it looks creamy and smooth.

With a whisk, beat the egg yolks and water together in a medium-size saucepan over low to medium heat for about 2 minutes until they thicken and become smooth. You must whisk continuously. Start ladling in the butter, whisking all the while. Continue until you have used all the butter except the fatty layer on the bottom of the pan. Discard that, and season the sauce with the lemon juice, salt and pepper.

You can make this 2–3 hours ahead of time and keep it warm in a bain-marie.

# HOLLANDAISE IN THE PROCESSOR

1 pound butter
4 egg yolks
3 tablespoons water
1 teaspoon lemon juice
Salt, white pepper

**SERVES 4–8**

*This recipe for Hollandaise is the same as the preceding one, except that you bind the sauce in the processor. It is a very sure way to make this sauce work.*

Melt the butter and beat the egg yolks and water together exactly as in the preceding recipe. Pour the egg yolk mixture into the food processor bowl and scrape in any extra from the pan with a rubber spatula. Slowly ladle the melted butter into the bowl, and at the same time turn the machine on and off several times for about half a minute. When most of the butter is absorbed (see preceding recipe), season the sauce with the lemon juice, salt and pepper.

*Variations:* Add at the end, for *Hollandaise with mustard:* 2 tablespoons Dijon mustard; *with basil:* 2 tablespoons wine vinegar and 2 tablespoons freshly chopped basil (use a little more pepper, preferably freshly ground); *with Armagnac:* 2 tablespoons Armagnac and 1 tablespoon chopped chives; *with tomatoes:* 1 tablespoon tomato paste; 1 tablespoon chopped sun-dried tomatoes; ½ fresh tomato, peeled and chopped finely; 6 leaves fresh tarragon, chopped.

1 small zucchini or ½ a large
  one
1 scallion
½ pound butter
1 egg
4 basil leaves
Salt, white pepper

*SERVES 4*

# ZUCCHINI SAUCE
## Sauce à la courgette

*Serve this sauce with fish, steamed lobster, shrimp or hot vegetable salad.*

Cut the ends off the zucchini and cut it into small pieces. Steam for about 8–10 minutes.

Trim the scallion and cut it into 3 pieces. Melt the butter. Place the steamed zucchini into the bowl of a food processor and add the egg, scallion and basil leaves. Process for about half a minute, then slowly add the melted butter through the top feeder hole. Season with 2 pinches salt and 1 large pinch pepper; serve immediately.

½ zucchini
2 scallions
½ clove garlic (optional)
2 branches thyme (or tarragon
  or coriander)
5 large basil leaves
1½ cups peanut or olive oil
Salt, white pepper

*SERVES 4*

# FRESH HERB SAUCE
## Sauce aux fines herbes

*This sauce goes well with any white fish, salmon, shellfish, veal, lamb or chicken. It can be served warm or cold. It is nice with cold roast beef for a picnic.*

Cut the half zucchini into pieces by cutting it in half lengthwise, then slicing the halves crosswise. Steam the pieces for 8 minutes.

Trim and chop the scallions; mash and chop the garlic, if used. Strip the thyme leaves from the branches. Drain the zucchini and put into a food processor. Add the thyme, basil, scallions and garlic, and process briefly. Add the oil slowly through feeder tube. Season with a small pinch of salt and a pinch of pepper. Sauce will keep for 2 days in the refrigerator.

# ORANGE SAUCE
*Sauce à l'orange*

*This is my favorite sauce. Made with the duck stock base as in this recipe, it is lovely with duck or roast chicken. You can also make it with veal stock for veal and beef dishes, or as a special sauce for red snapper, mullet or salmon.*

1 navel orange
1½ cups duck stock (p. 220)
1 teaspoon Grand Marnier
Salt, white pepper
1½ tablespoons butter,
    softened

*SERVES 4*

Grate the rind of the orange. Cut off the remaining orange peel and section out the orange from between the membranes. You should have about 10–12 sections.

Reduce the duck stock, Grand Marnier, salt and pepper in a heavy saucepan over medium heat for about 5 minutes. Add the orange sections and grated orange rind, and cook for another 5 minutes. Finish the sauce with butter and serve immediately.

# MOREL SAUCE
*Sauce aux morilles*

*I am giving you this recipe that uses dried morels because you can buy them all year. To taste this sauce at its very best, however, I suggest you look for fresh morels from Oregon during their season— late spring and early summer. Made with lamb stock, this sauce is for lamb dishes; if made with duck stock, serve it with duck. If you make it with veal stock, as in this recipe, it is a lovely sauce for fish, such as salmon, bass or red snapper, as well as for veal and beef recipes.*

2 ounces dried morels
2 cups veal stock (p. 219)
2 tablespoons port
1 tablespoon cognac
Salt, white pepper
1½ tablespoons butter,
    softened

*SERVES 4*

Soak the dried morels in warm water for 10 minutes. Cut off the foot end of the stems. Squeeze out the water with your hands. Place the morels, veal stock, port and cognac in a heavy saucepan over medium heat. Season with salt and pepper, and reduce liquid to almost half the original amount, about 8 minutes. Fresh morels do not need as much cooking, so add them halfway through the reduction. Finish the sauce with butter and serve immediately.

*Note:* This sauce can also be made with Paris mushrooms (cèpes), chanterelles, pleurottes or shiitaki. When the mushrooms are small, they need not be cut; if they are large, cut them in half vertically.

½ *cup fish velouté (p. 227)*
*1 cup heavy cream*
*3 cooked asparagus spears*
*2 tablespoons white wine*
*Salt, white pepper*
*A pinch of freshly grated
nutmeg*
*1½ tablespoons butter,
softened*

*SERVES 4*

# ASPARAGUS SAUCE
## Sauce aux asperges

*The following 4 sauces are built on a base of fish velouté (velouté
made with fish stock) and are good with broiled or roasted fish.*

Pour the fish velouté and cream into a small, heavy pot and reduce
by half over medium heat for about 10 minutes.

Cut off the white ends of the asparagus and discard. Cut the remainder of the asparagus into julienne strips; they do not have to be
extremely thin. Add the asparagus strips and white wine to the velouté
and cream. Season with 2 pinches salt, pepper and the nutmeg. Finish
the sauce with the butter and serve immediately.

½ *cup fish velouté (p. 227)*
*1 cup heavy cream*
*2 slices smoked salmon*
*2 scallions*
*3 basil leaves*
*2 tablespoons white wine*
*Salt, white pepper*
*1½ tablespoons butter,
softened*

*SERVES 4*

# SMOKED SALMON SAUCE
## Sauce au saumon fumé

*This sauce is a beautiful accompaniment to salmon and almost all
white fish.*

Pour the fish velouté and cream into a small, heavy pot and reduce
by half over medium heat for about 10 minutes.

Chop the smoked salmon slices into small pieces; you should have
about 2½ tablespoons. Chop the scallions, using both green and white
parts. Chop the basil leaves finely. Add the salmon, scallions and basil
to the velouté-and-cream reduction. Season with white wine, salt and
pepper, and cook for another 5 minutes, stirring the sauce occasionally
with a spatula or a wooden spoon. Finish the sauce with butter and
serve.

# PARSLEY SAUCE
## Sauce persil

*Parsley sauce goes nicely with a poached chicken breast as well as with any white fish, salmon or lobster.*

Pour the fish velouté and cream into a small, heavy pot and reduce by half over medium heat for about 10 minutes.

Chop the parsley; do not do this in the food processor, you will lose some of the taste. Cut the crusts off the bread and cut the slices into small squares. In a heavy frying pan, over high heat, sauté the bread in the oil until brown. Turn once or twice during the browning. Pour off all the remaining fat and reserve the croutons on a paper towel, dish towel or brown paper bag.

Add the chopped parsley to the velouté-and-cream reduction; add the wine and lemon juice, and season with a pinch of salt and pepper and the cumin. Finish the sauce with butter and ladle it over the fish. Sprinkle with the croutons and serve immediately.

*½ cup fish velouté (p. 227)*
*1 cup heavy cream*
*4 generous tablespoons chopped parsley*
*2 slices white bread*
*⅓ cup oil*
*2 tablespoons white wine*
*½ tablespoon lemon juice*
*Salt, white pepper*
*2 pinches ground cumin*
*1½ tablespoons butter, softened*

*SERVES 4*

# CHAMPAGNE SAUCE
## Sauce champagne

*This is a very light sauce for fish that can be enhanced by the addition of mushrooms or fresh herbs.*

Reduce the velouté, champagne and heavy cream by half over medium heat. Season with salt and pepper to taste. Finish the sauce with butter and serve immediately.

*Variations:* Steam oyster mushrooms (pleurottes) very briefly, about 1 minute, and chop them finely. Add them to the sauce halfway through the reduction for Champagne Sauce with Mushrooms. Or add finely chopped fresh herbs such as basil, thyme, tarragon.

*2–3 teaspoons fish velouté (p. 227)*
*1 cup champagne (or dry white wine)*
*1 cup heavy cream*
*Salt, white pepper*
*1 tablespoon butter, softened*

*SERVES 4*

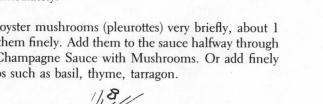

# LOBSTER SAUCE BASE
*Base sauce homard*

*When this sauce base is reduced and finished with butter or cream, it is a perfect, elegant sauce for all white fish or shellfish, for veal or chicken.*

*2–3 head and thorax parts from live lobsters (see Note)*
*1 large onion*
*3 cloves garlic*
*1 leek*
*½ carrot*
*1 tomato*
*2 tablespoons oil*
*1 bouquet garni (p. 182)*
*1 tablespoon flour*
*2 tablespoons tomato paste*
*2 cups white wine*
*4 cups water or chicken stock*
*4 cups fish stock (p. 227) (or chicken or beef consommé)*
*Sea salt, white pepper*

*YIELD: approximately 2 cups*

Place the lobster parts on your work surface stomach side down; with a strong, sharp knife, cut them in half through the length of the back. Peel the onion and cut it into thin slices. Mash the garlic cloves; cut the leek, carrot and tomato into large pieces. (It is not necessary to peel these vegetables, but remember to wash the leek thoroughly.)

Sweat the onion in the oil in a medium-size saucepan over medium heat. After about 1–2 minutes, add the lobster pieces, mix them around once and cook over high heat for 4–5 minutes. Dump in the vegetables and the bouquet garni, mix them around and cook another 2–3 minutes.

Add the flour and tomato paste, mix vigorously and cook until the lobster pieces turn bright red and the flour and tomato paste dry out and form a crust on the bottom of the pan. Pour in the white wine, water or chicken stock, and the fish stock, and season with 1 pinch of sea salt (or 2 pinches regular salt) and pepper. Bring sauce to a boil, skim off the scum, reduce the heat and cook slowly for 45 minutes. Skim several times.

Remove the sauce from the stove and put the lobster pieces in the bowl of a food processor and process for less than half a minute. (Be sure to cover the processor or you will have a very messy kitchen!) Return to the sauce and cook for 10 minutes longer. (See *Note*.)

Strain the sauce through a fine-meshed sieve and reduce for another 30 minutes. The sauce will keep for 1 week in the refrigerator or much longer in the freezer. Divide it into small containers for storing.

*Note:* I realize it is not always easy to obtain the head and thorax part of live lobsters. If your fish man will not sell them to you and you have no need for 3 whole lobsters, substitute 1 whole live lobster. Separate the head and thorax from the tail (leave the tail whole), and cut off the claws. Split the head section in half as directed. You will now have 5 pieces of lobster for the sauce. The tail meat is delicious cooked in this way; remove it from the pan 10 minutes after the liquid comes to a boil.

It is not absolutely necessary to run the lobster pieces through the food processor before the final 10 minutes of cooking, but I feel it adds to the taste.

If you are going to all the trouble to make this sauce, you might like to make it in large quantity to store in your freezer. In that case use 12 lobster heads, 2 carrots, 2 onions, 2 leeks, ½ whole head garlic, 2 tomatoes, 6 tablespoons tomato paste, 8 tablespoons flour, 6 cups white wine, 6 cups water, 10 cups fish stock or consommé.

# MADRAS SAUCE

## Sauce madras

*Madras Sauce always makes me think of sunny Caribbean islands. The mixture of spices makes it an interesting sauce for any white fish, salmon, lobster, chicken and even veal.*

Bring the lobster sauce base to a boil. Add the curry powder, saffron, port and cognac. Reduce for about 3 minutes over medium heat. Finish the sauce with butter and serve immediately.

*1 cup Lobster Sauce Base (p. 234)*
*¼ teaspoon curry powder*
*1 pinch saffron threads*
*1 tablespoon port*
*1 tablespoon cognac or brandy*
*1 tablespoon butter, softened*

**SERVES 4**

# CAVIAR SAUCE

## Sauce caviar

*Adding caviar to a recipe is a certain way to create an elegant dish. A little bit goes a long way as you can see in this recipe, which uses only 1 tablespoon of caviar. Serve this sauce with broiled fish, such as sole, salmon, bass, red snapper, etc.*

Slice the carrot, blanch briefly and cut it into large dice. Cut the ends off the snow peas and cut them into medium-size pieces.

Reduce the white wine, vodka, cream and fish stock by half over medium-high heat. Add the vegetables and reduce for 1–2 minutes longer. Heat the caviar in the sauce for a very brief time, a bare 20 seconds. Season with a small pinch of salt and a pinch of white pepper, and serve immediately.

*½ small carrot*
*6 snow peas*
*2 tablespoons white wine or champagne*
*1 tablespoon vodka*
*1½ cups heavy cream*
*4 tablespoons fish stock (p. 222)*
*1 tablespoon caviar*
*Salt, white pepper*

**SERVES 4**

# WARM SAUCE WITH HARD-BOILED EGGS

## Sauce tiède aux oeufs durs

*You can serve this sauce warm as given here or at room temperature with boiled meat, fish or vegetables.*

Peel the eggs and chop them finely with a knife; do not mash them with a fork. Put the chopped egg into a small bowl.

Whisk the mustard and vinegar together, then add the oil and whisk quickly to mix it in. Season with a large pinch of salt and a small pinch of pepper. Pour into a small saucepan and heat slowly, just to warm.

Chop the cornichons and capers together, and add them to the eggs along with the scallion, garlic and parsley. Whisk in the warm oil mixture, the Tabasco and the basil leaves. Serve warm. You can keep this sauce 2–3 days in the refrigerator.

*2 hard-boiled eggs*
*2 tablespoons French-style mustard (seedless)*
*2 tablespoons red wine vinegar*
*1 cup oil*
*Salt, white pepper*
*4 small cornichons (French pickles)*
*1 generous teaspoon capers*
*2 tablespoons chopped scallion*
*¼ teaspoon chopped garlic*
*2 generous tablespoons chopped parsley*
*2 drops Tabasco*
*2 basil leaves, chopped*

**SERVES 4–6**

# *MAYONNAISE*

*When I give cooking classes, I am always surprised when people tell me how hard it is to make mayonnaise; I think it is very easy! Try this recipe and see if you agree. If you are making this mayonnaise as a base for one of the following sauces, I suggest a neutral oil like peanut, safflower or corn oil. If it is to be served fresh, use a fine olive oil.*

1 tablespoon Dijon mustard
1 egg yolk
1½ cups oil
1 teaspoon lemon juice
Salt, white pepper

YIELD: approximately 1½
    cups

Whisk the mustard and egg yolk together in a bowl until well blended. Add the oil very, very slowly, whisking continuously. (If you are using a metal bowl, it helps to place a dish towel under the bowl to keep it from turning.) Add the lemon juice and 2 pinches salt and a pinch of pepper at the end. If the mayonnaise separates during the mixing, pour in a few drops of boiling water and whisk vigorously.

This mayonnaise will keep in the refrigerator for 3 days. Whisk in 2 tablespoons water and a few drops lemon juice just before using.

# *MAYONNAISE IN THE PROCESSOR*

2 eggs
2 tablespoons mustard
1⅔ cups oil
1 tablespoon lemon juice
Salt, white pepper
2 tablespoons water (optional)

YIELD: approximately 1½
    cups

Break the eggs into the processor bowl and add the mustard. Start processing. With the motor running, slowly pour in the oil. Season with the lemon juice, 2 pinches of salt and 1 pinch pepper at the end. If you like a softer mayonnaise, add 2 tablespoons water.

# *GREEN SAUCE*
*Sauce verte*

*This sauce is lovely with cold fish, shellfish or cold meat.*

2 eggs
2 tablespoons mustard
1⅔ cups oil
1 tablespoon lemon juice
Salt, white pepper
2 tablespoons water (optional)
½ cup spinach leaves
1 bunch scallions (green tops
    only)
6 parsley sprigs
10 fresh basil leaves
1 clove garlic (optional)

YIELD: approximately 2 cups

Use the first 6 ingredients to make mayonnaise according to directions for Mayonnaise in the Processer (above); do not remove the mayonnaise from the processor bowl.

Wash and dry the spinach leaves. Chop the spinach, scallion tops, parsley and basil coarsely, and add them to the mayonnaise. Add the peeled garlic clove if you like the taste. Process briefly.

# TARTARE SAUCE
## Sauce tartare

*Serve this sauce with cold meat or as a dip for raw vegetables, or heat it to accompany the organ meats of game.*

Finely chop the cornichons, capers and scallions. Mix all the ingredients together, seasoning carefully. If the mayonnaise is already well seasoned, you will only want to add a very little more salt and pepper.

This sauce will keep 1–2 days in the refrigerator. If you plan to keep it, however, I advise you to blanch the onion first, because raw onion might ferment and cause you problems.

*3 small cornichons (French pickles)*
*1 teaspoon capers*
*3 scallions*
*1 generous cup mayonnaise (p. 236)*
*2 teaspoons chopped onion*
*2 teaspoons chopped parsley*
*1 teaspoon lemon juice*
*Salt, white pepper*

*SERVES 4*

# COCKTAIL SAUCE
## Sauce cocktail

*This is nice with cold meats and vegetable terrines as well as with cold fish and shellfish, especially shrimp.*

Chop the scallions. Mix all the ingredients together, seasoning carefully to your taste with salt and pepper, because the mayonnaise is already seasoned. This sauce will keep for 2–3 days in the refrigerator.

*2 scallions*
*1 cup mayonnaise (p. 236)*
*1 generous teaspoon chopped parsley*
*1 tablespoon finely chopped chives*
*1 teaspoon cognac*
*1 teaspoon Armagnac or scotch*
*⅓ cup tomato ketchup*
*Salt, white pepper*

*SERVES 4*

# ROUILLE SAUCE
## Rouille

*Rouille is a traditional Provençal sauce made from a base of mashed potatoes and is usually served with bouillabaisse. I think you will find this adaptation easy to make; it is delightful with cold fish or cold pork. Mayonnaise made with olive oil is the best base for rouille.*

Mash the garlic clove and chop it. Mix all ingredients together, seasoning with 2 pinches salt and 2 pinches cayenne pepper. Let rest at least 10 minutes before serving. You can keep this sauce 1 day in the refrigerator.

*1 clove garlic*
*1 cup mayonnaise (p. 236)*
*⅓ teaspoon chopped saffron threads*
*½ teaspoon Pastis (anise liqueur)*
*¼ teaspoon paprika*
*Salt, cayenne pepper*

*SERVES 4*

½ tart apple (Granny Smith,
    etc.)
1 cup mayonnaise (p. 236)
1 teaspoon curry powder
1 pinch ground cumin
    (optional; see Note)
½ teaspoon finely chopped
    coriander leaves
½ teaspoon finely chopped
    parsley
Salt, white pepper

SERVES 4

# CURRY SAUCE
### Sauce curry

*This sauce is very refreshing in the summer with fish grilled on the barbecue or with cold meats. If you prepare it several hours before using, it will be better.*

Peel and core the apple and cut it into fine dice. Mix all ingredients together, seasoning with salt and pepper. Use the same day.

*Note:* I prefer a mild curry powder that is a yellow ocher color; if you wish a stronger curry, add small amounts of cumin to the curry powder.

1 teaspoon capers
1 teaspoon green peppercorns
1 cup mayonnaise (p. 236)
1 teaspoon chopped parsley
¼ teaspoon Worcestershire
    sauce
1 tablespoon chopped scallion

SERVES 4

# CAPER SAUCE
### Sauce aux câpres

*Serve with cold meats, cold fish; excellent to take on picnics.*

Chop finely the capers and green peppercorns. Mix all ingredients together. It is best to eat this sauce the same day.

2 slices soft white bread
2 tablespoons milk
1 tablespoon Dijon-style
    mustard
Salt, white pepper
1 cup oil

SERVES 4

# MAYONNAISE WITHOUT EGGS
### Mayonnaise sans oeuf

*This fragile mayonnaise is a useful sauce for anyone who cannot eat eggs. It must be served immediately, however; it will not keep.*

Remove the crusts from the bread and crumble the slices into a bowl. Soften them with the milk. Whisk in the mustard, 2 generous pinches salt, or more, and a pinch of pepper. Add the oil very slowly, whisking continuously.

# FRESH TOMATO SAUCE
*Sauce vierge*

*This fresh tomato sauce is nice with fish, meat or chicken, hot or cold. Served on thin puff pastry rounds, it makes delicate Tomato Tarts suitable for canapés or as an appetizer. (See Note.)*

Peel the tomatoes; squeeze out the water and seeds, and chop finely. (Do not chop in the food processor.) Finely chop the basil leaves, garlic clove and scallions.

Squeeze the lemon juice into a bowl and season with 2 generous pinches salt, a pinch or so of pepper. Whisk to mix in the salt and pepper, then add the tomatoes. Whisk again. Add the basil, garlic and scallions, whisking after each addition to incorporate thoroughly. Whisk in the oil. This sauce will keep in the refrigerator for 3 days; it can be frozen.

*Note:* To serve as Tomato Tarts, prepare as directed, using only 2 tablespoons of oil. Roll out puff pastry or Short Pastry (p. 185) and cut into 3-inch rounds. Spoon the sauce onto the pastry rounds and cook 15–20 minutes in a 350°–400° oven.

*4 tomatoes*
*6 large basil leaves*
*1 large clove garlic*
*2 scallions*
*Juice of 1 lemon*
*Salt, white pepper*
*4 tablespoons oil*

*SERVES 4*

# WHIPPED SOUR CREAM SAUCE
*Sauce aigre au fouet*

*This and the 2 following sour cream sauces are good in the summer on cold fish, shellfish or meat.*

Whisk the sour cream and cream together vigorously for about 2 minutes. Season with the cumin, nutmeg gratings, lime rind and a pinch of salt and pepper. Chop the peppers into very small dice and add it and the parsley to the sauce. This sauce should be made fresh; it does not hold well.

*2 generous tablespoons sour cream*
*5 tablespoons heavy cream*
*A pinch of ground cumin*
*Gratings of a whole nutmeg*
*Grated rind of 1 lime*
*Salt, white pepper*
*1 small piece red pepper*
*1 small piece green pepper*
*1 tablespoon chopped parsley*

*SERVES 4*

# SOUR CREAM SAUCE WITH HORSERADISH AND SALMON ROE
*Sauce aigre au raifort et caviar rouge*

Mix the ingredients together, seasoning with a pinch of salt and pepper. This sauce keeps 2–3 days, covered, in the refrigerator.

*2 generous tablespoons sour cream*
*2 teaspoons horseradish*
*2 teaspoons salmon roe*
*1 tablespoon chopped scallion*
*Salt, white pepper*

*SERVES 4*

2 tablespoons sour cream
2 tablespoons heavy cream
2 tablespoons red wine
    vinegar
1 tablespoon chopped parsley
1 tablespoon chopped scallion
1 tablespoon chopped fresh
    basil
Salt, freshly ground black
    pepper

SERVES 4

# SOUR CREAM AND VINEGAR SAUCE

*Sauce aigrellette*

Whisk the sour cream, cream and vinegar together. Add the other ingredients, seasoning with a pinch of salt and several grindings of black pepper. This sauce keeps 2–3 days, covered, in the refrigerator.

# MENUS

*Spring Menu*
Clear Vegetable and Lobster Pâté
Veal in an Envelope with Coriander
Fruit Compote

*Summer Menu*
Cucumber Soup
Bass with Fresh Tomatoes
Maple Syrup Ice Cream with Pecans
Tulips

*Fall Menu*
Brandade of Cod My Way
Pheasant and Cabbage
Caramelized Apple Tart

*Winter Menu*
Pistou Soup
Old-Fashioned Red Snapper in the Oven
Orange Tart

*Hunter's Menu*
Lean Pheasant and Veal Pâté in Lettuce
Ribs of Venison with Red Cabbage
Hot Grapefruit

*Fisherman's Menu*
   Mussel Salad
   Trout Poached in Vinegar
      or
   Bluefish with Pineapple
   Chocolate Tart with Pine Nuts

*Picnic Menu*
   Chicken Salad
   Eggplant Caviar
   Stuffed Zucchini
   Apple Compote
   Crispy Cookies
   Watermelon Jam
   Orange Wine

*Flower Menu*
   Spring Salad with Nasturtiums
   Chicken Fricandeau with Violets
   Crêpes with Rose Petals and Syrup of Poppies

*Improvisation Menu* or *What to Cook When You Have Nothing in the Refrigerator*
   Crispy Tuna
   Onion Omelette
   Apples in the Oven, Farm Style

*Valentine Menu*
   Hearts of Salad
   Salmon with Hearts of Artichoke
   Valentine Tarts

*Children's Menu*
   Strawberry Soup
   Chicken Legs Like a Little Leg of Lamb
   Rice Pudding

### Suggestions for Diet Menus

The following recipes are appropriate for those who are on a diet where they wish very little fat, cream, butter or sugar. I think you will find them tasty and interesting.

Light Canapés with Artichoke Hearts
Zucchini Soup with Nutmeg
Steamed Filets of Sole
Flounder in the Steamer with Cinnamon
Bass Cooked in Tea
Steamed Skate with Oranges
Red Mullet Cooked in an Envelope
Steamed Lobster with Tomato Sauce
Warm Lobster and Asparagus Salad
Mussel Salad
Steamed Cornish Game Hen
Quail in the Steamer
Lamb Chops in the Steamer
Veal in an Envelope with Coriander
Desserts Without Sugar:
   Hot Grapefruit
   Fruit Compote
   Apple Tart with Plum Sauce

# INDEX

Anchovy(ies)
  Butter, 177
  red snapper with, 75
Anise Bread, 200
Appetizers, 21–29
Apple(s)
  chicken breast with calvados and,
      116–17
  Compote, 190
    and Plum Compote, 191
    in the Oven, Farm Style, 191
  Tart
    caramelized, 186
    with Plum Sauce, 196
Artichoke
  hearts
    light canapés with, 19
    salmon with, 72
  Ragoût, 154
Asparagus, 155
  Crêpe, 156
  salad and warm lobster, 96
  salmon with, 72–73
  Sauce, 232
  Soup, 42
  Tart, 155

Baby Lamb, 129
Baked Eggs with Lettuce, 54–55
Basil Bread, 200
Bass
  Cooked in Tea, 70–71
  with Fresh Tomatoes, 69

  with Passion Fruit, 68–69
  with Peppers, 68
  in Puff Pastry, 70
Beans
  broad, 156
  dried, 156
  green, 156
  quail with, 143
Beets in Red Wine, 157
Black Fruit Jam, 206
Blue cheese, potatoes filled with, 16
Bluefish
  braised, 91
  with Pineapple, 90
Bouillabaisse, chilled, 50–51
Bouillon, shrimp in spicy, 97
Bouquet Garni, 182
Braised Bluefish, 91
Braised Veal Chops, 132
Brandade of Cod My Way, 86–87
Bread, 197–201
  a few tips on, 198
  anise, 200
  basic recipe, 199
  basil, 200
  garlic, 200
  marbled, with orange, 201
  onion, 199
  walnut, 200
Brie with Cabbage, 23
Broad Beans, 156
Brochettes, monkfish, 81
Butter, 176
  anchovy, 177

cold béarnaise, 178
garlic, 177
green, 177
honey, 178
lemon or lime, sauce, 228
onion, 177
red, 228
salted, 178
scallion, soft-shell crabs with, 101
spicy, 178

Cabbage
brie with, 23
envelopes, 157
foie gras and, 36
chicken poached with, 113
pheasant and, 144
red
skate with, 79
venison with, 150–51
Cake
carrot, 158
Calf's Liver
with Endive, 133
Packages, 134
with Scallions, 133
Calvados and apples, chicken breasts
with, 116–17
Canapés, 15–19
light, with artichoke hearts, 19
Provençal, 17
Caper Sauce, 238
Caramel
Custard with Brown Sugar, 192
riz au, 190
Caramelized Apple Tart, 186
Carrot(s), 158
Cake, 158
Cornish Game Hen with, 122
puree of celery root and peas, 158
red snapper with, 73
Cauliflower
Pancake, 159
sautéed, 159
Soup and Curry, 39
Caviar, 33
Crêpes, 34
eggplant, 27, 28
red, sauce with horseradish, 239
Sauce, 235
Wrapped in Lettuce, 34
Celery, 159
Celery Root Puree, 159

with carrots and peas, 158
Champagne, 211
Sauce, 233
Cheese
blue, potatoes filled with, 16
brie with cabbage, 25
Tart, 23
zucchini with, 169
Chicken, 109–26
breast
with Beer, 117
with Calvados and Apples, 116–17
and Liver, 119
with Pineapple and Strawberries,
118
with Whiskey, 118
Fricandeau with Violets, 181
Fricassee with Lemon and Lime, 116
Legs Like a Little Leg of Lamb, 114
old-fashioned roast, 111
poached, 112
with cabbage, 113
with creme, 113
Provençal, 115
Salad, 120
Sausage, 25
Stock, 221
Wings Minute, 119
Chicken Liver
chicken breast with, 119
Custard, 25
Chilled Bouillabaisse, 50–51
Chocolate
Cobblestones, 188
Napoleons, 189
Tart with Pine Nuts, 187
Clam Soup, 45
Clear Vegetable and Lobster Pâté, 27
Cocktail
Pierre's, 214
Sauce, 237
Cold Béarnaise Butter, 178
Cold Stuffed Vegetables, 29
Cod
brandade of, 86–87
in Court Bouillon with Garlic
Mayonnaise, 88
with Vegetables, 87
Compote
apple, 190
and plum, 191
fruit, 195
Consommé, Sisto's, 42–43
Cookies,

crispy, 193
small sweet, 194
tulips, 193
Corn Condiment with Vinegar, 173
Cornish Game Hen(s)
with Carrots, 122
Fritters, 123
steamed, 122
Stuffed with Shrimp, 120–21
Court bouillon, cod in, 88
Crab, 100
soft-shell
mousse, 102
sautéed, 101
with scallion butter, 101
Creamy Puree of Potatoes, 166
Crêpes, 184–85
asparagus, 156
caviar, 34
in the Processor, 184–85
with Rose Petals and Syrup of
Poppies, 181
Crispy Cookies, 193
Crispy Duck Fat Salad, 126
Crispy Eggs, 55
Crispy Potato, 167
Crispy Tuna, 24
Cucumber(s), 160
soup, 48
Culinary vocabulary, 13–14
Curry
sauce, 238
soup, cauliflower and, 39
Custard
caramel with brown sugar, 192
chicken liver, 25

Desserts, 183–96
Desserts without Sugar, 194
Dried Beans, 156
Drinks, nonalcoholic, 214
Duck, 123
Conserve, 125
Salad with Pear, 24
fat, crispy, salad, 126
quick, breast stew with vegetables,
124–25
roast, with figs, 124
Stock, 220

Egg Whites
poached, with peppers, 164–65

in the Steamer, 184
Eggplant
caviar, 27, 28
in the oven, 160
Soup, 46
with Tomatoes, 160
Eggs, 53–56
baked, with lettuce, 54–55
crispy, 55
hard-boiled, warm sauce with, 235
Onion Omelette, 56
Poached in White Wine, 54
stuffed, 56
*See also* Egg Whites
Endive, 161
calf's liver with, 133

Farm soup, 40
Few Tips on Bread, A, 198
Figs, roast duck with, 124
Filet of Pheasant, 145
Filet of Sole and Smoked Salmon,
64–65
Filet of Sole in the Steamer, 64
Fish, 57–91
cooked whole, 71
how to filet, 60
seven ways to cook, 59
stock, 222–23
three cuts, 59
three ways to prepare filets for
cooking, 61
*See also specific types*
Flounder
with Capers and Lemon, 65
and Potatoes, 66
in the Steamer with Cinnamon, 66
with Sweet Garlic, 67
Foie Gras, 34–35
and Cabbage, 36
hot, 35
salad, 36
Fresh Herb Sauce, 230
Fresh Tomato Sauce, 239
Fried Polenta, 165
Fritters
cornish game hen, 123
shellfish, 18
vegetable, 18
Frosty Marmalade, 207
Fruit(s)
Compote, 195
jam, black, 206

passion, 17
    bass with, 68–69
Vinaigrette, 175
wine with, 211–12


Game, 139–51
Garlic
    Bread, 200
    Butter, 177
    flounder with sweet, 67
    mayonnaise, cod with, 88
    Soup, 38
Gazpacho, 49
Gigot of Rabbit, 148
Glazed Turnips, 169
Grapefruit
    hot, 194–95
    soup, melon and, 46
Green Beans, 156
Green Butter, 177
Green Cabbage Envelopes, 157
Green Sauce, 236
Green Tomato Jam, 207
Grilled Rabbit Breast, 146–47


Hearts of Salad, 22
Herb sauce, fresh, 230
Herbs, Spices and Flowers, 179–82
Hollandaise, 229
    in the Processor, 229
Honey Butter, 178
Horseradish, and salmon roe, sour
    cream sauce with, 239
Hot Foie Gras, 35
Hot Grapefruit, 194–95
Hot Wine, 213


Ice cream, maple syrup, with pecans,
    192
Infusion, 214


Jam(s), 203–08
    black fruit, 206
    green tomato, 207
    melon, 205
    peach, 204–5
    pineapple, 205
    plum and pear, 206
    vegetable, 208
    watermelon, 206

Kitchen equipment, 11


Labels, the (for wine), 211
Lamb
    baby, 129
    chops
        quick, with shallots, 129
        in the steamer, 129
    light, pâté, 26
    soft leg of, 130
    Stock, 220
Lean Pheasant and Veal Pâté in
        Lettuce, 26
Leek
    base, potato and, 47
    Mousseline, 162
    and truffles, ragoût of, 162
    and zucchini, little doormat of, 161
Lemon or Lime Butter Sauce, 228
Lettuce
    baked eggs with, 54–55
    caviar in, 34
    veal and pheasant pâté in, 26
Light Canapés with Artichoke Hearts,
        19
Light Lamb Pâté, 26
Light Ragoût of Potatoes and Truffles,
        33
Light Vinaigrette, 175
Lime, or lemon, butter sauce, 228
Little Doormat of Leek and Zucchini,
        161
Liver, *see* Calf's liver; Chicken, breast;
        chicken liver; Foie gras
Lobster, 94–95
    and vegetable pâté, clear, 27
    Medallions, 18
    Sauce Base, 234
    steamed, with tomato sauce, 96
    with Tarragon, 95
    warm, and asparagus salad, 96


Mackerel
    Rillettes, 88–89
    rolls, steamed, 89
Madras Sauce, 235
Maple Syrup Ice Cream with Pecans,
        192
Marbled Bread with Orange, 201
Marigolds, vinegar with, 172
Marmalade
    frosty, 207

orange, 207
Mayonnaise, 236
  garlic, cod with, 88
  in the Processor, 236
  without Eggs, 238
Meat, 127–37
Melon
  and Grapefruit Soup, 46
  Jam, 205
Menus, 241–43
Molded Red Mullet, 83
Monkfish
  Brochettes, 81
  Masquerading as a Little Leg of
    Lamb, 82
  Stew with Anise, 80–81
Morel(s)
  Sauce, 231
  sautéed, 162
  Stuffed with Scallop Mousse, 163
Mousse
  scallop, morels stuffed with, 163
  of Soft-Shell Crab, 102
Mousseline, leek, 162
Muffins, 201
Mullet, red, 83
  cooked in an envelope, 84
  meunière with basil, 82
  molded, 83
Mushrooms, scallops with oyster, 107
  *See also* Morels
Mussel(s), 103
  Gratin, 103
  and Rice, 103
  Salad, 104
  Soup with Saffron, 44
My Bread (Basic Recipe), 199


Napoleons, chocolate, 189
Nasturtiums, spring salad with, 180
Nonalcoholic Drinks, 214
Noodles, sweetbread with, 136


Oils, 173–74
Old-Fashioned Red Snapper in the
    Oven, 74–75
Old-Fashioned Roast Chicken, 111
Omelette, onion, 56
Onion(s), 163
  Bread, 199
  Butter, 177
  Omelette, 56

skate with, 80
Orange(s)
  marbled bread with, 201
  Marmalade, 207
  Sauce, 231
  steamed skate with, 78
  Tart, 186
  Wine, 212
Oyster(s), 105
  Gratin with Truffles, 105
  and Vegetable Salad, 105


Pancake
  cauliflower, 159
  potato, 166
  seafood, 23
Parmentier, 47
Parsley Sauce, 233
Passion Fruit, 17
  bass with, 68–69
Pastry, short, 185
Pâté
  lean pheasant and veal, in lettuce, 26
  light lamb, 26
  small, of peppers, 164
  vegetable and lobster, clear, 27
Pâte brisée, 185
Peach
  Jam, 204–5
  Wine, 212
Pears
  Duck Conserve Salad with Slices of,
    24
Peas, puree of carrots, celery root and,
    158
Pecan(s)
  maple syrup ice cream with, 192
  Pie, 188
  spicy, 17
Peppers
  bass with, 68
  poached egg whites with, 164–65
  polenta soufflé with red, 166
  small pâté of, 164
Pheasant
  and Cabbage, 144
  filet of, 145
  lean, and veal pâté in lettuce, 26
  roast, 146
Philosophy of cooking, 10
Pie
  pecan, 188
  rabbit, quick, 148–49

Pierre's Cocktail, 214
Pigeon
    Salad, 142
    stuffed, 140–41
Pineapple
    bluefish with, 90
    Jam, 205
    and strawberries, chicken breast with,
        118
Pink Radish Soup, 48
Pistou Soup, 41
Plum
    apple and, compote, 191
    and Pear Jam, 206
    sauce, apple tart with, 196
Poached Chicken, 112
    with Cabbage, 113
    with Cream, 113
Poached Egg Whites with Peppers,
    164–65
Poached Filets of Sole, 62
Polenta
    fried, 165
    Soufflé, with Red Pepper, 166
Poppies, syrup of, 215
    crêpes with rose petals and, 181
Potato(es)
    creamy puree of, 166
    crispy, 167
    Filled with Blue Cheese, 16
    flounder and, 66
    Forestières, 167
    and Leek Base (for soup), 47
    mashed, shrimp and, 99
    Pancake, 166
    ragoût of, and truffles, 33
    smoked red, 16
Presentation, 11
Provençal, chicken, 115
Pudding, rice, 190
Puff pastry, bass in, 70
Pumpkin, sweet, 168
Puree of Carrots, Celery Root and Peas,
    158

Quail
    with Beans, 143
    in the Steamer, 143
Quick Duck Breast Stew With
        Vegetables, 124–25
Quick Lamb Chops with Shallots, 129
Quick Quenelles of Red Snapper, 74
Quick Rabbit Pie, 148–149

Rabbit
    breast, grilled, 146–47
    gigot of, 148
    quick, pie, 148–49
    Stock, 222
    wild, 149
Radish soup, pink, 48
Ragout
    artichoke, 154
    of leeks and truffles, 162
    of potatoes and truffles, light, 33
Raspberry, strawberry, or wine, 213
Red Butter, 228
Red Cabbage
    ribs of venison with, 150–51
    skate with, 79
Red Mullet, 83
    Cooked in Envelope, 84–85
    Meunière with Basil, 82
    molded, 83
Red Snapper
    with Anchovies, 75
    with Carrots, 73
    old fashioned, in the oven, 74–75
    quick quenelles of, 74
    Risotto, 76
Ribs of Venison, with Red Cabbage,
    150–51
Rice
    mussels and, 103
    Pudding, 190
Rillettes, mackerel, 88–89
Risotto, red snapper, 76
Roast Duck with Figs, 124
Roast Pheasant, 146
Rose petals, crêpes with, and syrup of
        poppies, 181
Rouille Sauce, 237

Salad
    chicken, 120
    crispy duck fat, 126
    duck conserve, 24
    hearts of, 22
    hot foie gras, 36
    mussel, 104
    oyster and vegetable, 105
    smoked trout, 78
    spring, with nasturtiums, 180
    pigeon, 142
    sweetbread in a, 137
    warm lobster and asparagus, 96
Salmon, 72

with Asparagus, 72–73
with Hearts of Artichoke, 72
roe, sour cream sauce with
    horseradish and, 239
smoked
    filet of sole and, 64–65
    potatoes with, 16
    sauce, 232
Salsify, 168
Salted Butter, 178
Sauce(s), 225–40
    asparagus, 232
    caper, 238
    caviar, 235
    champagne, 233
    cocktail, 237
    curry, 238
    fresh herb, 230
    fresh tomato, 239
    green, 236
    hollandaise, 229
        in the processor, 229
    lemon or lime butter, 228
    lobster, base, 234
    Madras, 235
    mayonnaise, 236
        in the processor, 236
        without eggs, 238
    morel, 231
    orange, 231
    parsley, 233
    plum, apple tart with, 196
    red butter, 228
    rouille, 237
    smoked salmon, 232
    sour cream
        with horseradish and salmon roe,
        239
        and vinegar, 240
        whipped, 239
    tartare, 237
    tomato, fresh, 239
        lobster with, 96
    velouté, 227
    walnut, 174
    warm, with hard-boiled eggs, 235
    zucchini, 230
Sausage, chicken, 25
Sauteed Cauliflower, 159
Sauteed Morels, 162
Sauteed Soft-Shell Crabs, 101
Scallion butter, soft-shell crabs with,
    101
Scallop(s), 106

with Fresh Tomatoes, 106
mousse, morels stuffed with, 163
with Oyster Mushrooms, 107
Seafood Pancake, 23
Shellfish, 93–107
    Fritters, 18
    *See also specific types*
Short Pastry, 185
Shrimp
    Cornish game hens stuffed with,
        120–21
    and Mashed Potatoes, 99
    Soufflé, 98
    Soup, 44–45
    in Spicy Bouillon, 97
    and Vegetable Stew, 99
Sisto's Consomme, 42–43
Skate, 78
    with Onions, 80
    with Red Cabbage, 79
    steamed, with oranges, 78
Sliced Turnips, 169
Small Pâté of Peppers, 164
Small Sweet, A, 194
Smoked Red Potatoes, 16
Smoked Salmon Sauce, 232
Smoked Trout Salad, 78
Snapper
    quick quenelles of red, 74
    red, with anchovies, 75
    red, with carrots, 73
    red, risotto, 76
Snow Peas, 163
Soft Leg of Lamb, 130
Soft-Shell Crabs
    mousse of, 102
    sauteed, 101
    with scallion butter, 101
Sole
    how to filet, 60
    filet of
        poached, 62
        and smoked salmon, 64–65
        in the steamer, 64
    Soufflé, 63
Soufflé
    polenta, with red pepper, 166
    shrimp, 98
    sole, 63
Soup(s), 37–51
    asparagus, 42
    Bouillabaisse, chilled, 50–51
    cauliflower and curry, 39
    clam, 45

consommé, 42–43
cucumber, 48
eggplant, 46
farm, 40
garlic, 38
Gazpacho, 49
melon and grapefruit, 46
mussel, with saffron, 44
pink radish, 48
pistou, 41
potato and leek base, 47
shrimp, 44–45
strawberry, 49
Vichyssoise, 48
zucchini, with nutmeg, 47
Sour Cream Sauce
with horseradish and salmon roe, 239
whipped, 239
Sour Cream and Vinegar Sauce, 240
Spicy Butter, 178
Spicy Pecans, 17
Spinach, 168
Spring Salad with Nasturtiums, 180
Steamed Cornish Game Hens, 122
Steamed Lobster with Tomato Sauce,
   96
Steamed Mackerel Rolls, 89
Steamed Skate with Orange, 78
Stew
quick duck breast with vegetables,
   124–25
monkfish, with anise, 80–81
shrimp and vegetable, 99
Stock(s), 217–23
chicken, 221
duck, 220
fish, 222–23
lamb, 220
rabbit, 222
veal, 219
vegetable, 223
Strawberry(ies)
pineapple and, chicken breast with,
   118
or Raspberry Wine, 213
Soup, 49
Stuffed Breast of Veal, 132–33
Stuffed Eggs, 56
Stuffed Pigeon, 140–41
Stuffed Zucchini, 170
Sweetbread, 136
with Fresh Noodles, 136
in a Salad, 137
Sweet Pumpkin, 168

Syrup of Poppies, 215
crêpes with rose petals and, 181

Tart(s)
apple
carmelized, 186
with plum sauce, 196
asparagus, 155
cheese, 23
chocolate, with pine nuts, 187
orange, 186
Valentine, 187
vegetable, 22
Tartare Sauce, 237
Tomato(es)
bass with fresh, 69
eggplant with, 160
fresh, sauce, 239
green, jam, 207
Provençal, 168
fresh, 239
lobster with, 96
scallops with fresh, 106
Trout, 76
Poached in Vinegar, 76–77
smoked, salad, 78
Stuffed with Vegetables, 77
Truffle(s), 32
oysters gratin with, 105
ragoût
of leeks and, 162
of potatoes and, 33
turnover with, 32–33
Vinaigrette, 175
Truffles, Caviar and Foie Gras, 31–36
Tulips, 193
Tuna, crispy, 24
Turnips
glazed, 169
sliced, 169
Turnover with Truffles, 32–33

Valentine Tarts, 187
Veal, 131
breast, stuffed, 132–33
chops, braised, 132
in an Envelope with Coriander, 131
Kidney
in Red Wine, 135
with Watercress, 134
and pheasant pâté in lettuce, 26
Stock, 219

*See also* Calf's liver; Sweetbreads
Vegetable(s), 153–70
  cod with, 87
  cold stuffed, 29
  fritters, 18
  Jam, 208
  and lobster pâté, clear, 27
  and oyster salad, 105
  soup
    farm, 40
    pistou, 41
  stew
    quick duck breast, with, 124–25
    shrimp and, 99
  Stock, 223
  Tart, 22
  trout stuffed with, 77
  Wine without Alcohol, 215
  *See also specific types*
Velouté, 227
Venison
  ribs of, with red cabbage, 150–51
  wild bird stuffed with, 151
Vichyssoise, 48
Vinaigrette, 174
  fruit, 175
  light, 175
  without Oil, 176
  truffle, 175
Vinaigrettes, Oils and Butters, 171–78
Vinegar, 172
  corn condiment with, 173
  with Marigolds, 172
  sour cream and, sauce, 240
Violet(s)

chicken fricandeau with, 181
  Wine, 213
Vocabulary, culinary, 13–14

Walnut
  Bread, 200
  Sauce, 174
Warm Lobster and Asparagus Salad, 96
Warm Sauce with Hard-Boiled Eggs,
  235
Watercress, veal kidneys with, 134
Watermelon Jam, 206
Whipped Sour Cream Sauce, 239
Wild bird
  stuffed with venison, 151
  *See also specific types*
Wild Rabbit, 149
Wine(s)
  with Fruit, 211–12
  hot, 213
  labels, 211
  orange, 212
  peach, 212
  strawberry or raspberry, 213
  vegetable, without alcohol, 215
  violet, 213
Wines and Other Drinks, 209–15

Zucchini
  with Cheese, 169
  leek and, little doormat of, 161
  Sauce, 230
  soup with nutmeg, 47
  stuffed, 170